THE PHILOSOPHICAL WRITINGS

The Philosophy of Disenchantment.
& The Anatomy of Negation.

EDGAR SALTUS

WITH A FOREWORD BY
CHIP SMITH

UNDERWORLD AMUSEMENTS

ISBN: 978-0-9885536-4-4

Designed and Edited by Kevin I. Slaughter

The Philosophy of Disenchantment was first published in 1885.
The Anatomy of Negation was first published in 1886.

Foreword ©2014 by Chip Smith,
who is also a publisher:
www.NineBandedBooks.com

Underworld Amusements
www.UnderworldAmusements.com

CONTENTS

Foreword.

FOREWORD.

EDGAR SALTUS WAS BORN IN 1855. HE DIED IN 1921. HE WROTE quite a few books during the years intervening, and it seems there is a percolating consensus—among vested scholars, in any case—that his oeuvre has since been woefully neglected. I won't argue with that appraisal. I'm a reasonably well-read plebe, yet Saltus had escaped my notice until a couple of years ago when I caught a passing reference to his work in Thomas Ligotti's pessimistically pitched lit-crit treatise, *The Conspiracy against the Human Race*. And the truth is I might never have followed the lead had I not been contacted by Kevin Slaughter in late 2012 with the news that he planned to reprint two "nonfiction Saltus books" under his (also woefully neglected) Underworld Amusements publishing venture. When Kevin asked if I would consider writing an introduction, I reasonably suggested that the task should fall on someone familiar with the literature. I was disposed to reconsider, however, when I began reading *The Philosophy of Disenchantment* and found myself wanting to throw the thing across the room because it's just that fucking good. Scholarly introductions tend to be stuffy and overwrought, anyway. With no academic reputation to secure or uphold, I am at liberty to share a catechumen's enthusiasm for the double-shot on offer.

If you want the full effect, read *Anatomy of Negation* first. It's a solid book—a surefooted, if somewhat idiosyncratic, study of the antitheistic impulse as expressed and developed from antiquity to modernity. Tracing the roots of worldly skepticism to the Vedic sage Kapila ("the first serious thinker who looked up into the archaic skies and declared them to be void"), Saltus provides a deftly ornamented account of such atheistic rumblings that may be descried in the texture of Buddhist and Epicurean thought, turning his sights in course on those pre- and post-Enlightenment "slayers of superstition" who endeavored to break the spell of Christian mysticism. Montaigne figures prominently as one who "refused to take a step beyond the actual," and Spinoza receives due favor for his "three-fold" negations ("He denied the existence of an extra-mundane Deity; he denied that man is a free agent; and he denied the doctrine of final causes").

While modern readers may register disappointment that Saltus' curatorial labors would never be updated to account for the philosophical turn signaled by Nietzsche's rise, his contextual discussion of the ever-ascendant Arthur Schopenhauer serves just as well to distinguish his project from that of a lesser contrarian. Describing the great pessimist as "an idealist who saw the inutility of dream," Saltus correctly apprehends Schopenhauer's concept of Will as an antecedent expression of the central tenet of Darwinian theory. More important, Saltus grasped the deeper implications for the cause of human well-being in a universe at once disenchanted and governed by inchoate force. Paraphrasing the philosopher Eduard von Hartmann in relevant context, Saltus writes—not for the first time—in anticipation of contemporary antinatalism:

> The interest of the Unconscious is opposed to our own.
> It is to our advantage not to live; it is to the advantage
> of the Unconscious that we should do so, and that oth-
> ers should be brought into existence through us. The
> Unconscious, therefore, in the furtherment of its aims,
> has surrounded man with such illusions as are capable
> of deluding him into a belief that life is a pleasant thing
> well worth the living.

While *Negation* proceeds as an episodically paced, biograph-
ically annotated intellectual history that plots and, by interne-
cine turns, celebrates the dethronement of the transcendental
temptation in its various and sundry cross-cultural guises, the
author's editorial investment is made clearest in the book's
closing chapter, "The Poet's Verdict," where Saltus captures the
human predicament with apposite measures of resignation and
flair:

> There is no answer to any appeal. The best we can do,
> the best that has ever been done, is to recognize the
> implacability of the laws that rule the universe, and
> contemplate as calmly as we can the nothingness from
> which we are come and into which we shall all disap-
> pear.

It is instructive, I think, to contrast what dim solace Saltus
summons before the void with the cheery—and frankly credulous—optimism incessantly being trumpeted in contemporary
iterations of what has recently been branded the "New Atheism." Examples of such rose-tinted sentiment are amply supplied in the writings of the movement's chief expositor, Richard
Dawkins, whose fast and loose atheistic polemics come adorned
with curiously exultant paeans to the life-affirming wonders of

the natural universe into which we are assuredly and emphatically privileged to have been cast. Dawkins' bestseller, *The God Delusion*, is so littered with awestruck Panglossianism that the philosopher David Benatar (whose signature work, *Better Never to Have Been: The Harm of Coming into Existence*, Saltus might have relished) was motivated to pen an incisive demurral[*] taking the New Atheist doyen to task for embracing the "gospel of secular optimism without feeling the need to engage seriously with philosophical pessimism–the ultimate delusion buster."

Saltus, of course, suffered no such delusion. Time to flip your bookmark to *The Philosophy of Disenchantment*.

Disenchantment was Published in 1885, only a year before *The Anatomy of Negation* (which it resembles in its formal trajectory). Saltus would later describe it—one assumes with a self-effacing wink—as "the gloomiest and worst book ever published." Like its deicidal counterpart, *Disenchantment* proceeds as a richly embellished study of a perennial species of heterodoxy, in this instance: the case of pessimism, or such deep or cosmic pessimism as that bearing on the grim conclusion that—again anticipating philanthropic strains of contemporary antinatalism—"the world is a theatre of misery in which, were the choice accorded, it would be preferable not to be born at all."

Saltus evinces competence and grace throughout, charting and amplifying the minor chords of miserablism that have been sounded in terms philosophical and poetic for millennia. We are reminded of the public disturbance aroused by Hegesias of Cyrene, who may have been the first Western thinker to consign happiness to the rank of "pure illusion" and who rejoined the Socratic exaltation of knowledge with a plaintive echo of Buddhist resignation, declaring "Contentment is not to be relied on, and even wisdom cannot preserve us from the treachery and insecurity of the perceptions." We are introduced anew to

---

[*]   BENATAR, D. 2008. The optimism delusion. Think, 16 (Winter) : 19-22

the poet and essayist Giacomo Leopardi, whose contemptuous indictments of the "sinister and terrible mystery of life" gave shape to the "muffled discontent" of ages, transforming the restive churn of a formless pessimistic sensibility into "one clear note of eloquent arraignment."

Prominence of stature is perforce accorded to Arthur Schopenhauer, "The High Priest of Pessimism," to whom Saltus devotes expansive biographical attention and in whose philosophy he locates the conception of life as "a motiveless desire, a constant pain and continued struggle, followed by death, and so on, in *secula seculorum*, until the planet's crust crumbles to dust." As if to flirt with the endgame, Saltus appends his treatment of Schopenhauerian negation with a discursive—and desultorily critical—account of the proto-extinctionist ideas of his personal contemporary, Eduard von Hartmann, an evolutionary pessimist who held "the idea that happiness is obtainable in this life" to be "the first and foremost of illusions" and who blackly averred that the ascent of human consciousness would—and should—ultimately resolve in the (presumably voluntary) cessation of "every form of existence."

Considered as discrete works, *The Philosophy of Disenchantment* and *Anatomy of Negation* stand as valuable contributions to the literature of philosophical pessimism and supernatural skepticism respectively. Taken together, the effect is alchemic—and volatile. For the outspoken modern atheist who feels an abiding need to promote his pet disbelief as sport, cosmic pessimism is a jagged shard that threatens to blunt the only salve he has yet on offer. However it may be qualified, the enthronement of meaning is today tacitly encouraged by self-imagined freethinkers who, in their effusive appeals to reason, disdain to consider that the vaunted sense of life's purpose could in the next breath be revealed as yet another paper-thin conceit—or, in deeper acid, as the final precious article of phantom nonsense that pulses after the armor of so many impotent spooks has been penetrated and dismantled. In what wreckage remains, every boast and sneer will ring hollow.

Saltus dwelled in that wreckage. Understanding what was at stake, he stood atop the corpse mound of fallen gods and he sifted through the rot to unlay the deep nest of demons still as-quirm in the minds of mortals who once dreamed of angels. He dissected and exploded every cherished myth and he burned what hope remained. The char of deflagrated hope now resides at the margins of a sprawling disquisition that may finally be considered as intellectual backdrop to the shadow inquest that has continued apace, whether in the amoral perturbations of the natural sciences or in the outcast voices of those who have since staged protest against the reigning chorus of optimism. You can compile a list where Zapffe and Lovecraft and Cioran hold place, or you can go all in, settling at the grimly extrapolat-ed declaration of Ligotti (the contemporary nihilist who, from a century's distance, Saltus most resembles), *videlicet*, "The uni-verse is *malignantly useless.*"

Saltus did well enough for his time. He limned the dreari-est sentiments of the ages in crystalline prose that fairly scintil-lates with lyrically inflected insight. He was an entrancing writ-er. And though his work may remain to languish in obscurity along with the work of so many other forgotten thinkers and litterateurs, what's sure is that a dreadful thrill awaits those in-trepid truth seekers who venture beyond the lonely footnote to receive the bleak verdict of an overlooked miserablist, and per-haps, a kindred spirit.

Chip Smith
January, 2014

The Philosophy of Disenchantment.

In Arkadien geboren sind wir Alle...
                    —Schiller

CHAPTER ONE.

The Genesis of Disenchantment.

THE TRITE AND COMMONPLACE QUESTION OF CONTENTMENT and dissatisfaction is a topic which is not only of every-day interest, but one which in recent years has so claimed the attention of thinkers, that they have broadly divided mankind into those who accept life off-hand, as a more or less pleasing possession, and those who resolutely look the gift in the mouth and say it is not worth the having.

Viewed simply as systems of thought, the first of these two divisions is evidently contemporaneous with humanity, while the second will be found to be of purely modern origin; for from the earliest times man, admittedly and with but few exceptions, has been ever accustomed to regard this world as the best one possible, and through nearly every creed and sect he has considered happiness somewhat in the light of an inviolable birthright.

Within the last half century, however, there has come into being a new school, which, in denying the possibility of any happiness, holds as first principle that the world is a theatre of misery in which, were the choice accorded, it would be preferable not to be born at all.

In stating that this view of life is of distinctly modern origin, it should be understood that it is so only in the systematic form which it has recently assumed, for individual expressions of discontent have been handed down from remote ages, and any one who cared to rummage through the dust-bins of literature would find material enough to compile a dictionary of pessimistic quotation.

For these pages but little rummaging will be attempted, but as the proper presentation of the subject demands a brief account of the ideas and opinions in which it was cradled, a momentary examination of general literature will not, it is believed, cause any after-reproach of time misspent.

To begin, then, with Greece, whose literature has precedence over all others, it will be remembered that in former days, when the citizen expended the greater part of his activity for the common good, the poets in like manner sang of national topics, the gods, the heroes, and the charms of love. There was, therefore, little opportunity for the expression of purely personal ideas, and the whole background of the poetry of antiquity is in consequence brilliant with optimistic effect. Nevertheless, here and there, a few complaints crop out from time to time. Homer, for instance, says that man is the unhappiest wight that ever breathed or strutted, and describes his ephemeral existence in a wail of gloomy hexameters.

Then, too, there is the touching Orphean distich, which runs:—

> "From thy smile, O Jove, sprang the gods,
> But man was born of thy sorrow."

Pindar in one of his graceful odes compared men to the shadows of a dream, while the familiar quotation, "Whom the gods love die young," comes to us straight from Menander.

With the peculiar melancholy of genius, that in those favored days seems more a presentiment than the expression of a general conception, Sophocles, in his last tragedy, says that not to be born at all is the greatest of all possible benefits, but inasmuch as man has appeared on earth, the very best thing he can do is to hurry back where he came from.

In spite, too, of the general tendency of thought, sentiments not dissimilar are to be found in Æschylus and Euripides, while something of this instinctive pessimism was expanded into a quaint and national custom by the Thracians, who, according to Herodotus, met birth with lamentations, but greeted death with salvos and welcoming festivals.

With but few exceptions the early philosophers considered death not as a misfortune, but as an advantage. Empedocles taught that the sojourn on earth was one of vexatious torment, an opinion in which he was firmly supported by Heraclitus, and even Plato, whose general drift of thought was grandly optimistic, said in the *Apology*, "If death is the withdrawal of every sensation, if it is like a sleep which no dream disturbs, what an incomparable blessing it must be! for let any one select a night passed in undisturbed and entire rest, and compare it with the other nights and days that have filled his existence, and then from his conscience let him answer how many nights and days he has known which have been sweeter and more agreeable than that. For my part I am sure that not the ordinary individual alone, but even the great King of Persia would find such days and nights most easy to enumerate."

The doctrine of Epicurus held, in substance, that the moment it was no longer possible to delight the senses death became a benefit, and suicide a crowning act of wisdom. The teaching of the Socratic school and its offshoots amounted, in brief, to the idea that the only admissible aim of life was the pursuit and attainment of absolute knowledge. Absolute knowledge, however, being found unattainable, the logical culmination of their doctrine was delivered by Hegesias, in Alexandria, in the third century before the Christian era. This disciple of Socrates argued that as there was a limit to the knowable, and happiness was a pure illusion, a further prolongation of existence was useless. "Life seems pleasing only to the fool," he stated; "the wise regard it with indifference, and consider death just as acceptable." "Death," he added, "is as good as life; it is but a supreme renunciation in which man is freed from idle complaints and long deceptions. Life is full of pain, and the pangs of the flesh gnaw at the mind and rout its calm. In countless ways fate intercepts and thwarts our hopes. Contentment is not to be relied on, and even wisdom cannot preserve us from the treachery and insecurity of the perceptions. Since happiness, then, is intangible we should cease to pursue it, and take for our goal the absence of pain; this condition," he explained, "is best obtained in making ourselves indifferent to every object of desire and every cause of dislike, and above all to life itself. In any event," he concluded, "death is advantageous in this, it takes us not from blessings but from evil."*

This curious mixture of pessimism and theology was, it is said, delivered with such charm of persuasive grace and eloquence that several of his listeners put his ideas into instant practice, and that the city might be preserved from the contagion of suicide, King Ptolemy felt himself obliged to prevent this seductive misanthrope from delivering any further harangues.

Literature has the same tendency to repeat itself as history, and as the Romans took much of their culture and many of their ideas from Greece, the tone of their principal writers is only dissimilar to those already quoted in that with the fall of their religion, the decline of the empire and the universal intoxication of the senses, the pessimist element became somewhat

---

*   Zeller, *Philosophie der Griechen.*

accentuated. It would be an idle task, however, to attempt to cite even a fraction of the cheerless distress which pervades the Roman classics, and it will perhaps suffice for the moment to note but a passage or two, which bear directly upon the subject.

Seneca, for instance, whose insight was as clear and whose understanding was as unclouded as any writer with whom the world is acquainted, sent his letters down the centuries freighted with such ideas as these: "Death is nature's most admirable invention." "There is no need to complain of particular grievances, for life in its entirety is lamentable." "No one would accept life were it not received in ignorance of what it is."

Pliny, also, is very quotable. "Nature's most pleasing invention," he says, "is brevity of life." And he adds, "No mortal is happy, for even if there is no other cause for discontent there is at least the fear of possible misfortune."

Then, too, Petronius, the poet of the Roman orgy, opening and closing his veins, toying with death, as with a last and supreme delight, is of familiar, if repulsive, memory.

English literature is naturally as well stocked with individual expressions of distaste for existence as that of Rome. The poets, nearly one and all, from Chaucer to Rossetti, have told their sorrow in a variety of more or less polished metre, and even Macpherson was careful, in dowering his century with another bard, to put thoughts into Ossian's verse which would not have been unfitting in a Greek chorus.

In speaking of the world, Chaucer had already said,—

"Here is no home, here is but a wilderness,"

when Sir Thomas Wyatt, enlarging on the theme, repeated,—

"Wherefore come death and let me dye."

The delicate muse of Samuel Fletcher found—

"Nothing's so dainty sweet, as lovely melancholy,"

and Shakespeare's depressing lines on the value of life are familiar to every schoolboy.

Dryden wrote,—

> "When I consider life, 't is all a cheat;
> Yet, fooled with hope, men favour the deceit,
> Trust on and think to-morrow will repay;
> To-morrow's falser than the former day."

All of which was afterwards summed up in the well-known line,—

> "Man never *is* but always *to be* blessed,"

while Thomson noted—

> ... "all the thousand, nameless ills
> That one incessant struggle render life."

Keats, and especially Byron, wrote stanza after stanza of enervating sadness. Moore's dear gazelle is nowadays a familiar comparison. Shelley's tremulous sensibility forbade his finding any charm in life, and we none of us need to be reminded that Poe's soul was sorrow-laden.

But the poets are not alone in their tale of the deceptions of life; the moralists and essayists, too, have added their quota to the general budget, and it is not simply the value of life that has been questioned by many of the best writers; there has been also a certain surprise expressed that man should care to live at all. Indeed, the "I see no necessity" of the wit, to the beggar imploring aid that he might live, is the epigram of the thoughts of a hundred scholars.

In France, pessimism cannot be said to have been ever regarded otherwise than as an intellectual curiosity. The Frenchman, it is true, not infrequently lapses into a cynical indifference; yet the value of life is as a rule so evident to him, that he seldom vouchsafes more than a passing shrug to any theory of disparagement. In the first place, death, to which the hat is gravely raised, has never been in France a polite or welcome topic; moreover, French literature, while lawless enough in other respects, has left its readers generally unprepared to view the world as a fiasco, in which misery is the one immense success. The trouvères and troubadours sang to the mediæval châtelaine little else than the praise of love, with here and there the account of some combat, to show what they might do were they put to the test. Later, Villon told gently of the *neiges d'antan*, Ronsard aimed a dart or two at fate, and Rabelais's laugh was sometimes very near to tears; but, broadly speaking, the French asked of their writers little else than wit,—if they could not give them that, then should they hold their peace.

The delicate irony of *Candide* had, therefore, when appreciated, something almost novel in its savor; and, indeed, it may fairly be said that it was not until the blight of Byron had been cheerfully translated, that the French were in any measure prepared to understand Rolla and the pathetic beauties of De Musset's verse. Pascal, Helvetius, and other writers of desultory depression had of course already appeared. Maupertuis had found no difficulty in showing that life held more pain than pleasure, while Chamfort's conclusions on the same subject were as luminous as they were gloomy; and yet it is difficult to say that the gall with which these authors dashed their pages served otherwise than as a condiment to fresher and less flavored works. Baudelaire, the poet of boredom, praying for a new vice that should wrest life into some semblance of reality, was in consequence almost a novelty, and not a perfectly satisfactory one at that. It is therefore only within the last ten years or so that pessimism has in any wise attracted the notice of French thinkers, and the attention which has recently been paid to it is due partly to Leconte de Lisle, and partly to a surge of German thought.

During the eighteenth century the majority of the scholars who represented the culture of Germany were faithfully following the optimist theories of Leibnitz and Wolf. The doctrine that the world was the best one possible, supported as it was by official theology and strictly in accord with the deism of Pope and Paley, was very generally and unhesitatingly accepted. Indeed, there is no apparent reason why it should not have been. The Minnesingers doubtless had formulated some few complaints, but then these literary vagrants had already begun to form part of mythology, and besides, poets are all more or less prone to discontent and voluble of sorrow. Beyond the classics of Greece and Rome there was, therefore, no precedent for pessimistic thought. German literature, strictly speaking, did not begin until Lessing's advent, and before that the theatre, with its Hans Wurst and its Pickleherring, had offered only a succession of the broadest farce.

The calm and quiet which the Germans then enjoyed was ruffled, if at all, only by some confused echoes of the *obiter dicta* which Voltaire's royal disciple was pleased to disseminate, but it is probable that the better part of this ferocious gayety was drowned in crossing the Rhine, and, in any event, it was too delicately pungent to do more than disturb the placid current of their thought.

Later, when Kant appeared, the effect of his philosophy was very much like a successful treatment of cataract on the eyes of the whole nation. "Happiness," he insisted in the *Kritik der Urtheilskraft*, "has never been attained by man, for he is unable to find contentment in any possession or enjoyment, ...and were he called upon to fashion a system of happiness for his fellows he would be unable to do so, for happiness is in its essence intangible." "No one," he added elsewhere, "has a right conception of life who would care to prolong it beyond its natural duration, for it would then be only the continuation of an already tiresome struggle."

After this the teaching of Leibnitz slowly disappeared, and though a certain amount of optimism necessarily subsisted, the tendency of thought veered to the opposite direction. Fichte, Kant's immediate successor, declared, in direct contradiction to Leibnitz, that this world was the worst one possible, and was only consoled by thinking he could raise himself by the aid of pure thought into the felicity of the "supersensible." "Men," he says, "in the vehement pursuit of happiness grasp at the first object which offers to them any prospect of satisfaction, but immediately they turn an introspective eye and ask, 'Am I happy?' and at once from their innermost being a voice answers distinctly, 'No, you are as poor and as miserable as before.' Then they think it was the object that deceived them, and turn precipitately to another. But the second holds as little satisfaction as the first.... Wandering then through life, restless and tormented, at each successive station they think that happiness dwells at the next, but when they reach it happiness is no longer there. In whatever position they may find themselves there is always another one which they discern from afar, and which but to touch, they think, is to find the wished delight, but when the goal is reached discontent has followed on the way and stands in haunting constancy before them."[*]

Schelling expressed himself more guardedly. As professional pantheist, he seemed to think that anything not rigidly vague and inaccessible was inconsistent with his philosophy. Still there was probably a secret revolt, some propelling impulse to deny his own syllogisms, and to bathe for once in some clear stream of common sense. In the *Nachtwachen*, which he published under the pseudonym of Bonaventura, this incentive is evidently, though unsuccessfully, at work. It may be that the force of hab-

---

[*]   *Werke, v.* p. 408, *et seq.*

it was too strong, but at any rate this rhapsody, which was intended to be a confession of the combat that he had waged with his belief, and a recognition of the immedicable misery of life, brings with it something of that impression of delirium which Poe and Doré not infrequently suggest.

Nor was Hegel hostile to pessimism; he regarded it as an inevitable phase of universal evolution, and indeed its dawn as a science had then already broken.

Meanwhile the poets had not been idle. Herder and Schiller had already attested the bitterness of life to unreluctant ears, and the number of suicides that were directly traceable to the appearance of Werther and his sorrows was instructively large. This phase of sentimentalism, which immediately preceded the riotous rebirth of the Romantic school, was not without its influence on Heine's verse, and in some measure affected the literary tone of the day.

It would, however, be erroneous to suppose that the poets of this epoch were more agitated by the impression of universal worthlessness of life than were their classic predecessors. The distress of Werther, as that of Lara and of Rolla, was not the pain of suffering humanity; it was in each case merely the poet's complacent analysis of his own exceptional nature and personal grievances; it was the expression of the inevitable surprise of youth, which notes for the first time reality's unsuspected yet yawning indifference to the ideal, and the stubborn disaccord between aspiration and fact. It was indeed very beautiful and elegiac, and yet so fluent in its polished melancholy that somehow it did not at all times seem to have been really felt. In any case, it was not a theory of common woe, and lacked that clear conception of the universality of suffering, which the less exalted minds of the philosophers had already signaled, but for which no one as yet had been able to suggest a remedy.

It was about this time that an action was being instituted

against humanity by a young Italian, the Count Giacomo Leopardi, and the muffled discontent which for centuries had been throbbing through land and literature was raised by his verse into one clear note of eloquent arraignment.

Now, in most countries there is a provision which inhibits a judge from hearing a cause which is pleaded by one of his connections, for it is considered that the scales of justice are so delicately balanced, that their holder should be preserved from any biasing influence, however indirect; for much the same reason, there are few communities that permit a man to sit in judgment on his own case. Some knowledge of Leopardi himself, therefore, will be of service in deciding whether the verdict which he brought against the world should be accepted without appeal, or returned as vitiated by extraneous circumstances.

Leopardi passed a joyless boyhood at Recanti, one of those maddeningly monotonous Italian towns whose unspeakable dreariness is only attractive when viewed through the pages of Stendhal. The unrelaxing severity of an austere and pedant father curbed, as with a bit, every symptom of that haphazard gayety which is incident to youth. At once precocious and restive, deformed yet inflammable, he was necessarily enervated by the exasperating dullness of his life, and chafed, too, by the rigid poverty to which his father condemned him. As he grew up, his mind, richly stored with the wealth of antiquity, rioted in a turbulency of imagination which, unable to find sympathetic welcome without, consumed itself in morbid distrust within, and led him at last from fervid Catholicism down the precipitate steps of negation.

He was not much over twenty before excessive study had well-nigh ruined such health as he once possessed. The slightest application was wearisome both to eye and brain. He wandered silently about the neighboring forests, seeking solitude not only for the sake of solitude, but also perhaps for the suggestions, at once soothing and rebellious, which solitude always whispers to him who courts her truly. At other times he sat hour by hour in a state as motionless as that of catalepsy. "I am so much overcome," he wrote to a friend, "by the nothingness that surrounds me, that I do not know how I have the strength to answer your letter. If at this moment I lost my reason, I think that my insanity would consist in sitting always with eyes fixed, open-mouthed, without laughing or weeping, or changing place. I have no longer the strength to form a desire, be it even for death."

The Muse, however, would have none of this; she flaunted her peplum so seductively before him that, a little later, when he had been visited by some semblance of returning health, he resisted no longer, and delivered himself up to her, heart and soul.

The present century, especially during its earlier decades, has been racked with a great glut of despondent verse; but no batch of poets, however distressed, has been able, at any time, to catch and cling to such a persistent monotone of complaint as that which runs through every line of Leopardi's verse. To quote De Musset:—

> "*Les plus désespérés sont les chants les plus beaux,*
> *Et j'en sais d'immortels qui sont de purs sanglots.*"

His odes, his adjurations to Italy, and his elegies are, one and all, stamped with such unvarying and changeless despair, that their dominant motive seems not unlike that tower which René, finding alone in the desert, compared to a great thought in a mind ravaged by years and by grief. His theory of life never altered; he resumed it in a distich,—

> ..."*Arcano é tutto*
> *Fuor che il nostro dolor.*"

It may be said, and with justice perhaps, that it was the invalid body, aggravating and coexisting with a mind naturally morbid, that afterwards wrote of the *gentilezza del morir*, but it was the thinker, conquering the ills of the flesh, who later whispered to the suffering world the panacea of patience and resignation.

In Leopardi there is none of the vapid elegance and gaudy vocabulary of French verse; technically, he wrote in what the Italians call *rime sciolte*, and he charms the reader as well through a palpitant sincerity as evident and continuous inspiration. Now, the educated Italian turns naturally to rhyme; any incident holds to him the germ of a sonnet, and there is perhaps no other country in the world so richly dowered with patriotic *canzoni* as this joyously unhappy land. But of all who have sounded this eloquent chord, not one has done so with the masculine originality and fervor of expression that Leopardi reached in his ode to Italy, in which, in a resounding call to arms, he exclaims:—

"Let my blood, O gods! be a flame to Italian hearts."

Italian hearts, however, had other matters to attend to, and Leopardi's magnificent invocation was barely honored with a passing notice. For that matter, his poetry, in spite of its resonant merit, has, through some inexplicable cause, been generally ignored; and while it resembles no other, it has never, so to speak, been in vogue.

As has been seen, he was a lover of solitude; indeed, it would not be an exaggeration to say that he was glued to it; and in the isolation which he partly made himself, and which was partly forced upon him, he watched the incubation of thought very much as another might have noted the progress of a disease. A life of this description, even at best, is hardly calculated to awaken much enthusiasm for every-day matters, and it was not long before Leopardi became not only heartily sick of the commonplace aspects of life, but contemptuous, too, of those who lived in broader and more active spheres.

Poetically untrammeled, and of advanced views on all subjects, he regarded erudition as the simple novitiate of the man of letters, or in other words, as a preparation which renders the intelligence supple and pliant; and in one of those rare moments, when the timid approach of ambition was seemingly unnoticed, he caressed the pleasing plan of attacking Italian torpor with reason, passion with laughter, and of becoming, in fact, the Plato, the Shakespeare, and the Lucian of his epoch. To Giordani, his mentor, he wrote: "I study night and day, so long as my health permits; when it prevents me from working, I wait a month or so, and then begin again. As I am now totally different from that which I was, my plan of study has altered with me. Everything which savors of the pathetic or the eloquent wearies me beyond expression. I seek now only the true, the real, which before was so repulsive. I take pleasure in analyzing the misery of men and things, and in shivering as I note the sinister and terrible mystery of life. I see very clearly that when passion is once extinguished, there subsists in study no other source of pleasure save that of vain curiosity, whose satisfaction, however, is not without a certain charm."

But Leopardi was so essentially the poet that, in spite of his growing disdain of the pathetic and the eloquent, he became not infrequently the dupe of his own imagination. That which he took for the fruit of deduction was probably little more than ordinary hypochondria, and in turning as he did to other work, he was never able to free himself entirely from the jealous influence of the muse.

He was, from a variety of causes, very miserable himself, and his belief in universal misery amounted very nearly to a mania. His logic reduced itself to the paraphrase of an axiom, "I am, therefore I suffer," and the suffering which he experienced was not, he was very sure, limited solely to himself. It was, he considered, the garment and appanage of every sentient being. In this he was perfectly correct, but his error consisted in holding all cases to be equally intense, and in imagining that means might be devised which would at once do away with or, at least, lessen the evil. Patience and resignation he had already suggested, but naturally without appreciable success; indeed, the regeneration of man, he clearly saw, was not to be brought about through verse, and he turned therefore to philosophy with a fixity of purpose, which was strengthened by the idea that he could work therein another revolution. This was in 1825. Leopardi at that time was in his twenty-seventh year, and the task to which he then devoted himself was, he said, to be the sad ending of a miserable life. His intention was to run the bitter truth to earth, to learn the obscure destinies of the mortal and the eternal, to discover the wherefore of creation, and the reason of man's burden of misery. "I wish," he said, "to dig to the root of nature and seek the aim of the mysterious universe, whose praises the sages sing, and before which I stand aghast."

Forthwith, then, in the *Operette Morale*, Leopardi began a resolute, if poetic, siege against every form of illusion. His philosophy, however, provoked no revolution, nor can it be even said that he discovered any truth more bitter than the old new ones, which antiquity had unearthed before him. His work, nevertheless, sent the old facts spinning into fresh and novel positions, and is to be particularly admired for the artistic manner in which it handles the most stubborn topics. The starting point of each of his arguments is that life is evil; to any objection, and the objections that have been made are countless, Leopardi has one invariable reply, "All that is advanced to the contrary is the result of illusion." "But supposing life to be painless," some one presumably may interject, whereupon Leopardi, with the air of an oracle, too busy with weighty matters to descend to chit-chat on the weather, will answer tersely, "Evil still."

It is useless for the practical man of the day, who knows the price of wheat the whole world over before he has tasted his coffee, and who digests a history of the world's doings and misdoings each morning with his breakfast,—it is useless for him to say, as he invariably does:—Why, this is rubbish, look at modern institutions, look at progress, look at science; for if he listens to Leopardi he will learn that all these palpable advantages have, in expanding activity, only aggravated the misery of man. In other words, that the sorrows of men and of nations develop in proportion to their intelligence, and the most civilized are in consequence the most unhappy.

Indeed, Leopardi's philosophy is nothing if not destructive; he does not aim so much to edify as to undermine. According to his theory the universe is the resultant of an unconscious force, and this force, he teaches, is shrouded in a vexatious mystery, behind which it is not given to man to look. In one of his dialogues, certain mummies resurrect for a quarter of an hour and tell in what manner they died. "And what follows death?" their auditor asks, eagerly. But the quarter of an hour has expired and the mummies relapse into silence.

In another fantastic scene, an Icelander, convinced that happiness is unattainable, and solely occupied in avoiding pain, has, in shunning society, found himself in the heart of the Sahara, face to face with Nature. This Icelander, who, by the way, singularly resembles Leopardi, had found but one protection against the ills of life, and that was solitude; but wherever he wandered he had been pursued by a certain malevolence. In spite of all he could do, he had roasted in summer and shivered in winter. In vain he had sought a temperate climate: one land was an ice-field, another an oven, and everywhere tempests or earthquakes, vicious brutes or distracting insects. In short, unalloyed misery. Finding himself, at last, face to face with Nature he took her to task, demanding what right she had to create him without his permission, and then, having done so, to leave him to his own devices? Nature answers that she has but one duty, and that is to turn the wheel of the universe, in which death supports life, and life death. "Well, then," the obstinate Icelander asks, "tell me at least for whose pleasure and for what purpose this miserable universe subsists?" But before Nature can enlighten her embarrassing questioner, he is surprised by two famished lions and conveniently devoured.

The moral of all this is not difficult to find. Life, such as it is, is all this is accorded. Beyond it there is only an impenetrable silence. The blue of the heavens is pervasive, but void. The hope of ultramundane felicity is, therefore, an illusion, and man is to seek such happiness as is possible only in this life. But if it be asked what the possibilities of earthly happiness are, Leopardi is quick to tell his reader that there are none at all.

As has been seen, he regarded life as an evil; and he insisted in so regarding it, not only as a whole, but in each of its fractional divisions. This idea is quaintly expressed in a dialogue between a sorcerer and a demon, the latter having been presumably summoned with an incantatory blue flame. The demon is somewhat sulky at first, and asks why he has been disturbed. Is it wealth that the sorcerer wishes? Is it glory or grandeur? But the sorcerer has neither greed nor ambition.

"Do you wish me to procure for you a woman as captiously capricious as Penelope?"

The sorcerer probably smiles, for he answers wittily:—

"Do you think I need the aid of a devil for that?"

Thus outfaced, the demon begs to know in what manner he may be of service.

"I simply want one moment of happiness," the sorcerer answers.

But Mephisto declares, on his word as a gentleman, that such a thing is impossible, because the desire for happiness is insatiable, and no one can be happy so long as it is unsatisfied.

"Well, then?" the sorcerer asks, moodily querulous.

"Well, then," answers the demon, "if you think it worth while to give me your soul before the time, behold me ready to oblige you."

Since happiness, then, is intangible, the wisest thing to do is to try to be as little unhappy as possible. One of the chief opponents to such a state of being is evidently discontent, and this, Leopardi hints, should be routed at any cost, and the yawning spectre of ennui flung with it into fettered exile. In the warmth of these instructions it is curious to note how Leopardi turns on himself, so to speak, and recommends as cure-all the very activity which he had before proscribed. In his dialogue between Columbus and Gutierrez, the navigator admits to his discouraged companion that the success of the undertaking is far from certain; "but," he adds, "even if no other benefit accrue from our voyage, it will be an advantage at least in this; it has for a certain time delivered us from boredom; it has made us love life, and appreciate, moreover, many things of which otherwise we would have thought nothing."

It should not, however, be supposed that Leopardi had no higher rule of life than that which is circumscribed in the narrow avoidance of discontent. That man has certain duties to perform, he frequently admitted, but he denied that he owed any to the unconscious and tyrannical force which had given him life. "I will never kiss," he said, "the hand that strikes." Any obligation to society was equally out of the question. "Society," he noted in the *Pensieri*, "is a league of blackguards against honest men." Man's duties are to himself alone; and the essence of Leopardi's ethics (as, indeed, of all other ethics) is held simply in the recommendation that virtue and self-esteem be preserved. "To thine own self be true," Polonius had said long before, and to this Leopardi had nothing to add.

The illusions which hamper life have been so clearly and thoroughly analyzed by other thinkers, whose conclusions will be found to constitute the groundwork of the subsequent part of this monograph, that it will be unnecessary at this stage to examine any of Leopardi's theories on this subject, save such, perhaps, as may seem to contain original views. He had, as has been intimated, a thorough contempt for life: "It is," he said, "fit but to be despised." *Nostra vita a che val, sola a spregiarla.* He was, in consequence, well equipped to combat the illusion which leads so many to imagine that were their circumstances different, they would then be thoroughly content. This idea is presented with vivacious ingenuity in a dialogue between a man peddling calendars and a passer-by.

It runs somewhat as follows:—

"Calendars! New calendars!"

"For the coming year?"

"Yes, sir."

"Do you think the year will be a good one?"

"Yes, indeed, sir."

"As good as last year?"

"Better, sir,—better."

"As year before last?"

"Much better, sir."

"But wouldn't you care to have the next year like any of the past years?"

"No, sir, I would not."

"For how long have you been selling calendars?"

"Nearly twenty years, sir."

"Well, which of these twenty years would you wish to have like the coming one?"

"I? I really don't know, sir."

"Can't you remember any one year that seemed particularly attractive?"

"I cannot, indeed, I cannot."

"And yet life is very pleasant, isn't it?"

"Oh, yes, sir, we all know that."

"Would you not be glad to live these twenty years over again?"

"God forbid, sir."

"But supposing you had to live your life over again?"

"I would not do it."

"But what life would you care to live? mine, for instance, or that of a prince, or of some other person?"

"Ah, sir, what a question!"

"And yet, do you not see that I, or the prince, or any one else, would answer precisely as you do, and that no one would consent to live his life over again?"

"Yes, sir, I suppose so."

"Am I to understand, then, that you would not live your life over again?"

"No, sir, truly, I would not."

"What life would you care for, then?"

"I would like, without any other condition, such a life as God might be pleased to give me."

"In other words, one which would be happy-go-lucky, and of which you would know no more than you do of the coming year."

"Exactly."

"Well, then, that is what I would like too; it is what every one would like, and for the simple reason that up to this time there is no one whom chance has not badly treated. Every one agrees that the misery of life outbalances its pleasure, and I have yet to meet the man who would care to live his old life over. The life which is so pleasant is not the life with which we are personally acquainted; it is another life, not the life that we have lived, but the life which is to come. Next year will treat us all better; it will be the beginning of a happy existence. Do you not think it will?"

"Indeed, I hope so, sir."

"Show me your best calendar."

"This one, sir; it is thirty soldi."

"Here they are."

"Thank you, sir, long life to you, sir. Calendars! new calendars!"

There are few scenes as clever as this, and fewer still in which irony and humor are so delicately blended; and yet, notwithstanding its studied bitterness, there is little doubt that its author clearly perceived that life does hold one or two incontestable charms.

In speaking of glory, Pascal noted in his *Pensées* that even philosophers seek it, and those who wrote it down wished the reputation of having written it down well. To this rule Leopardi was no exception; he admitted as much on several occasions; and even if he had not done so, the fact would have been none the less evident from the burnish of his verse and the purity of his prose, which was not that of a writer to whom the opinion of others was indifferent. In the essay, therefore, in which he attacks the illusion of literary renown, he reminds one forcibly of Byron hurrying about in search of the visible isolation which that simple-minded poet so seriously pursued; and yet while no other writer, perhaps, has been more thoroughly given to *pose* than the author of *Childe Harold*, there are few who have been so entirely devoid of affectation as Leopardi. The comparative non-success of his writings, however, was hardly calculated to make him view with any great enthusiasm the subject of literary fame; and as, moreover, he considered it his mission to besiege all illusions, he held up this one in particular as a seductive chimera and attacked it accordingly.

In the *Ovvero della Gloria*, he says reflectively: "Before an author can reach the public with any chance of being judged without prejudice, think of the amount of labor which he expends in learning how to write, the difficulties which he has to overcome, and the envious voices which he must silence. And even then, what does the public amount to? The majority of readers yawn over a book, or admire it because some one else has admired it before them. It is the style that makes a book immortal; and as it requires a certain education to be a judge of style, the number of connoisseurs is necessarily restricted. But beyond mere form there must also be depth, and as each class of work presupposes a special competence on the part of the critic, it is easy to see how narrow the tribunal is which decides an author's reputation. And even then, is it one which is thoroughly just? In the first place, the critic, even when competent, judges—and in that he is but human—according to the impression of the moment, and according to the tastes which age or circumstances have created. If he is young, he likes brilliance; old, he is unimpressionable. Great reputations are made in great cities, and it is there that heart and mind are more or less fatigued. A first impression, warped in this way, may often become final; for if it be true that valuable works should be re-read, and are only appreciated with time, it is also true that at the present time very few books are read at all. Supposing, however, the most favorable case: supposing that a writer, through the suffrage of a few of his contemporaries, is certain of descending to posterity as a great man,—what is a great man? Simply a name, which in a short time will represent nothing. The opinion of the beautiful changes with the days, and literary reputations are at the mercy of their variations; as to scientific works, they are invariably surpassed or forgotten. Nowadays, any second-rate mathematician knows more than Galileo or Newton." Genius, then, is a sinister gift, and its attendant glory but a vain and empty shadow.

The life of Leopardi, as told by his biographers, is poetically suggestive of the story of the pale Armide, who burned the palace that enchanted her; and the similarity becomes still more noticeable when he is found hacking and hewing at the illusion of love. Personally considered, Leopardi was not attractive; he was undersized, slightly deformed, near-sighted, prematurely bald, nervous, and weak; and though physical disadvantages are often disregarded by women, and not infrequently inspire a compassion which, properly tended, may warm into love, yet when the body, weak and infirm as was his, encases the strength and lurid vitality of genius, the unlovable monstrosity is complete. Indeed, in this respect, it may be noted that while the love of a delicate-minded woman for a coarse and stupid ruffian is an anomaly of daily repetition, there are yet few instances in which genius, even when strong of limb, has succeeded in inspiring a great and enduring affection.

Against Leopardi, then, the house of love was doubly barred. When he was about nineteen, he watched the usual young girl who lives over the way, and with a *naïveté* which seems exquisitely pathetic he made no sign, but simply watched and loved. The young lady does not appear to have been in any way conscious of the mutely shy adoration which her beauty had fanned into flame, and at any rate paid no attention to the sickly dwarf across the street. She sat very placidly at her window, or else fluttered about the room humming some old-fashioned air. This went on for a year or more, until finally she was carried away in a rumbling coach, to become the willing bride of another.

This, of course, was very terrible to Leopardi. Through some inductive process, which ought to have been brought about by the electric currents which he was establishing from behind the curtain, he had in his lawless fancy made quite sure that his love would sooner or later be felt and reciprocated. When, therefore, from his hiding place he saw the bride depart in maiden ignorance of her conquest, and entirely unconscious of the sonnets which had been written in her praise, the poet's one sweet hope faded slowly with her.

This pure and sedate affection remained vibrant in his memory for many years, and formed the theme of so many reveries and songs that love finally appeared to him as but another form of suffering. In after life, when much of the luster of youthful candor had become dull and tarnished, he besieged the heart of another lady, but this time in a bolder and more enterprising fashion. His suit, however, was unsuccessful. It may be that he was too eloquent; for eloquence is rarely captivating save to the inexperienced, and the man who makes love in rounded phrases seems to the practiced eye to be more artistic than sincere. At all events, his affection was not returned. The phantom had passed very close, but all he had clutched was the air. He was soon conscious, however, that he had made that mistake which is common to all imaginative people: it was not the woman he loved, it was beauty; not woman herself, but the ideal. It was a conception that he had fallen in love with; a conception which the woman, like so many others, had the power to inspire, and yet lacked the ability to understand. This time Leopardi was done with love, and forthwith attacked it as the last, yet most tenacious, of all illusions. "It is," he said, "an error like the others, but one which is more deeply rooted, because, when all else is gone, men think they clutch therein the last shadow of departing happiness. *Error beato,*" he adds, and so it may be, yet is he not well answered by that sage saying of Voltaire, "*L'erreur aussi a son mérite*"?

It was in this way that Leopardi devastated the palace from whose feasts he had been excluded. At every step he had taken he had left some hope behind; he had been dying piecemeal all his life; he was confessedly miserable, and this not alone on account of his poverty and wretched health, but chiefly because of his lack of harmony with the realities of existence. The world was to him the worst one possible, and he would have been glad to adorn the gate of life with the simplicity of Dante's insistent line,—

"*Lasciate ogni speranza voi ch'entrate.*"

"There was a time," he said, "when I envied the ignorant and those who thought well of themselves. Today, I envy neither the ignorant nor the wise, neither the great nor the weak; I envy the dead, and I would only change with them."

This, of course, was purely personal. Toward the close of his life he recognized that his judgment had been in a measure warped by the peculiar misfortunes of his own position, but in so doing he seemed almost to be depriving himself of a last, if sad, consolation. Nor did he ever wholly recant, and it is in the conception of the universality of misery which stamped all his writings, and which, even had he wished, he was then power-less to alter, that his relation to the theoretic pessimism of today chiefly rests.

As a creed, the birthplace of pessimism is to be sought on the banks of the Ganges, or far back in the flower-lands of Nepaul, where the initiate, with every desire lulled, awaits Nirvana, and murmurs only, "Life is evil."

Now, as is well known, in every religion there is a certain metaphysical basis which is designed to supply an answer to man's first question; for while the animal lives in undismayed repose, man of all created things alone marvels at his own ex-istence and at the destruction of his fellows. To his first ques-tion, then, What is life and death? each system attempts to offer a perfect reply; indeed, the temples, cathedrals, and pagodas clearly attest that man at all times and in all lands has contin-ually demanded that some reply should be given, and it is per-haps for this very reason that where other beliefs have found fervent adherents, neither materialism nor skepticism have been ever able to acquire a durable influence. It is, however, curious to note that in attempting the answer, nearly every creed has given an unfavorable interpretation to life. Aside from the glorious lessons of Christianity, its teaching, in brief, is that the world is a vale of tears, that nothing here can yield any real satisfaction, and that happiness, which is not for mortals, is solely the recompense of the ransomed soul. To the Brahmin, while there is always the hope of absorption in the Universal Spirit, life meanwhile is a regrettable accident. But in Buddhism, which is perhaps the most naïve and yet the most sublime of all religions, and which through its very combination of simplicity and grandeur appeals to a larger number of adherents than any other, pessimism is the beginning, as it is the end.

To the Buddhist there is reality neither in the future nor in the past. To him true knowledge consists in the perception of the nothingness of all things, in the consciousness of—

> "The vastness of the agony of earth,
> The vainness of its joys, the mockery
> Of all its best, the anguish of its worst;"

and in the desire to escape from the evil of existence into the entire affranchisement of the intelligence. To the Buddhist,—

> ..."Sorrow is
> Shadow to life, moving where life doth move."

The Buddhist believes that the soul migrates until Nirvana is attained, and that in the preparation for this state, which is the death of Death, the nothingness of a flame extinguished, there are four degrees. In the first, the novitiate learns to be implacable to himself, yet charitable and compassionate to others. He then acquires an understanding into the nature of all things, until he has suppressed every desire save that of attaining Nirvana, when he passes initiate into the second degree, in which judgment ceases. In the next stage, the vague sentiment of satisfaction, which had been derived from intellectual perfection, is lost, and in the last, the confused consciousness of identity disappears. It is at this point that Nirvana begins, but only begins and stretches to vertiginous heights through four higher degrees of ecstasy, of which the first is the region of infinity in space, the next, the realm of infinity in intelligence, then the sphere in which nothing is, and, finally, the loss of even the perception of nothing. When Death is dead, when all have attained Nirvana, then, according to the Buddhist, the universe will rock forevermore in unconscious rest.

In brief, then, life to the Christian is a probation, to the Brahmin a burden, to the Buddhist a dream, and to the pessimist a nightmare.

CHAPTER TWO.

The High Priest of Pessimism.

ARTHUR SCHOPENHAUER, THE FOUNDER OF THE PRESENT school, was born toward the close of the last century, in the now mildewed city of Dantzic. His people came of good Dutch stock, and were both well-to-do and peculiar. His grandmother lost her reason at the death of her husband, a circumstance as unusual then as in more recent years; his two uncles passed their melancholy lives on the frontiers of insanity, and his father enjoyed a reputation for eccentricity which his end fully justified.

This latter gentleman was a rich and energetic merchant, of educated tastes and excitable disposition, who, when well advanced in middle life, married the young and gifted daughter of one of the chief magnates of the town. Their union was not more unhappy than is usually the case under similar circumstances, his time being generally passed with his ledger, and hers with the poets.

With increasing years, however, his untamable petulance grew to such an extent that he was not at all times considered perfectly sane, and it is related that on being visited one day by a lifelong acquaintance, who announced himself as an old friend, he exclaimed, with abrupt indignation, "Friend, indeed! there is no such thing; besides, people come here every day and say they are this, that, and the other. I don't know them, and I don't want to." A day or two later, he met the same individual, greeted him with cheerful cordiality, and led him amiably home to dinner. Shortly after, he threw himself from his warehouse to the canal below.

He had always intended that his son, who was then in his sixteenth year, should continue the business; and to prepare him properly for his duties he had christened him Arthur, because he found that name was pretty much the same in all European languages, and furthermore had sent the lad at an early age first to France, and then to England, that he might gain some acquaintance and familiarity with other tongues.

The boy liked his name, and took naturally to languages, but he felt no desire to utilize these possessions in the depressing atmosphere of commercial life, and after his father's death loitered first at the benches of Gotha and then at those of Göttingen.

Meanwhile his mother established herself at Weimar, where she soon attracted to her all that was brilliant in that brilliant city. Goethe, Wieland, Fernow, Falk, Grimm, and the two Schlegels were her constant guests. At court she was received as a welcome addition, and such an effect had these surroundings upon her imagination, that in not very many years she managed to produce twenty-four compact volumes of criticism and romance.

During this time her son was not idle. Thoroughly familiar with ancient as with modern literature, he devoted his first year at Göttingen to medicine, mathematics and history; while in his second, which he passed in company with Bunsen and William B. Astor, he studied physics, physiology, psychology, ethnology and logic; as these diversions did not quite fill the hour, he aided the flight of idle moments with a guitar.

He was at this time a singularly good-looking young man, possessing a grave and expressive type of beauty, which in after years developed into that suggestion of majestic calm for which the head of Beethoven is celebrated, while to his lips there then came a smile as relentlessly implacable as that of Voltaire.

From boyhood he had been of a thoughtful disposition, finding wisdom in the falling leaf, problems in vibrating light, and movement in immobility. Already he had wrung his hands at the stars, and watched the distant future rise with its flouting jeer at the ills of man. In this, however, there was little of the cheap sentimentalism of Byron, and less of the weariness of Lamartine. His griefs were purely objective; life to him was a perplexing riddle, whose true meaning was well worth a search; and as the only possible solution of the gigantic enigma seemed to lie in some unexplored depth of metaphysics, he soon after betook himself to Berlin, where Fichte then reigned as Kant's legitimate successor. But the long-winded demonstrations that Fichte affected, his tiresome verbiage, lit, if at all, only by some trivial truism or trumpery paradox, bored Schopenhauer at first well-nigh to death, and then worked on his nerves to such an extent that he longed, pistol in hand, to catch at his throat, and cry, "Die like a dog you shall; but for your pitiful soul's sake, tell me if in all this rubbish you really mean anything, or take me simply for an imbecile like yourself." For Schopenhauer, it should be understood, had passed his nights first with Plato and then with Kant; they were to him like two giants calling to one another across the centuries, and that this huckster of phrases should pretend to cloak his nakedness with their mantle seemed to him at once indecent and absurd.

Schelling pleased him no better; he dismissed him with a word,—mountebank; but for Hegel, Caliban-Hegel as he was wont in after years to call him, his contempt was so violent that, with a prudence which is both amusing and characteristic, he took counsel from an attorney as to the exact limit he might touch in abusing him without becoming amenable to a suit for defamation. "Hegel's philosophy," he said, "is a crystallized syllogism; it is an abracadabra, a puff of bombast, and a wishwash of phrases, which in its monstrous construction compels the mind to form impossible contradictions, and in itself is enough to cause an entire atrophy of the intellect." "It is made up of three fourths nonsense and one fourth error; it contains words, not thoughts;" and then, rising in his indignation to the heights of quotation, he added, "'Such stuff as madmen tongue and brain not.'" Time, it may be noted, has to a great extent indorsed Schopenhauer's verdict. The tortures of Fichte, Schelling, and Hegel linger now in the history of philosophy very much as might the memory of a nightmare, and except in a few cobwebbed halls the teachings of the three sophists may safely be considered as a part of the inexplicable past.

It should not, however, be supposed that because he found the philosophy of the moment so little to his taste he necessarily squandered his time; on the contrary, he turned to Aristotle and Spinoza for consolation, and therewith followed sundry lectures in magnetism, electricity, ichthyology, amphiology, ornithology, zoölogy, and astronomy, all of which he enlivened with rapid incursions to the rich granaries of Rabelais and Montaigne, and moreover gave no little time to the study of the religion and philosophy of India.

It was at this time characteristic of the man, that while his appearance, wealth, and connections would have formed an open letter to the best society in Berlin, which was then heterogeneously agreeable, or even to the worst, which is said to have been charming, he preferred to pass his leisure hours in scrutinizing the animals in the Zoölogical Gardens, and in studying the inmates of the State Lunatic Asylum.

In this *cità dolente* his attention was particularly claimed by two unfortunates who, while perfectly conscious of their infirmity, were yet unable to master it; in proof of which, one wrote him a series of sonnets, and the other sent him annotated passages from the Bible.

In the second year of his student life at Berlin the war of 1813 was declared, and Schopenhauer was in consequence obliged to leave the city before he had obtained his degree. He prepared, however, and forwarded to the faculty at Jena an elaborate thesis, which he entitled the "Quadruple Root of Conclusive Reason,"—a name which somewhat astounded his mother, who asked him if it were something for the apothecary,—and meanwhile prowled about Weimar meditating on the philosophy which he had long intended to produce. He visited no one but Goethe, took umbrage at his mother's probably harmless relations with Fernow, treated her to discourse not dissimilar to that which Hamlet had addressed to his own parent, received his degree from Jena, and then went off to Dresden, where he began to study women with that microscopic eye which he turned on all subjects that engaged his attention.

The result of these studies was an essay on the metaphysics of love, which he thereupon attached to his budding system of philosophy; an axiom to the effect that women are rich in hair and poor in thought; and the same misadventure that befell Descartes.

His life at Dresden was necessarily much less secluded than that to which he had been hitherto accustomed; he became an *habitué* at the opera and comedy, a frequent guest in literary and social circles, and, as student of men and things, he went about disturbing draperies and disarranging screens, very much as any other philosopher might do who was bent on seeing the world.

Meanwhile, he was not otherwise idle: the morning he gave to work, and in the afternoon he surrendered himself to Nature, whom he loved with a passionate devotion, which increased with his years. The companionship of men was always more or less irksome to him; and while it was less so perhaps at this time than at any other, it was nevertheless with a sense of relief that he struck out across the inviting pasture-lands of Saxony, or down the banks of the Elbe, and left humanity behind, in search of that open-air solitude which is Nature's nearest friend.

In the companionship of others he was constantly seeking a trait or a suggestion, some hint capable of development; when in the world, therefore, he flashed a lantern, so to speak, at people, and then passed them by; but in the open country he communed with himself, and strolled along, note-book in hand, jotting down the thoughts worth jotting very much after the manner that Emerson is said to have recommended.

With regard to the majority of men, it will not seem reckless to say that their end and aim is happiness and self-satisfaction; but however trite the remark may be, it may still perhaps serve to bring into relief something of Schopenhauer's distinctive purpose. It would, of course, be foolish to assert that he did not care for his own happiness, and disregarded his own satisfaction, for of these things few men, it is imagined, have thought more highly. If his ideas of happiness diverged widely from those generally received as standards, it has but little to do with the matter in hand, for the point which is intended to be conveyed is simply that above all other things, beyond the culture of self, that which Schopenhauer cared for most was truth, and that he pursued it, moreover, as pertinaciously as any other thinker whom the world now honors. Whether he ran it to earth or not, the reader must himself decide; indeed, it was very many years before any one even heard that he had been chasing it at all. Of late, however, some of the best pickets who guard the literary outposts from Boston to Bombay have brought a very positive assurance that he did catch it, and, moreover, held it fast long enough to wring out some singularly valuable intimations.

In hurrying along after his quarry, Schopenhauer became convinced that life was a lesson which most men learned trippingly enough, but whose moral they failed to detect; and this moral, which he felt he had caught on the wing, as it were, he set about dissecting with a great and sumptuous variety of reflection.

Wandering, then, on the banks of the Elbe, massing his thoughts and arranging their progression, his system slowly yet gradually expanded before him. He wrote only in moments of inspiration, yet his hours were full of such moments; little by little he drifted away from the opera and his friends into a solitude which he made populous with thought, and in this manner gave himself up so entirely to his philosophy that one day, it is reported, he astonished an innocent-minded gate-keeper, who asked him who he was, with the weird and pensive answer, "Ah! if I but knew, myself!"

Meanwhile his work grew rapidly beneath his hands, and when after four years of labor and research *Die Welt als Wille und Vorstellung* was so far completed as to permit its publication, he read it over with something of the same unfamiliarity which he would have experienced in reading the work of another author, though, doubtless, with greater satisfaction.

Fascinated with its merits, he offered the manuscript to Brockhaus, the Leipsic publisher. "My book," he wrote, "is a new system of philosophy, but when I say new I mean new in every sense of the word; it is not a restatement of what has been already expressed, but it is in the highest degree a continuous flow of thought such as has never before entered the mind of mortal man. It is a book which, in my opinion, is destined to rank with those which form the source and incentive to hundreds of others."

Brockhaus, familiar with the proverbial modesty of young

authors, lent but an inattentive ear to these alluring statements, and accepted the book solely on account of the reputation which Schopenhauer's mother then enjoyed; a mark of confidence, by the way, which he soon deeply regretted. "It is so much waste paper," he said, dismally, in after years; "I wish I had never heard of it." He lived long enough, however, to change his mind, and in 1880 his successors published a stout little pamphlet containing the titles of over five hundred books and articles, of which the *World as Will and Idea* formed the source and incentive. "*Le monde,*" Montaigne has quaintly noted, "*regorge de commentaires, mais d'auteurs il en est grand chierté.*"

Schopenhauer's philosophy first appeared in 1818; but while it was still in press, its author, like one who has sprung a mine and fears the report, fled away to Italy, where he wandered about from Venice to Naples bathing his senses in color and music. He associated at this time very willingly with Englishmen, and especially with English artists and men of letters. Germans and Americans he avoided, and as for Jews, he not only detested them, but expressed an admiring approval of Nebuchadnezzar, and only regretted that he had been so lenient with them. "The Jews are God's chosen people, are they?" he would say, "very good; tastes differ, they certainly are not mine." In this dislike he made no exception, and scenting in after years some of the *fœtor judaicus* on Heine and Meyerbeer, he refused them the attention which others were only too glad to accord. Schopenhauer's distaste, however, for everything that savored of the Israelite will be perhaps more readily understood when it is remembered that the Jews, as a race, are optimists, and their creed, therefore, to him, in his consistency, was like the aggressive flag to the typical bull.

With the Germans he had another grievance. "The Germans," he said, "are heavy by nature; it is a national characteristic, and one which is noticeable not only in the way they carry themselves, but in their language, their fiction, their conversation, their writings, their way of thinking, and especially in their style and in their mania for constructing long and involved sentences. In reading German," he continued, "memory is obliged to retain mechanically, as in a lesson, the words that are forced upon it, until after patient labor a period is reached, the keynote is found, and the meaning disentangled. When the Germans," he added, "get hold of a vague and unsuitable expression which will completely obscure their meaning, they pat themselves on the back; for their great aim is to leave an opening in every phrase, through which they may seem to come back and say more than they thought. In this trick they excel, and if they can manage to be emphatic and affected at the same time, they are simply afloat in a sea of joy. Foreigners hate all this, and revenge themselves in reading German as little as possible.... Wherefore, in provision of my death, I acknowledge that on account of its infinite stupidity I loathe the German nation, and that I blush to belong thereto."

At various *tables-d'hôte* Schopenhauer had encountered traveling Yankees, and objected to them accordingly. "They are," he said, "the *plebs* of the world, partly, I suppose, on account of their republican government, and partly because they descend from those who left Europe for Europe's good. The climate, too," he added, reflectively, "may have something to do with it." Nor did Frenchmen escape his satire. "Other parts of the world have monkeys; Europe has Frenchmen, *ça balance*."

But with Englishmen he got on very well, and during his after life always talked to himself in their tongue, wrote his memoranda in English, and read the "Times" daily, advertisements and all.

Meanwhile Schopenhauer held his hand to his ear unavailingly. From across the Alps there came to him no echo of any report, only a silence which was ominous enough to have assured any other that the fusee had not been properly applied. But to him it was different; he had, it is true, expected a reverberation which would shake the sophistry of all civilization, and when no tremor came he was mystified, but only for the moment. He had been too much accustomed to seek his own dead in the great morgue of literature not to know that any man, who is to belong to posterity, is necessarily a stranger to his epoch. And that he was to belong to posterity he had no possible doubt; indeed he had that prescience of genius which foresees its own future, and he felt that however tightly the bushel might be closed over the light, there were still crevices through which it yet would shine, and from which at last some conflagration must necessarily burst.

It was part of the man to analyze all things, and while it cannot be said that the lack of attention with which his philosophy had been received left him entirely unmoved, it would be incorrect to suppose that he was then sitting on the pins and needles of impatience.

Deeply reflective, he was naturally aware that as everything which is exquisite ripens slowly, so is the growth of fame proportioned to its durability. And Schopenhauer meant to be famous, and this not so much for fame's sake, as for the good which his fame would spread with it. He could therefore well afford to wait. His work was not written especially to his own epoch, save only in so far as his epoch was part of humanity collectively considered. It did not, therefore, take him long to understand that as his work was not tinted with any of the local color and fugitive caprices of the moment, it was in consequence unadapted to an immediate and fictitious vogue. Indeed, it may be added that the history of art and literature is eloquent with the examples of the masterpieces which, unrewarded by contemporary appreciation, have passed into the welcome of another age; and of these examples few are more striking than that of the absolute indifference with which Schopenhauer's philosophy was first received.

It was presumably with reflections of this nature that Schopenhauer shrugged his shoulders at the inattention under which he labored, and wandered serenely among the treasuries and ghosts of departed Rome.

About this time an incident happened which, while not possessing any very vivid interest, so affected his after life as to be at least deserving of passing notice. Schopenhauer was then in his thirty-first year. On coming of age, he had received his share of his father's property, some of which he securely invested, but the greater part he deposited at high interest with a well-known business house in Dantzic. When leaving for Italy, he took from this firm notes payable on demand for the amount which they held to his credit, and after he had cashed one of their bills, learned that the firm was in difficulties. Shortly after, they suspended payment, offering thirty per cent. to those of their creditors who were willing to accept such an arrangement, and nothing to those who refused.

All the creditors accepted save Schopenhauer, who, with the wile of a diplomat, wrote that he was in no hurry for his money, but that perhaps if he were made preferred creditor he might accept a better offer. His debtors fell into the trap, and offered him first fifty, and then seventy per cent. These offers he also refused. "If," he wrote, "you offer me thirty per cent. when you are able to pay fifty, and fifty per cent. when you are able to pay seventy, I have good reason to suspect that you can pay the whole amount. In any event, my right is perennial. I need not present my notes until I care to. Settle with your other creditors, and then you will be in a better position to attend to me. A wise man watches the burning phœnix with a certain pleasure, for he well knows what that crafty bird does with its ashes. Keep my money, and I will keep your drafts. When your affairs are straightened either we will exchange, or you will be arrested for debt. I am, of course, very sorry not to be able to oblige you, and I dare say you think me very disagreeable, but that is only an illusion of yours, which is at once dispelled when you remember that the money is my own, and that its possession concerns my lifelong freedom and well-being. You will say, perhaps, that if all your creditors thought as I do, it would be deuced hard for me. But if all men thought as I do, not only would more be thought, but there would probably be neither bankrupts nor swindlers. Machiavelli says, *Giacchè il volgo pensa altrimente*,—although the common herd think otherwise,—*ma nel mondo non é se non volgo*,—and the world is made up of the common herd,—*e gli pocchi ivi luogo trovano*,—yet the exceptions take their position,—*dove gli molti stare non possono*,—where the crowd can find no foot-hold."

By the exercise of a little patience, and after a few more dagger thrusts of this description, Schopenhauer recovered the entire amount which was due him, together with the interest in full. But the danger which he had so cleverly avoided gave him, so to speak, a retrospective shock; the possibility of want had brushed too near for comfort's sake. He was thoroughly frightened; and in shuddering at the cause of his fright he experienced such a feeling of insecurity with regard to what the future might yet hold that he determined to lose no time in seeking a remunerative shelter. With this object he returned to Berlin, and as *privat-docent* began to lecture on the history of philosophy.

Hegel was then in the high tide of his glory. Scholars from far and near came to listen to the man who had compared himself to Christ, and said, "I am Truth, and teach truth." In the *Reisebilder*, Heine says that in the learned caravansary of Berlin the camels collected about the fountain of Hegelian wisdom, kneeled down, received their burden of precious waters, and then set out across the desert wastes of Brandenburg.

At that time not to bend before Hegel was the blackest and most wanton of sins. To disagree with him was heretical, and as few understood his meaning clearly enough to attempt to controvert it, it will be readily understood that in those days there was very little heresy in Berlin.

Among the few, however, Schopenhauer headed the list. "I write to be understood," he said; and indeed no one who came in contact with him or with his works had ever the least difficulty in seizing his meaning and understanding his immense disgust for the "pachyderm hydrocephali, pedantic eunuchs, apocaliptic retinue *della bestia triumphante*," as in after years, with gorgeous emphasis, he was wont to designate Hegel and his clique. The war that he waged against them was truly Homeric. He denounced Hegel in a manner that would have made Swinburne blush; then he attacked the professors of philosophy in general and the Hegelians in particular, and finally the demagogues who believed in them, and who had baptized themselves "Young Germany."

For the preparation of such writings as theirs he had a receipt, which was homeopathic in its simplicity. "Dilute a minimum of thought in five hundred pages of nauseous phraseology, and for the rest trust to the German patience of the reader." He also suggested that for the wonder and astonishment of posterity every public library should carefully preserve in half calf the complete works of the great philosophaster and his adorers; and, considering very correctly that philosophers cannot be hatched like bachelors of arts, he further recommended that the course in philosophy should be cut from the University programmes, and the teaching in that branch be limited to logic. "You can't write an *Iliad*," he said, "when your mother is a dolt, and your father is a cotton nightcap."

There are few debts which are so faithfully acquitted as those of contempt; and as Schopenhauer kicked down every screen, tore off every mask, and jeered at every sham, it would be a great stretch of fancy to imagine that he was a popular teacher. But this at least may be said: he was courageous, and he was strong of purpose. In the end, he dragged Germany from her lethargy, and rather than take any other part in Hegelism than that of spectre at the feast, he condemned himself to an almost life-long obscurity. If, therefore, he seems at times too bitter and too relentless, it should be remembered that this man, whom Germany now honors as one of her greatest philosophers, fought single-handed for thirty years, and routed the enemy at last by the mere force and lash of his words.

But in the mean time, while Hegel was holding forth to crowded halls, his rival, who, out of sheer bravado, had chosen the same hours, lectured to an audience of about half a dozen persons, among whom a dentist, a horse-jockey, and a captain on half pay were the more noteworthy. Such listeners were hardly calculated to make him frantically attached to the calling he had chosen, and accordingly at the end of the first semester he left the empty benches to take care of themselves.

Early in life Schopenhauer wrote in English, in his note-book, "Matrimony—war and want!" and when the *privat-docent* had been decently buried, and the crape grown rusty, he began to consider this little sentence with much attention. As will be seen later on, he objected to women as a class on purely logical grounds,—they interfered with his plan of delivering the world from suffering; but against the individual he had no marked dislike, only a few pleasing epigrams. During his Dresden sojourn, as in his journey to Italy, he had knelt, in his quality of philosopher who was seeing the world, at many and diverse shrines, and had in no sense wandered from them sorrow-laureled; but all that had been very different from assuming legal responsibilities, and whenever he thought with favor of the *petits soins* of which, as married man, he would be the object, the phantom of a milliner's bill loomed in double columns before him.

Should he or should he not, he queried, fall into the trap which nature has set for all men? The question of love did not enter into the matter at all. He believed in love as most well-read people believe in William Tell; that is, as something very inspiring, especially when treated by Rossini, but otherwise as a myth. Nor did he need Montaigne's hint to be assured that men marry for others and not for themselves. The subject, therefore, was somewhat complex: on the one side stood the attention and admiration which he craved, and on the other an eternal farewell to that untrammeled freedom which is the thinker's natural heath.

The die, however, had to be cast then or never. He was getting on in life, and an opportunity had at that time presented itself, a repetition of which seemed unlikely. After much reflection, and much weighing of the pros and cons, he concluded that it is the married man who supports the full burden of life, while the bachelor bears but half, and it is to the latter class, he argued, that the courtesan of the muses should belong. Thereupon, with a luxury of reminiscence and quotation which was usual to him at all times, he strengthened his resolution with mental foot-notes, to the effect that Descartes, Leibnitz, Malebranche, and Kant were bachelors, the great poets uniformly married and uniformly unhappy; and supported it all with Bacon's statement that "he that hath wife and children has given hostages to fortune, for they are impediments to great enterprises, either of virtue or of mischief."

In 1831 the cholera appeared in Berlin, and Schopenhauer, who called himself a choleraphobe by profession, fled before it in search of a milder and healthier climate. Frankfort he chose for his hermitage, and from that time up to the day of his death, which occurred in September, 1860, he continued to live there in great peace and tranquility.

Schopenhauer should in no wise be represented as having passed his life in building dungeons in Spain. Like every true scholar he was, in the absence of his peers, able to live with great comfort with the dead. He was something of a Mezzofanti; he spoke and read half a dozen languages with perfect ease, and he could in consequence enter any library with the certainty of finding friends and relations therein. For the companionship of others he did not care a rap. He was never so lonely as when associating with other people, and of all things that he disliked the most, and a catalogue of his dislikes would fill a chapter, the so-called entertainment headed the obnoxious list.

He had taken off, one by one, the different layers of the social nut, and in nibbling at the kernel he found its insipidity so great that he had small approval for those who made it part of their ordinary diet. It should not, however, be supposed that this dislike for society and the companionship of others sprang from any of that necessity for solitude which is noticeable in certain cases of hypochondria; it was simply due to the fact that he could not, in the general run of men, find any one with whom he could associate on a footing of equality. If Voltaire, Helvetius, Kant, or Cabanais, or, for that matter, any one possessed of original thoughts, had dwelled in the neighborhood, Schopenhauer, once in a while, would have delighted in supping with them; but as agreeable symposiasts were infrequent, he was of necessity thrown entirely on his own resources. His history, in brief, is that of the malediction under which king and genius labor equally. Both are condemned to solitude; and for solitude such as theirs there is neither chart nor compass. Of course there are many other men who in modern times have also led lives of great seclusion, but in this respect it may confidently be stated that no thinker of recent years, Thoreau not excepted, has ever lived in isolation more thorough and complete than that which was enjoyed by this blithe misanthrope.

It is not as though he had betaken himself to an unfrequented waste, or to the top of an inaccessible crag; such behavior would have savored of an affectation of which he was incapable, and, moreover, would have told its story of an inability to otherwise resist the charms of society. Besides, Schopenhauer was no anchorite; he lived very comfortably in the heart of a populous and pleasant city, and dined daily at the best *table d'hôte*, but he lived and dined utterly alone.

He considered that, as a rule, a man is never in perfect harmony save with himself, for, he argued, however tenderly a friend or mistress may be beloved, there is at times some clash and discord. Perfect tranquility, he said, is found only in solitude, and to be permanent only in absolute seclusion; and he insisted that the hermit, if intellectually rich, enjoys the happiest condition which this life can offer. The love of solitude, however, can hardly be said to exist in any one as a natural instinct; on the contrary, it may be regarded as an acquired taste, and one which must be developed in indirect progression. Schopenhauer, who cultivated it to its most supreme expression, admitted that at first he had many fierce struggles with the natural instinct of sociability, and at times had strenuously combated some such Mephistophelian suggestion as,—

> "*Hör' auf, mit deinem Gram zu spielen,*
> *Der, wie ein Geier, dir am Leben frisst:*
> *Die schlechteste Gesellschaft lässt dich fühlen*
> *Dass du ein Mensch, mit Menschen bist.*"

But solitude, more or less rigid, is undoubtedly the lot of all superior minds. They may grieve over it, as Schopenhauer says, but of two evils they will choose it as the least. After that, it is presumably but a question of getting acclimated. In old age the inclination comes, he notes, almost of itself. At sixty it is well-nigh instinctive; at that age everything is in its favor. The incentives which are the most energetic in behalf of sociability then no longer act. With advancing years there arises a capacity of sufficing to one's self, which little by little absorbs the social instinct. Illusions then have faded, and, ordinarily speaking, active life has ceased. There is nothing more to be expected, there are no plans nor projects to form, the generation to which old age really belongs has passed away, and, surrounded by a new race, one is then objectively and essentially alone.

Then, too, many things are clearly seen, which before were as veiled by a mist. As the result of long experience very little is expected from the majority of people, and the conclusion is generally reached that not only men do not improve on acquaintance, but that mankind is made up of very defective copies, with which it is best to have as little to do as possible.

But beyond converting his life into a monodrama with reflections of this description, Schopenhauer considered himself to be a missionary of truth, and in consequence as little fitted for every-day companionship as missionaries in China feel themselves called upon to fraternize with the Chinese. It was the rule of his life to expect nothing, desire as little as possible, and learn all he could, and as little was to be expected and nothing was to be learned from the majority of the dull ruffians who go to the making of the census, it is not to be wondered that he trod the thoroughfares of thought alone and dismissed the majority of men with a shrug.

"They are," he said, "just what they seem to be, and that is the worst that can be said of them." Epigrams of this description were naturally not apt to increase his popularity. But for that he cared very little. He considered that no man can judge another save by the measure of his own understanding. Of course, if this understanding is of a low degree, the greatest intellectual gifts which another may possess convey to him no meaning; they are as colors to the blind; and consequently, in a great nature there will be noticed only those defects and weaknesses which are inseparable from every character.

But to such a man as Schopenhauer,—one who considered five sixths of the population to be knaves or blockheads, and who had thought out a system for the remaining fraction,—to such a man as he, the question of esteem, or the lack thereof, was of small consequence. He cared nothing for the existence which he led in the minds of other people. To his own self he was true, to the calling of his destiny constant, and he felt that he could sit and snap his fingers at the world, knowing that Time, who is at least a gentleman, would bring him his due unasked.

Schopenhauer's character was made up of that combination of seeming contradictions which is the peculiarity of all great men. He had the audacity of childhood and the timidity of genius. He was suspicious of every one, and ineffably kind-hearted. With stupidity in any form he was blunt, even to violence, and yet his manner and courtesy were such as is attributed to the gentlemen of the old school. If he was an egotist, he was also charitable to excess; and who shall say that charity is not the egotism of great natures? He was honesty itself, and yet thought every one wished to cheat him. To mislead a possible thief he labeled his valuables Arcana Medica, put his banknotes in dictionaries, and his gold pieces in ink bottles. He slept on the ground floor, that he might escape easily in case of fire. If he heard a noise at night he snatched at a pistol, which he kept loaded at his bedside. Indeed, he might have chosen for his motto, *"Je ne crains rien fors le dangier,"* and yet who is ever so foolish as a wise man? Kant's biography is full of similar vagaries, and one has but to turn to the history of any of the thinkers whose names are landmarks in literature, to find that eccentricities no less striking have also been recorded of them.

Voltaire said, *"On aime la vie, mais le néant ne laisse pas d'avoir du bon;*" and Schopenhauer, not to be outdone, added more massively, that if one could tap on the tombs and ask the dead if they cared to return, they would shake their heads. His views of life, however, and of the world in general, will be considered later on, and for the moment it is but necessary to note that he regarded happiness as consisting solely in the absence of pain, and laid down as one of the supreme rules for the proper conduct of life that discontent should be banished as far as possible into the outer darkness.

When, therefore, to this Emerson in black there came those moments of restlessness and dissatisfaction which visit even the most philosophic, he would argue with himself in a way which was almost pathetic, and certainly naïve; it was not he that was moody and out of sorts, it was some *privat-docent* lecturing to empty halls, some one who was abused by the Philistines, some defendant in a suit for damages, some one whose fortune was engulfed perhaps beyond recovery, some lover pleading to inattentive ears, some one attacked by one of the thousand ills that flesh is heir to; yet this was not he; these things truly he might have endured and suffered as one bears for a moment an ill-made shoe, but now the foot no longer ached; indeed, he was none of all this, he was the author of the *Welt als Wille und Vorstellung*, and what had the days to do with him!

But through all the intervening years the book had lain unnoticed on the back shelves of the Leipsic publisher; and Schopenhauer, who had at first been puzzled, but never disheartened, at the silence which had settled about it, became convinced that through the influence of the three sophists at Berlin, all mention of its merit had been suppressed from the start.

"I am," he said, "the Iron Mask, the Caspar Hauser of philosophy," and thereupon he pictured the Hegelians as looking admiringly at his system, very much as the man in the fairy tale looked at the genie in the bottle which, had he allowed it to come out, would carry him off. Truth, however, which is long-lived, can always afford to wait; and Schopenhauer, with something of the complacency of genius that is in advance of its era, held his fingers on the public pulse and noted the quickening which precedes a return to consciousness. Germany was waking from her torpor. Already the influence of Hegel had begun to wane; his school was split into factions, and his philosophy, which in solving every problem had left the world nothing to do but to bore itself to death, was slowly falling into disrepute. Moreover, the great class of unattached scholars and independent thinkers, who cared as little for University dogmas as they did for the threats of the Vatican, were earnestly watching for some new teacher.

Schopenhauer was watching too; he knew that a change was coming, and that he would come in with the change. He had but to wait. "My extreme unction," he said, "will be my baptism; my death, a canonization."

Meanwhile old age had come upon him unawares, but with it the rich fruition of lifelong study and reflection. The perfect tranquility in which he passed his days had been utilized in strengthening and expanding his work, and in 1843, in his fifty-sixth year, the second and complementary volume of his philosophy was completed.

Twelve months later he wrote to Brockhaus, his publisher:—

"I may tell you in confidence that I am so well pleased with this second volume, now that I see it in print, that I really think it will be a great success.... If, now, in return for this great work, you are willing to do me a very little favor, and one that is easily performed, I will beg you each Easter to let me know how many copies have been sold."

For two years he heard nothing, then in answer to a letter from him, Brockhaus wrote:—

"In reply to your inquiry concerning the sale of your book,

I can only tell you that, to my sorrow, I have made a very poor business out of it. Further particulars I cannot enter into."

"Many a rose," Schopenhauer murmured, as he refolded the note and turned to other things.

In 1850, when, after six years' daily labor, he had completed his last work, *Parerga und Paralipomena*, his literary reputation was still so insignificant that Brockhaus refused to publish it. Schopenhauer then offered it, unavailingly, to half a dozen other publishers. No one would have anything to do with it; the name which it bore would have frightened a pirate, and the boldest in the guild was afraid to examine its contents. "One thing is certain," said Schopenhauer, reflectively, "I am unworthy of my contemporaries, or they of me." The *Parerga*, however, in spite of the lack of allurement in its title, was not destined to wither in manuscript. After much reconnoitering a publisher was discovered in Berlin who, unwillingly, consented to produce it, and thereupon two volumes of the most original and entertaining essays were given to the public. For this work Schopenhauer received ten copies in full payment.

Meanwhile a few adherents had rallied about him. Brockhaus, in an attempt to make the best of a bad bargain, had marked the "Welt" down to the lowest possible price, and a few copies had in consequence fallen into intelligent hands. Among its readers there were some who came to Frankfort to make the author's acquaintance; a proceeding which pleased, yet alarmed Schopenhauer not a little.

One of them wrote to people with whom he was unacquainted, advising them to read the work at once. "He is a fanatic," said Schopenhauer, in complacent allusion to him, "a fanatic, that's what he is."

Dr. Gwinner, his subsequent biographer, whom he met about this time, was his apostle, while Dr. Frauenstadt, another Boswell, whose acquaintance he made at *table d'hôte*, he called his arch-evangelist, and, not without pathos, repeated to him Byron's seductive lines,—

> "In the desert a fountain is springing,
> In the white waste there still is a tree,
> And a bird in the solitude singing,
> That speaks to my spirit of thee."

These gentlemen, together with a few others, made up a little band of sturdy disciples, who went about wherever they could, speaking and writing of the merits of Schopenhauer's philosophy. But the first note of acclamation which, historically speaking, was destined to arouse the thinking world, came, curiously enough, from England.

In 1853 the "Westminster Review" published a long and laudatory article on Schopenhauer's philosophy; and this article Lindner, the editor of the *"Vossiche Zeitung,"* to whom Schopenhauer had given the title of *doctor indefatigabilis*, reproduced in his own journal. In the following year Dr. Frauenstadt published, in a well-written pamphlet* which only needed a little more order and symmetry to be a valuable handbook, a complete exposition of the doctrine; and the applause thus stimulated reëchoed all over Germany. The *Welt als Wille und Vorstellung*, the "World as Will and Idea," which for so many years had lain neglected, was dragged from its musty shelf like a Raphael from a lumber-room; and the fame to which Schopenhauer had not made a single step came to him as fame should, unsought and almost unbidden.

"My old age," he said, "is brighter now than most men's youth, for time has brought its roses at last; but see," he added, touching his silvered hair, "they are white."

From all sides now came evidences of the most cordial recognition. The reviews and weeklies published anecdotes about him and extracts from his works. Indeed, it was evident that the

---

* *Briefe über die Schopenhauer'sche Philosophie.*

Iron Mask had escaped, and that to Caspar Hauser light and air had at last been accorded. Thinkers, scholars, and philosophers, of all creeds and colors, became his attentive readers. Decorations were offered to him, which he unostentatiously refused. The Berlin Academy, within whose walls Hegel had reigned supreme, invited him to become one of its faculty. This honor he also declined. "They have turned their back on me all my life," he said, "and after my death they want my name to adorn their catalogues." His philosophy was lectured upon at Breslau, and the University of Leipsic offered it as a subject for a prize essay. All this was very pleasant. Much to his indignation, however, for he was by nature greatly disinclined to serve as pastime to an idle public, the *"Illustrirte Zeitung"* published his likeness, and added insult to injury by printing his name with two p's. Ah! how truly has it been said that fame consists in seeing one's name spelt wrong in the newspapers!

One of the most flattering manifestations of this sudden vogue was the curiosity of the public, the number of enthusiasts that visited him, and the eagerness with which artists sought to preserve his features for posterity. To all this concert of praise it is difficult to say that Schopenhauer lent a rebellious ear. The success of his philosophy of disenchantment enchanted him. He accepted with the seriousness of childhood the bouquets and sonnets which rained in upon him on his subsequent birthdays, and in his letters to Frauenstadt alluded to his ascending glory with innocent and amusing satisfaction:—

FRANKFORT, *September 23, 1854.*

...A fortnight ago, a Dr. K., a teacher, came to see me; he entered the room and looked so fixedly at me that I began to be frightened, and then he cried out, "I must look at you, I will look at you, I came to look at you." He was most enthusiastic. My philosophy, he told me, restored him to life. What next?...

June 29, 1855.

...B. called today; he had been here for twenty-four hours under an assumed name, and after many hesitations came in a closed carriage to pay his respects.... On taking leave, he kissed my hand. I screamed with fright....

August 17, 1855.

...My portrait, painted by Lunteschütz, is finished and sold. Wiesike saw it in time, and bought it while it was still on the easel. But the unheard-of part of the whole matter is that he told me, and Lunteschütz too, that he was going to build a temple on purpose for it. That will be the first chapel erected in my honor. Recitativo, "Ja, ja, Sarastro herrschet hier."* What will be said of me, I wonder, in the year 2100?...

September, 1855.

...Received a number of visits. Baehr, the Dresden painter and professor, came; he is a charming fellow, and pleased me very much. He knows all my works, and is full of them. He says, at Dresden every one is interested in them, especially the women, who, it appears, read me with passionate delight. Hornstein, a young composer, came also; he is a pupil of Richard Wagner, who, it seems, is also one of my students. Hornstein is still here, and pays me an exaggerated respect; for instance, when I want my waiter, he rises from table to summon him.... My portrait has been for a fortnight at the exposition. There has been a great crowd to see it. Von Launitz, the Frankfort Phidias, wants to take my bust....

December 23, 1855.

...A gentleman has written to me from Zurich to say that in the club to which he belongs my works are read with such admi-

---

* "Yes, yes, Sarastro reigns herein."—Air from the *Magic Flute.*

ration that the members are crazy to get a picture of me of any kind, nature, or description, and that the artist who takes it has but to forward it C. O. D.... You see that my fame is spreading like a conflagration, and not in arithmetical ratio either, but in geometric, and even cubic....

March 28, 1856.

...R., too, kissed my hand,—a ceremony to which I cannot accustom myself; yet it is one, I suppose, that forms part of my imperial dignity....

June 6, 1856.

...Becher sent his son and nephew here, and Baehr sent his son also, and that only that these young people may in their old age be able to boast that they had seen and spoken to me....

June 11, 1856.

...Professor Baehr, of Dresden, was here yesterday, and, penetrated with the most praiseworthy enthusiasm, wished to exchange his beautiful silver snuff-box for my forlorn old leather one. I refused, however. He told me of a certain Herr von Wilde, who was a perfect fanatic on the subject of my philosophy, and who, at the age of eighty-five, died with my name on his lips.

My Buddha, re-gilded, glittering on his pedestal, gives you his benediction.

August 14, 1856.

...Four pages and a half of Tallendier about me.[*] You have seen it, I suppose. French chatter, personal details, etc., but where the devil did he hear that I am "*tout etonné du bruit que font mes écrits dans le monde?*" I am so little astonished, that Emden told Nordwall, to the latter's intense surprise, that I had predicted to him my future celebrity fully twenty years ago....

---

[*]   An article in the *Revue des Deux Mondes.*

Now, mediocrity may, of course, be praised, but, as Balzac has put it, it is never discussed. And Schopenhauer, in the matter of discussion, came in for his full share. He was praised and abused by turn. Like every prominent figure, he made a good mark to fire at. Certain critics said that he had stolen from Fichte and Schelling everything in his philosophy that was worth reading, others abused him personally; and one writer, a woman with whom he had refused to converse, and who had probably expected to pay her hotel bill with the protocol of his conversation, wrote a quantity of scurrilous articles about him. But *censura perit, scriptum manet.* The criticisms are forgotten, while his work still endures and, moreover, grows each year into surer and stronger significance.

Among his visitors at the time was M. Foucher de Carsil, and the portrait which that gentleman subsequently drew of him is so graphic that it is impossible to resist the temptation of making the following extract:*—

"When I first saw him, in 1859, at the Hôtel d'Angleterre, at Frankfort, he was then an old man, with bright blue and limpid eyes. His lips were thin and sarcastic, and about them wandered a smile of shrewd intelligence. His high forehead was tufted on either side with puffs of white hair that gave to his physiognomy, luminous as it was with wit and malice, a stamp of nobility and distinction. His garments, his lace *jabot,* his white cravat, reminded me of that school of gentlemen who lived toward the close of the reign of Louis XV. His manners were those of a man accustomed to the best society; habitually reserved and timid even to suspicion, he rarely entered into conversation with any save his intimates and an occasional sympathetic traveler. His gestures were abrupt, and in conversation they became at once petulant and suggestive. He avoided discussions and combats in words, but he did so that he might the better enjoy the charm of familiar conversation. When he did speak, his imagi-

---

*   *Hegel et Schopenhauer.* Paris: Hachette et Cie.

nation embroidered on the heavy canvas of the German tongue the most subtle and delicate arabesques that the Latin, Greek, French, English, or Italian languages were capable of suggesting. Indeed, when he cared to talk, his conversation possessed swing and precision, and joined thereto was a wealth of citation, an exactitude of detail, and such tireless flow of wit, as held the little circle of his friends charmed and attentive until far into the night. His words, clear-cut and cadenced, captivated his listener wholly: they both pictured and analyzed, a tremulous sensitiveness heightened their fervor, they were precise and exact on every topic. A German, who had traveled extensively in Abyssinia, was so astonished at the minute details which he gave on the different species of crocodiles, and their customs, that he thought that in him he recognized a former companion.

"Happy are they who heard this last survivor of the conversationalists of the eighteenth century! He was a contemporary of Voltaire and of Diderot, of Helvetius and of Chamfort; his brilliant thoughts on women, on the part that mothers hold in the intellectual qualities of their children; his theories, profoundly original, on the connection between will and mind; his views on art and nature, on the life and death of the species; his remarks on the dull and wearisome style of those who write to say nothing, or who put on a mask and think with the thoughts of others; his pungent reflections on the subject of pseudonyms, and on the establishment of a literary censure for those journals which permitted neologisms, solecisms, and barbarisms; his ingenious hypotheses on magnetic phenomena, dreams, and somnambulism; his hatred of excess of every kind; his love of order; and his horror of obscurantism, '*qui, s'il n'est pas un péché contre le Saint Esprit en est un contre l'esprit humain,*' make for him a physiognomy entirely different from any other of this century."

A few tags and tatters of these conversations have been preserved by Dr. Frauenstadt,* and in them Schopenhauer is dis-

---

*   Arthur Schopenhauer. *Von ihm, Ueber ihn.* Berlin.

covered sprawled at ease, and expressing himself on a variety of topics with a *disinvoltura* and freedom of epithet which recalls the earlier essayists. With them, as with him, periphrasis was avoided. Spades were spades, not horticultural implements; and in one dialogue Frauenstadt compliments his master in having, in breadth and reach of his polemic, nothing in common with contemporary regard for ears polite. Citations of this class, however, may well be omitted. A thinker in slippers, and especially *in puris naturalibus*, is generally unattractive even to those the least given to prudishness. But beyond certain instances of this description, the scholar and man of the world is usually very discernible. At times he is profound, at others vivacious; for instance, he is asked what man would be if Nature, in making the last step which leads to him, had started from the dog or the elephant; to which he answers, in that case man would be an intelligent dog or an intelligent elephant, instead of being an intelligent monkey. As may be imagined, there was about Schopenhauer very little of the Sunday-school theologian, and religion was in consequence seldom viewed by him from an orthodox standpoint; when, therefore, Schleiermacher was quoted before him to the effect that no man can be a philosopher who is not religious, he observed very quietly, "No man who is religious can become a philosopher,—metaphysics are useless to him, and no true philosopher is religious; he is sometimes in danger, but he is not fettered, he is free." Elsewhere he said, "Religion and philosophy are like the two scales of a balance; the more one rises, the more does the other descend."

In Schopenhauer's opinion, the greatest novels were *Tristram Shandy*, *Wilhelm Meister*, *Don Quixote*, and the *Nouvelle Héloïse*. To *Don Quixote* he ascribed an allegorical meaning, but as an intellectual romance he preferred *Wilhelm Meister* to all others. He believed in clairvoyance, but not that man is a free agent; and it may be here noted that, according to the most recent scientific opinion, man is a free agent, *at most*, about once in twenty-four hours. "Everything that happens, happens necessarily," he would say; and it was with this maxim, of whose truth he had a variety of every-day examples, and with the aid of the theory of the ideality of time, that he explained second sight. "Everything is now that is to be," he said; "but with our ordinary eyes we do not see it; the clairvoyant merely puts on the spectacles of Time."

In the *Paränesen und Maximen*, in which Schopenhauer chats quietly with the reader and not with the disciple, many quaint and forcible suggestions are to be found. For instance, among other things, he says, "I accord my entire respect to any man who, when unoccupied, and waiting for something, does not immediately begin to beat a tattoo with his fingers, or toy with the object nearest his hand. It is probable that such a man has thoughts of his own." His advice, too, on the manner in which we should think and work is quite Emersonian in its directness. It was, it may be added, the manner in which he thought and worked, himself: "Have compartments for your thoughts and open but one of them at a time; in this way each little pleasure you may have will not be spoiled by some lumbering care; neither will one thought drive out another, and an important matter will not swamp a lot of smaller ones."

Such, vaguely outlined, was this great and interesting figure. With the appearance of the *Parerga* his work was done. He lived ten years longer in great seclusion, receiving only infrequent visits. "There, where two or three are gathered together," he would say, and suggested that his friends and believers should meet and consult without him. Such literary labor as he then performed consisted mainly in strengthening that which he had already written, and in making notes and suggestions for future editions. At the age of seventy-two he died, very peacefully though suddenly, leaving all his fortune to charitable purposes.

In these pages no attempt has been made to enter into the details of biography, for that pleasant task has been already well performed by other and better equipped pens. The present writer has therefore only sought to present such a view of Schopenhauer as might aid the general reader to a clearer understanding of the doctrine which he was the first to present, and which will be briefly considered in the next chapter.

CHAPTER THREE.

The Sphinx's Riddle.

IN THE MUNICH BEER HALLS, WHEN ONE STUDENT IS
heard laying down the law about something which he does not
understand to a companion who cares not a rap on the subject,
it is very generally taken for granted that the two are talking
metaphysics. Indeed, metaphysics has a bad name everywhere.
In itself, it suggests nothing very enticing, and even its nomenclature seems to bring with it a sort of ponderosity which is very
nearly akin to the repulsive.

This prejudice, of course, is not without its reason. The philosophers, nearly one and all, seem to have banded themselves
into a sort of imaginary freemasonry, whose portals they bar to
any one refusing to robe his thoughts in a garment of technical
speech. Moreover, at the very gateway of their guild there looms
before the timorous the fear of a hideous initiation, the cold
douche of logic, and the memorizing of hateful terms. There can
therefore be no stronger proof of Schopenhauer's ability than
that which is contained in the fact that he successfully eluded

all these stale abuses, and turned one of the heaviest kinds of writing into one of the most agreeable.

Indeed, Schopenhauer is not only one of the most profound thinkers of the essentially profound nineteenth century, but, what is still more noteworthy, he is an exceptionally fascinating teacher. His spacious theories and tangential flights are, of course, not such as charm the reader of the penny dreadful; but any one who is interested in the drama of evolution and the tragi-comedy of life will, it is believed, find in him a fund of curious information, such as no other thinker has had the power to convey.

He has, it is true, made the most of the worst; but beyond this reproach, but one other of serious import remains to be brought against him, and that is that though he has been dead and buried for very nearly a quarter of a century, he is still on the outer margin of his epoch. For this he is not, of course, entirely to blame. There are among thinkers many pleasant optimists still, who form a respectable majority; to be sure, a wise man once said that in considering a new subject the minority were always right; but, disregarding for the moment the fallacy of believing that this world is the best one possible, it cannot but be admitted that scientific pessimism is still in its infancy. It has yet many prejudices to disarm, and many errors of its own to correct. Like meaner things, it must mature. For this it has ample time.

Berkeley says that few men think, yet all have opinions; and it is now very frequently asserted that when more is thought, not only there will not be such a diversity of opinion, but at that time Pessimism, as the religion of the future, will begin its sway.

It has been elsewhere noted that the effect of Kant's philosophy was not dissimilar to that of a successful operation on cataract, and the aim of the *World as Will and Idea* is to place in the hands of those on whom that operation has been satisfactorily performed a pair of such spectacles as are suitable to convalescent eyes. Schopenhauer is therefore in a measure indebted to Kant, as also, it may be added, to Plato, and the sacred books of the Hindus.

In saying, however, that Schopenhauer is indebted to Kant, it is well to point out that Schopenhauer begins precisely where Kant left off. Kant's great merit consisted in distinguishing the phenomenon from the thing-in-itself, or in other words, in showing the difference between that which seems and that which is.* For the inaccessible thing-in-itself he had no explanation to offer. He called it the *Ding an sich*, regarded it as the result of an unintelligible cause, and then left it to be a bugbear to every student of his philosophy.

This unpleasant *Ding an sich* was exorcised, and well-nigh banished for good and all, by Fichte and Hegel; but Schopenhauer reëstablished the incomprehensible factor on a fresh basis, christened it "Will," and asserted it to be the creator of all that is, and at once independent, free, and omnipotent; in other words, the interior essence of the world of which Christ crucified is the sublime symbol. Thus disposed of, the *Ding an sich* may now be left to take care of itself, and the examination of the great theory begun.

Schopenhauer opens his philosophy with the formula, "The world is my idea;" a formula which, it may be noted, condenses in the fewest possible words all that is worth condensing of the idealism of Germany. Beginning in this manner it is evident that he proposes to show neither whence the world comes nor

---

*   This distinction of Kant's is not strictly original. Its germ is in Plato, and Voltaire set all Europe laughing at Maupertuis, who had vaguely stated that *"nous vivons dans un monde ou rien de ce que nous apercevons ne ressemble à ce que nous apercevons."* Whether Kant was acquainted or not with Maupertuis' theory is, of course, difficult to say; at any rate, he resurrected the doctrine, and presented idealism for the first time in a logical form.

whither it tends, nor yet why it is, but simply, *what it is*. The question has been asked before. According to Schopenhauer, the world is made up of two zones, the real and the ideal; and it may here be said that over the real and the ideal Schopenhauer successfully read the banns.

To return, however, to the opening formula. "The world is my idea" is a truth which holds good for everything that lives and thinks, but which, however, is appreciable only by man. When appreciated, it is at once clear that what we know is neither a sun nor an earth, for we have at best an eye which sees the one, and a hand which feels the other. In brief, we are unacquainted with either forms or colors; we have but senses which represent them to us, while objects exist for us merely through the medium of the intelligence. Indeed, as Schopenhauer has said, no other truth is more certain and less in need of proof than this,—that the whole world is simply the perception of a perceiver; in a word, idea.

Emerson says that the frivolous make themselves merry with this theory; and it must be admitted that at first it does not seem quite satisfactory to be told that the world in which we live is nothing more nor less than a cerebral phenomenon, which man carries with him to the tomb, and which, in the absence of a perceiver, would not exist at all. To arrive, however, at a clear understanding of the purely phenomenal existence of the exterior world, it will suffice to represent to one's self the world as it was when entirely uninhabited. At that time it was necessarily without perception. Later, there sprang up a great quantity of plants, upon which the different forces of light, air, humidity, and electricity acted according to their nature. If, now, it be remembered how impressionable plants are to these agents, and how thought leads by degrees to sensation and thence to perception, immediately then the world appears representing itself in time and space. Or, reverse the argument and imagine that the dream of the poet is realized, that nations have disappeared, and that every living thing has ceased to be, while beneath the sun's unchanging stare, and enveloped in the sky's bland, pervasive blue, the earth with her continents and archipelagoes continues to revolve in space. Under such circumstances it would naturally seem as though the universe subsisted still. But if the question is examined more closely, it will perhaps be admitted that these things remain as they are only on condition of being seen and felt. For supposing one spectator present, but of a different mental organization from our own, then the entire scene is changed; suppress him, and the whole spectacle tumbles into chaos.

This doctrine, as it will be readily understood, does not in any sense deny the reality of the world in the ordinary acceptation of the term; it maintains merely that every object is conditioned by its subject; or, to explain the theory less technically, it will be sufficient to reflect that for the world, or for anything else, to be an object, there must be some one as subject to think it; for instance, the dreamless sleep proves that the earth exists only to the thinking mind, and should all Nature be rocked in an eternal slumber, there could then be no question of an exterior world.

If it be asked in what this perception consists, which represents the exterior world, we find that it is limited to three fundamental concepts, that of time, space, and their concomitant causality; but inasmuch as time and space are the receptacle of every phenomenon, once their ideality is established, the ideality of the world is proven at the same moment, and with it the truth of the formula, "The world is my idea."

Now the ideality of time is established, according to Schopenhauer, by what is known in mechanics as the law of inertia. "For what," he asks in the *Parerga*, "does this law teach? Simply, that time alone cannot produce any physical action, that alone and in itself it alters nothing either in the repose or movement of a body. Were it either accidentally or otherwise inherent in things themselves, it would follow that its duration or brevity would affect them in a certain measure. But it does nothing of the sort; time passes over all things without leaving the slightest trace, for they are acted upon only by the causes that unroll themselves *in* time, but in no sense by time itself. When, therefore, a body is withdrawn from chemical action, as the mammoth in the ice fields, the fly in amber, and the Egyptian antiquities in their closed necropoli, thousands of years may pass and leave them unaffected. Indeed," he adds elsewhere, "the living toads found in limestone lead to the conclusion that even animal life may be suspended for thousands of years, provided this suspension is begun in the dormant period and maintained by special circumstances."

The *London Times*, 21st September, 1840, contains a notice to the effect that, at a lecture delivered by Mr. Pettigrew, at the Literary and Scientific Institute, the lecturer showed some grains of wheat which Sir G. Wilkenson had found in a grave at Thebes, where they must have lain for three thousand years. They were found in an hermetically sealed vase. Mr. Pettigrew had sowed twelve grains, and obtained a plant which grew five feet high, and the seeds of which were then quite ripe.

Many other instances are given of this absolute inactivity; for example, let a body once be put in motion, that motion is never arrested or diminished by any lapse of time; it would be never ending were it not for the reaction of physical causes. In the same manner a body in repose would remain so eternally did not physical causes put it in motion. It follows, therefore, that time is not a real existence, but only a condition of thought, or purely ideal.

In regard to the ideality of space, Schopenhauer says, "The clearest and most simple proof of the ideality of space is that we can never get it out of our thoughts, as we might anything else. We can fancy space as having no longer anything to fill it, we can imagine that everything within it has disappeared, we can represent it as being, between the fixed stars, an absolute void, but space itself we can never get rid of; whatever we do, however we turn, there it is in endless expansion. This fact certainly proves that space is a part of our intellect; or, in other words, that it is the woof of the tissue upon which the different objects of the exterior world apply themselves. As soon as I think of an object, space appears with it and accompanies every movement, every turn and *détour* of my thought, as faithfully as the spectacles on my nose accompany every movement, every turn and *détour* of my person, or just in the same manner as the shadow accompanies the body. If I notice that a thing accompanies me everywhere, and under all circumstances, I naturally conclude that it is in some way connected with me; as if, for instance, wherever I went I noticed a particular odor from which I could not escape. Space is precisely the same; whatever I think of, what ever I imagine, space comes first and yields its place to nothing. It must, therefore, be an integral part of my understanding, and its ideality in consequence must extend to everything that is thinkable."

Space and time being but the empty framework of phenomenal existence, something must fill them, and that something is causality, which, according to Schopenhauer, is synonymous with action and matter. Into these abstract regions, however, it is unnecessary to follow him any further. Suffice it to say that having shown in this way that one of the two zones of which the world is formed is but an effect of the perceptions, he passes therefrom to the world as it is.

Now there were many paths which might or might not have led him to the unravelment of the great secret which Kant gave up in despair, there were many ways which seemed to tend to a direct solution of the Sphinx's riddle, but the course which he chose, and which brought him nearer to the proper answer than any other system of which the world yet knows, may be fairly said to have been inspired by the spirit of truth, and as an inspiration given first to him of all men.

It was not mathematics that he selected to aid him in his search for the real, for whatever the subtleties of that science may be, it is still too superficial to contain an explorable depth. The natural sciences could aid him as little. Anatomy, botany, and zoölogy reveal, it is true, an infinite variety of forms, but these forms at best are but unrelated perceptions, a series of indecipherable hieroglyphics. Even etiology, when embracing the whole range of physical science, gives at most but the nomenclature, succession, and changes of inexplicable forces, without revealing anything of their inner nature. All these methods were smitten with the same defect,—they were all external, and offered not the essence of things, but only their image and description. To employ them, therefore, in a search for truth would, he said, be on a par with a man who, wandering about a castle looking vainly for the entrance, takes meanwhile a sketch of the façade. Such, however, he noted, is the method which all other philosophers have followed. He concluded, therefore, as man was not only a thinking being, to whom the world was merely an idea, but an individual riveted to the earth by a body whose affections were the starting-point of his intuitions, that reality would come to him, not from without, but from within. "For this body of man's is," he argued, "but an object among other objects; its movements and actions are unknown to the thinking being save as are the changes of the others, and they would be as incomprehensible to him as his own were not their signification revealed to him in another manner. He would see movements follow motives with the constancy of a natural law, and would as little understand the influence of the motive as the connection of any other effect with its cause. He could, if he chose, call it force, quality, or character, but that is all that he would know about it."

What, then, is the interior essence of every manifestation and of every action? What is that which is identical with the body to such an extent that to its command a movement always answers? What is that with which Nature plays, which works dumbly in the rock, slumbers in the plant, and awakes in man? Schopenhauer answers with a word, "Will." Will, he teaches, is a force, and should not be taken, as it is ordinarily, to mean simply the conscious act of an intelligent being. In Nature it is a blind, unconscious power; in man it is the foundation of being.

But before entering into an examination of the functions and vagaries of this force, of which everything, from a cataclysm to a blade of grass, is a derivative, it is well to inquire what its exact rank is. It has been already said that in man it was the foundation of being, but from very early times,—as a matter of fact, since the days in which Anaxagoras lived and taught,—the intellect has held, among all man's other attributes, a sceptre hitherto uncontested. If Schopenhauer, however, is to be believed, the supremacy hitherto accorded to it has been the result of error. The throne, by grace divine, belongs to Will. The intellect is but the prime minister, the instrument of a higher force, as the hammer is that of the smith.

If the matter be examined however casually, it will become at once clear that what we are most conscious of in effort, hope, desire, fear, love, hatred, and determination, are the workings and manifestations of Will. If the animal is considered, it will be seen that in the descending scale intelligence becomes more and more imperfect, while Will remains entirely unaffected. The smallest insect wants what it wants as much as man. The intellect, moreover, becomes wearied, while Will is indefatigable. Indeed, when it is remembered that such men as Swift, Kant, Scott, Southey, Rousseau, and Emerson have fallen into a state of intellectual debility, it is well-nigh impossible to deny that the mind is but a function of the body, which, in turn, is a function of the Will. But that which probably shows the secondary and dependent nature of the intelligence more clearly is its peculiar characteristic of intermittence and periodicity. In deep sleep, the brain rests, while the other organs continue their work. In brief, then, Intellect is the light and Will the warmth. "In me," Schopenhauer says, "the indestructible is not the soul, but rather, to employ a chemical term, the basis of the soul, which is Will."

Will, moreover, is not only the foundation of being, but, as has been noted, it is the universal essence. Schopenhauer points out the ascension of sap in plants, which is no easy problem in hydraulics, and the insect's marvelous anticipations of the future, and asks what is it all but Will? The vital force itself, he says, is Will,—Will to live,—while the organism of the body is but Will manifested, Will become visible.

As Schopenhauer describes it, Will is also identical, immutable, and free. Its identity is shown in inorganic life in the irresistible *tendency* of water to precipitate itself into cavities, the *perseverance* with which the loadstone turns to the north, the *longing* that iron has to attach itself to it, the violence with which contrary currents of electricity *try* to unite the *choice* of fluids, and in the manner in which they join and separate. In organic life, it is shown by the fact that every vegetable has a peculiar characteristic: one wants a damp soil, another needs a dry one; one grows only on high ground, another in the valley; one turns to the light, another to the water; while the climbing plant seeks a support. In the animal kingdom there exists another form, which is noticeable in the partly voluntary, partly involuntary movements of the lowest type. When, however, in the evolution of Will the insect or the animal seeks and chooses its food, then intelligence begins and volition passes from darkness into light.

Will, too, is immutable. It never varies; it is the same in man as in the caterpillar, for, as has been said, what an insect wants it wants as decidedly as does a man; the only difference is in the object of desire. The immutability of Will, moreover, is the base of its indestructibility; it never perishes, and for that matter what does? In the world of phenomena all things, it is true, seem to have a birth and a death, but that is but an illusion, which the philosopher does not share. Our true being, and the veritable essence of all things, dwell, Schopenhauer says, in a region where time is not, and where the concepts of birth and death are without significance. The fear of death, he adds parenthetically, is a purely independent sentiment, and one which has its origin in the Will to live. Briefly, it is an illusion which man brings with him when he is born, and which guides him through life; for notice that were this fear of death perfectly reasonable, man would be as uneasy about the chaos which preceded his existence as about that which is to follow it.

Let the individual die, however; the species is indestructible, for death is to the species as sleep is to the individual. The species contains the indestructible, the immutable Will of which the individual is a manifestation. It contains all that is, all that was, and all that will be.

"When we think of the future and of the coming generations, the millions of human beings who will differ from us in habits and customs, and we try in imagination to fancy them with us, we wonder from where they will spring, where they are now? Where is this fecund chaos, rich in worlds, that hides the generations that are to be? And where can it be save there, where every reality has been and will be,—here, in the present, and what it contains. And you, foolish questioner, who do not recognize your own essence, you are like the leaf on the tree which, withering in autumn, and feeling it is about to fall, laments at death, inconsolable at the knowledge of the fresh verdure which in spring will cover the tree once more. The leaf cries, 'I am no more.' Foolish leaf, where do you go? Whence do the fresh leaves come? Where is this chaos whose gulf you fear? See, your own self is in that force, interior and hidden, acting on the tree which, through all generations of leaves, knows neither birth nor death. And now tell me," Schopenhauer concludes, as though he were about to pronounce a benediction, "tell me, is man unlike the leaf?"

This doctrine, which teaches that through all there is one invariable, identical, and equal force, is the great problem whose solution was sought by Kant, and which he gave up in despair; it is the discovery which makes of Schopenhauer one of the foremost thinkers of the century, and one, it may be added without any unguarded enthusiasm, which will suffice to carry his name into other ages, somewhat in the same manner as the name of Columbus has descended to us.

"If we were to consider," he said, "the nature of this force which admittedly moves the world, but whose psychological examination is so little advanced that the most certain analytical results seem not unlike a paradox, we should be astonished at this fundamental verity which I have been the first to bring to light, and to which I have given its true name,—Will. For what is the world but an enormous Will constantly irrupting into life. Gravitation, electricity, heat, every form of activity, from the fall of an apple to the foundation of a republic, is but the expression of Will, and nothing more."

This doctrine of volition coincides, it may be noted, very perfectly with that of evolution, and it was not difficult for Schopenhauer to show that the more recent results of science were a confirmation of his philosophy. In the *Parerga*, which he wrote thirty years after the publication of his chief work, he says that during the early stages of the globe's formation, before the age of granite, the objectivity of the Will-to-live was limited to the most inferior forms; also that the forces were at that time engaged in a combat whose theatre was not alone the surface of the globe, but its entire mass, a combat too colossal for the imagination to grasp. When this Titan conflict of chemical forces had ended, and the granite, like a tombstone, covered the combatants, the Will-to-live, by a striking contrast, irrupted in the peaceful world of plant and forest. This vegetable world decarbonized the air, and prepared it for animal life. The objectivity of Will then realized a new form,—the animal kingdom. Fish and crustaceans filled the sea, gigantic reptiles covered the earth, and gradually through innumerable forms, each more perfect than the last, the Will-to-live ascended finally to man. This stage attained is, in his opinion, destined to be the last, for with it is come the possibility of the denial of the Will, through which the divine comedy will end.

This possibility of the denial of the Will, and the ransom of the world from its attendant misery thereby, will be explained later on, and for the moment it will be sufficient to note that Schopenhauer refused to admit that a being more intelligent than man could exist either here or on any other planet, for with enlarged intelligence he would consider life too deplorable to be supported for a single moment.

If, now, the foregoing arguments are admitted, and it is taken for granted that there are two separate and distinct hemispheres, one apparent and one real, one the world of perceptions and one the world of Will, there must necessarily be some connection between the two, some point at which they meet and join. This chasm Schopenhauer lightly bridges over with those ideas of Plato which the Middle Ages neglected, and which formed the banquet and the sustenance of the Renaissance: in fact, the eternal yet ever fresh suggestions that Nature offers to the artist, and which the sculptor with his chisel, the poet with his pen, the painter with his brush, resuscitate and explain anew.

It is, however, only in the purest contemplation that these suggestions can be properly received, and it is, of course, in genius that a preëminent capacity for such receptivity exists. For it is as if when genius appears in an individual, a larger measure of the power of knowledge falls to his lot than is necessary for the service of an individual will, and this superfluity, being free, becomes, as it were, the mirror of the inner nature of the world, or, as Carlyle puts it, "the spiritual picture of Nature." "This," Schopenhauer notes parenthetically, "explains the restless activity of the genius, for the present can rarely satisfy him, because it does not fill his thoughts. There is in him a ceaseless aspiration and desire for new and lofty things, and a longing to meet and communicate with others of similar status. The common mortal, on the other hand, filled with the hour, ends in it, and finding everywhere his like enjoys that satisfaction in daily life from which the genius is debarred."

The common mortal, the *bourgeois*, as it is the fashion to call him, turned out as he is daily by the thousand, manufactured, it would seem, to order, finds in his satisfied mediocrity no glimmer, even, of a spark that can predispose him to disinterested observation. Whatever arrests his attention does so only for the moment, and in all that appears before him he seeks merely the general concept under which it is to be brought, very much in the same manner as the indolent seek a chair, which then interests them no further.

And yet it is unnecessary to pore over German metaphysics to know that whoso can lose himself in Nature, and sink his own individuality therein, finds that it has suddenly become a suggestion, which he has absorbed, and which is now part of himself. It is in this sense that Byron says:—

> "Are not the mountains, waves, and skies a part
> Of me and of my soul, as I of them?"

This theory, it is true, is not that of all great poets, many of whom, as witness Shelley and Leopardi, did not see in the splendid face of Nature that they could not be absolutely perishable, and so selfishly mourned over their own weakness and her impassibility.

According to Schopenhauer, art should be strictly impersonal, and contemplation as calm as a foretaste of Nirvana, in which the individual is effaced and only the pure knowing subject subsists. This condition he praises with great wealth of adjective as the painless state which Epicurus, of refined memory, celebrated as the highest good, the bliss of the gods, for therein "man is freed from the hateful yoke of Will, the penal servitude of daily life ceases as for a Sabbath, the wheel of Ixion stands still." The cause of all this he is at no loss to explain, and he does so, it may be added, in a manner poetically logical and peculiar to himself. "Every desire is born of a need, of a privation, or a suffering. When satisfied it is lulled, but for one that is satisfied how many are unappeased! Desire, moreover, is of long duration, its exigencies are infinite, while pleasure is brief and narrowly measured. Even this pleasure is only an apparition, another succeeds it; the first is a vanished illusion, the second an illusion which lingers still. Nothing is capable of appeasing Will, nor of permanently arresting it; the best we can do for ourselves is like the alms tossed to a beggar, which in preserving his life today prolongs his misery to-morrow. While, therefore, we are dominated by desires and ruled by Will, so long as we give ourselves up to hopes that delude and fears that persecute, we have neither repose nor happiness. But when an accident, an interior harmony, lifting us for the time from out the infinite torrent of desire, delivers the spirit from the oppression of the Will, turns our attention from everything that solicits it, and all things seem as freed from the allurements of hope and personal interest, then repose, vainly pursued, yet ever intangible, comes to us of itself, bearing with open hands the plenitude of the gift of peace."

The fine arts, therefore, as well as philosophy, are at work on the problem of existence. Every mind that has once rested in impersonal contemplation of the world tends from that moment to some comprehension of the mystery of beauty and the internal essence of all things; and it is for this reason that every new work which grapples forcibly with any actuality is one more answer to the question, What is life?

To this query every masterpiece replies, pertinently, but in its own manner. Art, which speaks in the ingenuous tongue of intuition, and not in the abstract speech of thought, answers the question with a passing image, but not with a definite reply. But every great work, be it a poem, a picture, a statue, or a play, answers still. Even music replies, and more profoundly than anything else. Indeed, art offers to him who questions an image born of intuition, which says, See, this is life.

Briefly, then, contemplation brings with it that affranchisement of the intelligence, which is not alone a release from the trammels of the Will, but which is the law of art itself, and raises man out of misery into the pure world of ideas.

In the treatment of this subject, which in the hands of other writers has been productive of inexpressible weariness, Schopenhauer has given himself no airs. In what has gone before there has been, it must be admitted, no attempt to narrate history, and then pass it off as an explanation of the Universe. He has gone to the root of the matter, seized a fact and brought it to light, without any nauseous accompaniment of "Absolutes" or "Supersensibles." In view of the magnitude of the subject, it has been handled, I think, very simply, and that perhaps for the reason that simplicity is the *cachet* which greatness lends to all its productions. If in these pages it has seemed otherwise, the fault is not that of the master, but rather that of the clerk.

The question as to what the world is has been considered,

and the answer conveyed that Will, the essence of all things, is a blind, unconscious force which, after irrupting in inorganic life and passing therefrom through the vegetable and animal kingdom, reaches its culmination in man, and that the only relief from its oppressive yoke is found in art and impersonal contemplation. Taking these premises for granted, and admitting for a moment their corollary that life is a restless pain, it will be found that the sombre conclusion which follows therefrom has been deduced with an exactitude which is comparable only to the precision of a prism decomposing light.

Literature is admittedly full of the embarrassments of transition, and philosophy has naturally its attendant share. It is, of course, not difficult for the metaphysician to say, This part of my work is theoretical, and this, practical; but to give to the two that cohesion which is necessary in the unfolding of a single, if voluminous, thought is a feat not always performed with success. It is, therefore, no little to Schopenhauer's credit that he triumphantly connected the two in such wise that they seem as though fused in one, and after disposing of the world at large was able to turn to life and its attendant, pain.

Now in all grades of its manifestation, Will, he teaches, dispenses entirely with any end or aim; it simply and ceaselessly strives, for striving is its sole nature. As, however, any hindrance of this striving, through an obstacle placed between it and its temporary aim, is called suffering, and on the other hand the attainment of its end, satisfaction, well-being, or happiness, it follows, if the obstacles it meets outnumber the facilities it encounters, that having no final end or aim, there can be no end and no measure of suffering.

But does pain outbalance happiness? The question is certainly complex, and for that matter unanswerable save by a cumbersome mathematical process from which the reader may well be spared. The optimist points to the pleasures of life, the pessimist enumerates its trials. Each judges according to his lights. Schopenhauer's opinion goes without the telling, and as he gave his whole life to the subject his verdict may, for the moment, be allowed to pass unchallenged. Still, if the question is examined, no matter how casually, it will be seen, first, that there is no sensibility in the plant and therefore no suffering; second, that a certain small degree is manifested in the lowest types of animal life; third, that the capacity to feel and suffer is still limited, even in the case of the most intelligent insects; fourth, that pain of an acute degree first appears with the nervous system of the vertebrates; fifth, that it continues to increase in direct proportion to the development of the intelligence; and, finally, that as intelligence attains distinctness, pain advances with it, and what Mr. Swinburne calls the gift of tears finds its supreme expression in man. Truly, as Schopenhauer has expressed it, man is not a being to be greatly envied. He is the concretion of a thousand necessities. His life, as a rule, is a struggle for existence with the certainty of defeat in the end, and when his existence is assured, there comes a fight with the burden of life, an effort to kill time, and a vain attempt to escape ennui.

Nor is ennui a minor evil. It is not every one who can get away from himself. Schopenhauer could, it is true, but in so doing he noted that its ravages depicted on the human countenance an expression of absolute despair, and made beings who love one another as little as men do seek each other eagerly. "It drives men," he said, "to the greatest excesses, as does famine, its opposite extreme. Public precautions are taken against it as against other calamities, hence the historical *panem et circenses*. Want," he added, "is the scourge of the people as ennui is that of fashionable life. In the middle classes ennui is represented by the Sabbath, and want by the other days of the week."

In this way, between desire and attainment, human life rolls on. The wish is, in its nature, pain, and satisfaction soon begets satiety. No matter what nature and fortune may have done, no matter who a man may be, nor what he may possess, the pain which is essential to life can never be dodged. Efforts to banish suffering effect, if successful, only a change in its form. In itself it is want or care for the maintenance of life; and if in this form it is at last and with difficulty removed, back it comes again in the shape of love, jealousy, lust, envy, hatred, or ambition; and if it can gain entrance through none of these avatars, it comes as simple boredom, against which we strive as best we may. Even in this latter case, if at last we get the upper hand, we shall hardly do so, Schopenhauer says, "without letting pain in again in one of its earlier forms; and then the dance begins afresh, for life, like a pendulum, swings ever backward and forward between pain and ennui."

Depressing as this view of life may be, Schopenhauer draws attention to an aspect of it from which a certain consolation may be derived, and even a philosophic indifference to present ills be attained. Our impatience at misfortune, he notes, arises very generally from the fact that we regard it as having been caused by a chain of circumstances which might easily have been different. As a rule, we make little, if any, complaint over the ills that are necessary and universal; such, for instance, as the advance of age, and the death which must claim us all; on the contrary, it is the accidental nature of the sorrow that gives its sting. But if we were to recognize that pain is inevitable and essential to life, and that nothing depends on chance save only the form in which it presents itself, and that consequently the present suffering fills a place which without it would be occupied by another which it has excluded,—then, from convictions of this nature, a considerable amount of stoical equanimity would be produced, and the amount of anxious care which now pervades the world would be notably diminished. But fortifications of this description, however cunningly devised, form no bulwark against pain itself; for pain, according to Schopenhauer, is positive, the one thing that is felt; while on the other hand, satisfaction, or, as it is termed, happiness, is a purely negative condition. Against this theory it is unnecessary to bring to bear any great battery of argument; many thinkers have disagreed with him on this point, as they have also disagreed with his assertion that pleasure is always preceded by a want. It is true, of course, that unexpected pleasures have a delight whose value is entirely independent of antecedent desire. But unexpected pleasures are rare; they do not come to us every day, and when they do they cease to be pleasures; indeed, their rarity may in this respect be looked upon as the exception which confirms the rule. Ample proof, however, of the negativity of happiness is found in art, and especially in poetry. Epic and dramatic verse represent struggles, efforts, and combats for happiness; but happiness itself, complete and enduring, is never depicted. Up to the last scene the hero copes with dangers and battleaxes difficulties, whereupon the curtain falls upon his happiness, which, being completely negative, cannot be the subject of art. The idyl, it is true, professes to treat of happiness, but in so doing it blunders sadly, for the poet either finds his verse turning beneath his hands into an insignificant epic made up of feeble sorrows, trivial pleasures, and trifling efforts, or else it becomes merely a description of the charm and beauty of Nature. The same thing, Schopenhauer says, is noticeable in music. Melody is a deviation from the keynote, to which, after many mutations, it at last returns; but the keynote, which expresses "the satisfaction of the will" is, when prolonged, perfectly monotonous, and wearisome in the extreme.

From the logic of these arguments it is clear that Voltaire was not very far wrong when he said: "Happiness is but a dream, and only pain is real. I have thought so for eighty-four years, and I know of no better plan than to resign myself to the inevitable, and reflect that flies were born to be devoured by spiders, and man to be consumed by care."

To this conclusion the optimist will naturally object, but he does so in the face of history and experience, either of which is quite competent to prove that this world is far from being the best one possible. If neither of them succeeds in so doing, then let him wander through the hospitals, the cholera slums, the operating-rooms of the surgeon, the prisons, the torture-chambers, the slave-kennels, the battlefields, or any one of the numberless haunts of nameless misery; or, if all of these are too far, or too inconvenient, let him take a turn into one of the many factories where men and women, and even infants, work from ten to fourteen hours a day at mechanical labor, simply that they may continue to enjoy the exquisite delight of living.

Moreover, as Schopenhauer asks with grim irony, "Where did Dante find the materials for his 'Inferno' if not from this world; and yet is not his picture exhaustively satisfactory? To some minds it is even a trifle overcharged; but look at his Paradise; when he attempted to depict it he had nothing to guide him, this pleasant world could not offer a single suggestion; and so, being obliged to say something, and yet not knowing what to say, he palms off in place of a celestial panorama the instruction and advice which he imagines himself as receiving from Beatrice and the Saints."

Briefly, then, life, to the pessimist, is a motiveless desire, a constant pain and continued struggle, followed by death, and so on, in *secula seculorum*, until the planet's crust crumbles to dust.

Since, therefore, life is so deplorable, the deduction seems to follow that it is better to take the poet's advice:—

> "Count o'er the joys thine hours have seen,
>   Count o'er thy days from anguish free,
> And know, whatever thou hast been,
>   'Tis something better—not to be."

But here the question naturally arises, how is this annihilation to be accomplished? Through a vulgar and commonplace suicide? Not at all. Schopenhauer is far too logical to suggest a palliative so fruitless and clap-trap as that. For suicide, far from being a denial of the will to live, is one of its strongest affirmations. Paradoxical as it may seem, the man who takes his own life really wants to live; what he does not want are the misery and trials attendant on his particular existence. He abolishes the individual, but not the race. The species continues, and pain with it.

In what manner, then, can we decently rid ourselves, and all who would otherwise follow, of the pangs and torments of life? Schopenhauer will give the receipt in a moment; but to understand the method clearly, it is necessary to take a glance at the metaphysics of love.

We are told by Dr. Frauenstadt that Schopenhauer considered this portion of his philosophy to be "a pearl." A pearl it may be, but as such it is not entirely suited to an Anglo-Saxon setting; nevertheless, as it is important to gain some idea of what this clear-eyed recluse thought of the delicate lever which disturbs the gravest interests, and whose meshes entwine peer and peasant alike, a brief description of it will not be entirely out of place.

By way of preface it may be said that, save Plato, no other philosopher has cared to consider a subject so simple yet complex as this, and of common accord it has been relinquished to the abuse of the poets and the praise of the rhymesters. It may be, perhaps, that from its nature it revolted at logic, and that the seekers for truth, in trying to clutch it, resembled the horseman in the familiar picture who, over ditches and dykes, pursues a phantom which floats always before him, and yet is ever intangible. La Rochefoucauld, who was ready enough with phrases, admitted that it was indefinable; a compatriot of his tried to compass it with the epigram, *"C'est l'égoïsme à deux."* Balzac gave it an escutcheon. Every one has had more or less to say about it; and as some have said more than they thought, while others thought more than they said, it has been beribboned with enough comparisons to form an unportable volume, while its history, from Tatterdemalia to Marlborough House, is written in blood as well as in books.

Love, however, is the basis of religion, the mainstay of ethics, as well as the inspiration of lyric and epic verse. It is, moreover, the principal subject of every dramatic, comic, and classic work in India, Europe, and America, and the inexhaustible spring from whose waters the fecund lands of fiction produce fresh crops more regularly than the seasons. It is a subject never lacking in actuality, and yet one to which each century has given a different color. It is recognized as a disease, and recommended as a remedy. And yet what is it? There are poets who have said it was an illusion; but however it may appear to them, it is no illusion to the philosopher: far from it; its reality and importance increase in the ratio of its ardor, and whether it turns to the tragic or the comic, a love affair is to him, above all other early aims, the one which presents the gravest aspects, and the one most worthy of consideration; for all the passions and intrigues of today, reduced to their simplest expression and divested of all accompanying allurements, are nothing more nor less than the combination of the future generation.

"It is through this frivolity," Schopenhauer says, "that the *dramatis personæ* are to appear on the stage when we have made our exit. The existence of these future actors is absolutely conditioned on the general instinct of love, while their nature and characteristics depend on individual choice. Such is the whole problem. Love is the supreme will to live, the genius of the species, and nature, being highly strategic, covers itself, for the fulfillment of its aims, with a mask of objective admiration, and deludes the individual so cleverly therewith, that he takes that to be his own happiness which, in reality, is but the maintenance of the species."

The love affairs of today, therefore, instead of representing questions of personal joy or sorrow, are simply and solely a series of grave meditations on the existence and composition of the future generation. It is this grand preoccupation that causes the pathos and sublimity of love. It is this that makes it so difficult to lend any interest to a drama with which the question is not intermingled. It is this that makes love an every-day matter, and yet an inexhaustible topic. It is this that explains the gravity of the *rôle* it plays, the importance which it gives to the most trivial incidents, and above all, it is this that creates its measureless ardor. To quote Madame Ackermann:—

> "*Ces délires sacrés, ces désirs sans mesure,*
> *Déchaînés dans vos flancs comme d'ardents essaims,*
> *Ces transports, c'est déjà l'humanité future*
> *Qui s'agite en vos seins.*"

However disinterested and ideal an affection may seem, however noble and elevated an attachment may be, it is, from Schopenhauer's standpoint, simply Will projecting itself into the creation of another being; and the moment in which this new being rises from chaos into the *punctum saliens* of its existence is precisely that moment in which two young people begin to fancy each other. It is in the innocent union and first embrace of the eyes that the microbe originates, though, of course, like other germs, it is fragile and prompt to disappear. In fact, there are few phenomena more striking than the profoundly serious, yet unconscious, manner in which two young people, meeting for the first time, observe one another. This common examination, this mutual study, is, as has been stated, the meditation of the genius of the species, and its result determines the degree of their reciprocal inclination.

In comedy and romance the sympathies of the spectator are invariably excited at the spectacle of these two young people, and especially so when they are discovered defending their affection, or, to speak more exactly, the projects of the genius of the species, against the hostility of their parents, who are solely occupied with their individual interests. It is unquestionably for this reason that the interest in plays and novels centres on the entrance of this serene spirit, who, with his lawless aims and aspirations, threatens the peace of the other actors, and usually digs deep graves for their happiness. As a rule, he succeeds, and the climax, comformably with poetic justice, satisfies the spectator, who then goes away, leaving the lovers to their victory, and associating himself in the idea that at last they are happy, whereas, according to Schopenhauer, they have, in spite of the opposition of their parents, simply given themselves up as a sacrifice to the good of the species.

In tragedies in which love is the mainspring, the lovers usually die, because, as follows from the foregoing logic, they have been unable to triumph over those designs of which they were but the instruments.

As Schopenhauer adds, however, a lover may become comic as well as tragic, and this for the reason that in either case he is in the hands of a higher power, which dominates him to such an extent that he is, so to speak, carried out of himself, and his actions in consequence become disproportioned to his character. "Hence it is that the higher forms of love bring with them such poetic coloring, such transcendental and supernatural elevation, that they seem to veil their true end and aim from him completely. For the moment, he is animated by the genius of the species. He has received a mission to found an indefinite series of descendants, and, moreover, to endow them with a certain constitution, and form them of certain elements which are only obtainable from him and a particular woman. The feeling which he then has of acting in an affair of great importance transports the lover to such superterrestial heights, and garbs his material nature with such an appearance of immateriality that, however prosaic he may generally be, his love at once assumes a poetic aspect, a result which is often incompatible with his dignity."

In brief, the instinct which guides an insect to a certain flower or fruit, and which causes it to disregard any inconvenience or danger in the attainment of its end, is precisely analogous to that sentiment which every poet has tried to express, without ever exhausting the topic. Indeed, the yearning of love which brings with it the idea that union with a certain woman will be an infinite happiness, and that the inability to obtain her will be productive of insufferable anguish, cannot, according to Schopenhauer, be considered to have its origin in the needs of the ephemeral individual; it is in fact but the sigh of the genius of the species, who sees herein a unique opportunity of realizing his aims, and who in consequence is violently agitated.

Inasmuch as love rests on an illusion of personal happiness, which the supervising spirit is at little pains to evoke, so soon as the tribute is paid the illusion vanishes, and the individual, left to his own resources, is mystified at finding that so many sublime and heroic efforts have resulted simply in a vulgar satisfaction, and that, taking all things into consideration, he is no better off than he was before. As a rule, Theseus once consoled, Ariadne is forsaken, and had Petrarch's passion been requited his song would then have ceased, as that of the bird does when once its eggs are in the nest.

Every love-match, then, is contracted in the interest of the future generation, and not for the profit of the individual. The parties imagine, it is true, that it is for their own happiness; but, as Schopenhauer has carefully explained, owing to the instinctive illusion which is the essence of love they soon discover that they are not united to each other in any respect, and this fact becomes at once evident when the illusion which first joined them has at last disappeared. Hence it happens, Schopenhauer adds, that love-matches are usually unhappy, for they but assure the presence of the next generation at the expense of everything else, or, as the proverb runs, "*Quien se casa por amores ha de viver con dolores.*"

"If now," he concludes, "we turn our attention to the tumult of life, we find that all men are occupied with its torments, we see them uniting their efforts in a struggle with want and massing their strength against misery, and yet there, in the thick of the fight, are two lovers whose eyes meet, charged with desire! But why do they seem so timid, why are their actions so mysterious? It is because they are traitors who would perpetuate the pain which, without them, would soon come to that end which they would prevent, as others have done before them."

There can be but one objection to this novel theory, which, at least, has the merit of being thoroughly logical, as well as that of connecting a subject so intangible as love to the fundamental principle of the whole doctrine, and that is that it leaves those higher and purer realms of affection, of which most of us are conscious, almost entirely unvisited. This objection, however, loses much of its force when it is remembered that Schopenhauer gave to this division of his subject the title of "Metaphysics of Love," and in so doing sought solely to place the matter on a scientific basis. In this he has undoubtedly succeeded, and his explanation, if characteristic, is not for that reason necessarily unsound. In another essay,* which is narrowly connected with the one in hand, he takes the reader from the highest spheres of pure love to the foundation of ethics, and shows that both are derived from an identical sentiment, which he calls compassion.

And since grief is king, what better primate can he have than sympathy? To the thinker who sees joy submerged by pain, and

---

* "Das Fundament der Moral," contained in *Die beiden Grundprobleme der Ethik*. Leipsic: Brockhaus.

death rule uncontested, what higher sentiment can come than that of pity? Schopenhauer has, however, been very frequently blamed for giving this as the foundation of morality; to many it has seemed too narrow and incomplete, and an academy (that of Copenhagen) refused to crown his essay, for that very reason. But whatever objections may be brought against it, its originality at least is unattackable. In ancient philosophy, ethics was a treatise of happiness; in modern works, it is generally a doctrine of eternal salvation; to Schopenhauer, it is neither; for if happiness is unobtainable, the subject is necessarily untreatable from such a standpoint, and on the other hand, if morality is practiced in the hope of future reward, or from fear of future punishment, it can hardly be said to spring from any great purity of intention. With such incentives it is but a doctrine of expediency, and at best merely adapted to guide the more or less interested motives of human action; but as the detection of an interested motive behind an action admittedly suffices to destroy its moral value, it follows that the criterion of an act of moral value must be the absence of any egotistic or interested motive.

Schopenhauer points out that acts of this description are discernible in the unostentatious works of charity, from which no possible reward can accrue, and in which no personal interest is at work. "So soon," he says, "as sympathy is awakened the dividing line which separates one being from another is effaced. The welfare and misfortunes of another are to the sympathizer as his own, his distress speaks to him and the suffering is shared in common." Meanwhile this phenomenon, which he sees to be of almost daily occurrence, is yet one which reason cannot explain. All, even the most hard-hearted, have experienced it, and they have done so very often intuitively and to their own great surprise. Men, for instance, risk their lives spontaneously, without possible hope of gain or applause, for a total stranger. England, some years ago, paid twenty millions sterling to free the slaves in her colonies, and the motive of that grandiose action can certainly not be attributed to religion, for the New Testament does not contain a word against slavery, though in the days to which it refers slavery was universal.

It is pity, then, according to Schopenhauer, which is the base of every action that has a true moral value. "Indeed," he says, "the soundest, the surest guarantee of morality is the compassionate sympathy that unites us with everything that lives. Before it the casuist is dumb. Whoso possesses it is incapable of causing the slightest harm or injury to any one; rather to all will he be magnanimous, he will forgive, he will assist, and each of his actions will be distinguished by its justice and its charity." In brief, compassion "is the spontaneous product of nature, which, while independent of religion and culture, is yet so pervasive that everywhere it is confidently evoked, and nowhere counted among the unknown gods. It is compassion that makes the mother love best her feeblest child. Truly the man who possesses no compassion is outside of humanity."

The idea that runs through the whole subject, and which is here noted because its development leads to the logical climax of the entire philosophy, is that all love is sympathy, or, rather, all pure love is sympathy, and all love which is not sympathy is selfishness. Of course combinations of the two are frequently met; genuine friendship, for instance, is a mixture of both, the selfishness consisting in the pleasure experienced in the presence of the friend, and the sympathy in the participation in his joys and sorrows. With this theory as a starting-point, Schopenhauer reduces every human action to one, or sometimes to two, or at most three motives: the first is selfishness, which seeks its own welfare; the second is the perversity or viciousness which attacks the welfare of others; and the third is compassion, which seeks their good. The egotist has but one sincere desire, and that is the greatest possible amount of personal well-being. To preserve his existence, to free it from pain and privation, and even to possess every delight that he is capable of imagining, such is his end and aim. Every obstacle between his selfishness and his desires is an enemy to be suppressed. So far as possible he would like to possess everything, enjoy everything, dominate everything. His motto is, "All for me, nothing for you." When, therefore, the power of the state is eluded, or becomes momentarily paralyzed, all at once the riot of selfishness and perversity begins. One has but to read the "*Causes Célèbres,*" or the history of anarchies, to see what selfishness and perversity are capable of accomplishing when once their leash is loosed.

At the bottom of the social ladder is he whose desire for life is so violent that he cares nothing for the rights of others, and for a small personal advantage oppresses, robs, or kills. Above him is the man who never violates the rights of others,—unless he has a tempting opportunity, and can do so with every reasonable assurance of safety,—the respectable citizen who pays his taxes and pew-rent, and once in a while serves on the jury. On a higher level is he who, possessing a considerable income, uses but little of it for himself and gives the rest to the poor, the man who makes less distinction than is usually made between himself and others. Such an one is as little likely to let others starve while he himself has enough and to spare, as another would be to hunger one day that he might eat more the next. To a man of this description the veil of Mâyâ, which may be taken to mean the veil of illusions, has become transparent. He recognizes himself in every being, and consequently in the sufferer.

Let this veil of Mâyâ be lifted from the eyes of a man to such an extent that he makes no distinction at all between himself and others, and is not only highly benevolent, but ready at all times to sacrifice himself for the common good; then he has in him the holiness of the saint and the germ that may flower into renunciation. The phenomenon, Schopenhauer says, by which this change is marked is the transition from virtue to asceticism. In other words, it then no longer suffices for him to love others as himself; there arises within him a horror of the kernel and essence of the world, which recognizably is full of misery, and of which his own existence is an expression, and thereupon denying the nature that is in him, and ceasing to will anything, he gives himself up to complete indifferentism to all things.

Such, in outline, is Schopenhauer's theory of ethics, which, starting from the principle of kindness of heart, leads to the renunciation of all things, and, curious as the *dénouement* may appear, at last to universal deliverance.

In earlier pages the world has been explained to be utterly unsatisfactory, and it has been hinted that the suicide, were he delivered of his suffering, would gladly rehabilitate himself with life; for it is the form of life that the suicide repudiates, not life itself. But life, to be scientifically annihilated, should be abolished, not only in its suffering, but in its empty pleasures and happiness as well; its entire inanity should be recognized, and the whole root cut once and for all. In explaining in what manner this is to be accomplished, Schopenhauer carries his reader *bon gré, mal gré,* far off into the shadows of the Orient. On the one side is the lethargy of India, on the other China drugged with opium, while above all rises the fantasy of the East, the dogma of metempsychosis.

As has been seen, Schopenhauer holds that there is in every life an indestructible principle. This belief he shares with the Buddhist, the Brahmin, the ancient Druid, and the early Scandinavian; historically speaking, the doctrine is so old that a wise Anglican is reported to have judged it fatherless, motherless, and without genealogy. Properly speaking, however, this creed does not now insist that there is a transmigration of the soul, but rather, in accordance with recent esoteric teaching, it implies simply that the fruit of good and evil actions revives with the individual through a succession of lives, until the evil is outbalanced, the good is paramount, and deliverance is at last attained. In other words, the beautiful myth of the early faith is superseded by an absurd and awkward palingenesia.

Schopenhauer gives the name of Will to that force which, in Indian philosophy, is considered to resurrect with man across successive lives, and with which the horror of ulterior existences reappears. It is from this nightmare that we are summoned to awake, but in the summons we are told that the awakening can only come with a recognition of the true nature of the dream. The work to be accomplished, therefore, is less physical than moral. We are not to strangle ourselves in sleep, but to rise out of it in meditation.

"In man," says Schopenhauer, "the Will-to-live advances to consciousness, and consequently to that point where it can readily choose between its continuance or abolition. Man is the saviour, and all nature awaits its redemption through him. He is at once the priest and the victim."

If, therefore, in the succeeding generations the appetite for death has been so highly cultivated, and compassion is so generally practiced, that a widespread and united pity is felt for all things, then through asceticism, which the reader may construe universal and absolute chastity, that state of indifference will be produced in which subject and object disappear, and—the sigh of the egoist Will once choked thereby into a death-rattle—the world will be delivered from pain.

"It is this," Schopenhauer exclaims in his concluding paragraph, "that the Hindus have expressed in the empty terms of Nirvana, and reabsorption in Brahma. We readily recognize that what remains after the entire abolition of the Will is without effect on those in whom it still works; but to those in whom it has been crushed, what is this world of ours with its suns and stellar systems? Nothing."

In the preface to the second edition of the *Welt als Wille und Vorstellung*, Schopenhauer recommends that the work be read by the light of his supplementary essays. This task, beyond demanding an agility of pencil and some concentration, is otherwise one of the most morbidly agreeable that can be suggested. The sensation that comes with a first reading is that of an abrupt translation to the wonders of a world which heretofore may have been dimly perceived, but which then for the first time is visited and thoroughly explored. The perspective, it is true, holds no Edens; in the distance there are no Utopias; but when the journey is ended and the book laid aside, the peaks and abysses to which the reader has been conducted stand steadfast in memory, and the whole panorama of deception and pain groups itself in a retrospect as sudden and clear as that which attends the last moments of the drowning man.

And Schopenhauer is the least pedantic, and yet the most luminous of ciceroni: in pages which Hugo would not disavow, and of which the foregoing analysis can give at best but a bald and unsatisfactory idea, he explains each height and ruin with an untiring verve, and with an irony as keen and fundamental as Swift's. But beyond his charm as a stylist, and his exhaustive knowledge of life, he claims attention through his theory of the universal force, his originality in the treatment of ethics, and the profound ingenuity with which he attaches everything, from a globule to an adagio in B flat, to his general system.

It is said that philosophy begins precisely where science ends; the doctrine, therefore, which has just been considered is, in a measure, impregnable to criticism. Reduced to its simplest expression, it amounts briefly to this: an unknown principle— an x, which no term can translate, but of which Will, taken in the widest sense of Force, is the rendition the least inexact—explains the universe. The highest manifestation of Will is man; any obstacle it encounters is pain. Pain is the attendant of life.

Man, however, duped by the instinct of love, has nothing better to do than to prolong through his children the sorrowful continuation of unhappy generations. The hope of a future existence in a better world seems to be a consolation, but as a hope it rests on faith. Since life is not a benefit, chaos is preferable. Beyond suicide, which is not a philosophic solution, there are but two remedies for the misery of life; one, a palliative, is found in art and disinterested contemplation; the other, a specific, in asceticism or absolute chastity. Were chastity universal, it would drain the source of humanity, and pain would disappear; for if man is the highest manifestation of Will, it is permissible to assume that, were he to die out, the weaker reflections would pass away as the twilight vanishes with the full light.

All great religions have praised asceticism, and in consequence it was not difficult for Schopenhauer to cite, in support of his theory, a number of texts from the gnostics, the early fathers of the church, the thinkers, such as Angelius, Silesius, and Meister Eckhard, the mystics, and the quietists, together with pertinent extracts from the Bible and the sacred books of the Orient. But none of these authorities seem to have grasped the principle which, according to Schopenhauer, lies at the root of asceticism and constitutes its chief value. At best, they have seen in it but the merit of obedience to a fantastic law, the endurance of a gratuitous privation, or else they have blessed in celibacy the exaltation of personal purity and the renunciation of worldly pleasures. From the philosophic standpoint, however, the value of asceticism consists in the fact that it leads to deliverance, prepares the world for the annihilation of pain, and indicates the path to be pursued. Through his labors and sympathy the apostle of charity succeeds in saving from death a few families which, in consequence of his kindness, are condemned to a long misery. The ascetic, on the other hand, does far better; he preserves whole generations from life, and in two or three instances very nearly succeeded in saving the world. "The women," Schopenhauer says somewhere, "refused to join in the enterprise, and that is why I hate them."

If asceticism were practiced by all men, it follows that pain, so far as man is concerned, would cease in it. But is it permissible to assume that with the disappearance of man the world will vanish with him—in other words, if humanity dies out, that animality must necessarily follow after?

It is here, if anywhere, that Schopenhauer has blundered; the world is deplorably bad, let the optimist and thoughtless say what they will, and it would undoubtedly be very advantageous to have the whole universe tumble into sudden chaos; but that such a consummation is to be brought about by voluntary asceticism is, in the present state of society, and independent of the opposition of women, greatly to be doubted.

Schopenhauer has denied that a being superior to man could exist; if, then, the nineteenth century, which plumes itself on the mental elevation and culture of the age, and in looking back at the ignorance of earlier epochs considers itself the top of all creation,—if, then, the nineteenth century, in its perspicacity, refuses such a solution, there is little left for humanity to do save to bear the pains of life as it may, or, better still, with the resignation which Leopardi long ago suggested.

When, putting aside this eccentric theory of deliverance, the teaching of Schopenhauer is reviewed, it will, according to the nature of the reader, bring with it a warm approval or a horrified dissent. To some he will appear like an incarnation of the Spirit of Truth; to others like the skeleton in Goya's painting, which, leaning with a leer from the tomb, scrawls on it the one word, Nada,—nothing.

CHAPTER FOUR.

The Borderlands of Happiness.

IT WAS WITH SOMETHING OF THE LASSITUDE WHICH succeeds an orgy that Schopenhauer turned from the riot of the will and undertook to examine such possibilities of happiness as life may yet afford, and, as incidental thereto, the manner in which such possibilities may be most enjoyed.

To this subject he brought a sumptuous variety of reflections, which are summed up in a multi-colored essay, entitled "Lebensweisheit," or Conduct of Life, but in which, in spite of the luxury of detail and brilliancy of description, Schopenhauer almost unconsciously reminds the reader of a man who takes his constitutional at midnight, and preferentially when it rains.

The suggestions that occur to him are almost flamboyant in their intensity, and yet about them all there circles such a series of dull limitations that one somehow feels a sense of dumbness and suffocation, a longing to get away and rush out into an atmosphere less charged with sombre conclusions.

Concerning the baseness and shabbiness of every-day life

Schopenhauer has but little to say. He touches but lightly on its infinite vulgarity, while its occasional splendor is equally unnoticed. Indeed, he preaches not to redeem nor convert, but simply that his hearers may be in some measure enlightened as to the bald unsatisfactoriness of all things, and so direct their individual steps as to come as little in contact with avoidable misery as possible. To many it will, of course, seem quite appalling that a mind so richly receptive as his should have chosen such shaggy moorlands for habitual contemplation, when, had he wished, he might have feasted his eyes on resplendent panoramas. The moorlands, however, were not of his making; he was merely a painter filling in the landscape with objects which stood within the perspective, and if he happened upon no resplendent panoramas, the fault lay simply in the fact that he had been baffled in his attempt to find them.

Voltaire says, somewhere, "I do not know what the life eternal may be, but at all events this one is a very poor joke." In this sentiment Schopenhauer solemnly concurred. That which was a *boutade* to the one became a theory to the other, and it is to his treatment of this subject that the attention of the reader is now invited. The introduction which he gives to it, if not as light as the overture to a ballet, will, it is believed, still be found both interesting and instructive, while its conclusion and supplement form, it may be noted, an admitted part of that which is best of the modern essayists.

The first chapter opens with an enumeration of those possessions which differentiate the lot of man, and which in so doing form the basis of possible happiness. It has been said that the happiest land is the one which has little, if any, need of importations, and he notes that the man is most contented whose interior wealth suffices for his own amusement, and who demands but little, if anything, from the exterior world. Or, as Oliver Goldsmith has expressed it,—

"Still to ourselves in ev'ry place consigned
Our own felicity we make or find."

"In a world such as ours," Schopenhauer thinks, "he who has much to draw upon from within is not unlike a room in which stands a Christmas tree, bright, warm, and joyous, while all about are the snows and icicles of a December night."

That which a man is in himself, that which accompanies him into solitude, and which none can give him or take from him, is necessarily more essential than all that he may possess or all that he may appear in the eyes of others. The scholar, for instance, even when utterly alone feeds most agreeably on his own thoughts, and we are most of us very well aware that he whose intelligence is limited may ceaselessly vary his festivals and amusements without ever succeeding in freeing himself from the baleful weariness of boredom.

According to Schopenhauer, then, the supreme and all-important elements of earthly happiness are subjective possessions, such as a noble character, a capable mind, an easy disposition, and a well-organized and healthy body; and it is these gifts, he rightly insists, that should be cultivated and preserved, even at the expense of wealth and emolument. An easy disposition, however, is that which above all other things contributes most directly to contentment. Gayety of heart is, indeed, its own recompense, and he who is really gay has a reason for so being from the very fact that he is so. Supposing a man to be young, handsome, rich, and respected, the one question to be asked about him is, Is he light-hearted? On the other hand, if he is light-hearted, little does it matter whether he is young or old, straight-limbed or deformed, poor or rich; in any case he is contented. It is light-heartedness alone which is, so to speak, the hard cash of happiness; all the rest is but the note-of-hand; and in making this observation, he (Schopenhauer) is careful to point out that there is nothing that contributes so little to gayety as wealth, and nothing that contributes so much thereto as health. "It is in the lower classes, among the laborers, and particularly among the tillers of the soil, that gayety and contentment are to be found, while on the other hand, the faces of the great and the rich generally present an expression of sullen constraint. To thoroughly understand, however, how greatly happiness depends on gayety of disposition and the state of health, it is only necessary to compare the impression which the same circumstances and similar wants bring to us in days of health and vigor, with that which is paramount when through our condition we are predisposed to dullness and discontent. In brief, it is not the event itself, but the way in which we view it, that makes or unmakes our happiness." Or, as Epictetus said long ago, man is not moved by things, but by his opinion of them.

As a general rule, nine tenths of happiness may be said to rest on the state of health; when this is perfect, anything and everything may be a source of pleasure; in illness, on the other hand, nothing, no matter what its nature may be, is capable of affording any real enjoyment. It follows, therefore, that it is wanton stupidity to sacrifice health for any purpose, even for wealth and fame, and especially to passing and fugitive pleasures, however alluring they may appear.

The next class of possessions of which Schopenhauer treats is property; and in considering this division he seems not unlike that contented individual who, on seeing a quantity of objects exposed for sale, exclaimed pensively, "How much there is of which I have no need!"

Every man, it will be admitted, has his own horizon, beyond which his pretensions do not extend. They reach the edge, but they do not cross it. In other words, the absence of those possessions with which a man is unacquainted is in no sense a privation to him; and it is probably for this reason that the day-laborer bothers himself so little about the flaring wealth of the rich. Wealth, on the other hand, is like salt water; the more one drinks, the greater the thirst. But, even so, this grim philosopher was far from despising it. "It is a rampart against an incalculable number of discomforts; and it is in this manner that it should be viewed, instead of being considered, as is generally the case, in the light of a permission to procure a diversity of pleasure."

As a practical man, Schopenhauer saw nothing that could make his ink blush in repeatedly recommending the preservation of a fortune, made or inherited; "for even," he says, "if it simply suffices to permit its possessor to live without the necessity of labor, it is still an inappreciable advantage in that it brings with it an exemption from the general drudgery which is the ordinary lot of man. It is only on this condition that man is born free, master of his hour and his strength, and enabled to say each morning, 'The day is mine.' The difference, therefore, between him who has a thousand crowns a year and the landlord whose rent-roll runs into millions is infinitely less than the difference between the first and the man who has nothing."

If the man whose necessities are provided for is inclined to follow Schopenhauer's advice, he will, first of all, seek in repose and leisure the avoidance of every form of discomfort; especially will he seek to lead a tranquil and unpretentious existence which, so far as possible, will be sheltered from all intruders. After having for a certain time kept up relations with what is termed the world, he will prefer a retired life; and if he is of superior intelligence, he will give himself up to solitude. This he will do, because the more a man possesses in himself, the less he has need of the exterior world. Superiority of intelligence will therefore lead him to insociability; for, as Schopenhauer says, "It is precisely in solitude, where each of us is dependent on his own resources, that every one is brought face to face with his own individuality; there the imbecile in his purple groans beneath the weight of his miserable self, while he who is mentally gifted peoples and animates with his thoughts the most arid and desert region."

Now, it may be objected that contentment is not to be found in an idle folding of the hands behind a hedge set against vexation. Nor is this Schopenhauer's meaning. Wealth is but the means, not the source of contentment. It is not the certainty of an income that brings happiness, for its accompanying affranchisement from want carries the tenant to the opposite pole of misery, where gapes the hydra, ennui. And it is there that he whose necessities are provided for surely lands, unless he fills the hour with some one of the many elevated pursuits from which those who are obliged to work for their bread are in a great measure debarred.

The third and last class of possessions that Schopenhauer discusses is that which a man represents; or, in other words, the manner in which he appears to his neighbors. "There is," he says, "no superstition more universally dominant than that which leads us to attach a high value to the opinion of others; and whether it be that this superstition has its roots in our very nature, or that it has followed us up from the birth of society and civilization, it is none the less certain that it influences our conduct in a manner which is incommensurate, and hostile to our well-being. This influence may be traced from the point in which it shows itself beneath the anxious and servile deference to the *qu'en dira-t-on*, to that in which it drives the dagger of Virginius into his daughter's heart, or else to where it leads men to sacrifice their peace, their fortune, their wealth, and their lives, for the sake of posthumous renown."

The existence, however, which we lead in the minds of others is a possession, Schopenhauer has carefully explained, which, through a singular weakness, while highly prized is yet entirely unimportant to our happiness. Indeed, if the comparison be drawn between that which we are in reality and that which we are in the eyes of others, it will be seen that the first term of the comparison comprises our entire existence, for its sphere of action is in our own perceptions, while, on the other hand, that which we represent acts on other minds than our own, and in consequence has no direct existence for us, and an indirect one only so far as it may influence their conduct toward us. The wealthy, in their uttermost magnificence, can but say, "Our happiness is entirely outside of us; it dwells in the minds of others." Certainly, to a happiness of this description every thinker is indifferent, or will necessarily become so as he grows aware of the superficiality and dullness of mind, the narrow sentiments and limited ideas, the absurdity of opinion and numberless errors, which go to the making of his neighbor's brain. Indeed, it is generally sufficient to note with what contempt half-a-dozen imbeciles will speak of some distinguished man, to be quite ready to agree with Schopenhauer that in according a high value to the opinion of others we are paying them an honor which they in no sense deserve.

It is essential to our well-being to thoroughly understand the simple fact that each one lives but in his own particular skin and not in the opinion of others, and that, therefore, our actual condition as determined by health, temperament, intellect, wife, children, and home, is a hundred times more important than what it may please others to think about us; fame, of course, is very pleasant; so is glory; but, after all, what do they amount to? As has been seen, Leopardi snapped his fingers at them both. To him they were simply illusions. Schopenhauer goes more deeply into the subject, and explains with great opulence of detail and fantasy of adjective that glory and fame are founded on that which a man is in comparison to others; in other words, that their value is purely relative, and would disappear entirely if every one became that which a celebrity is already. It is not fame that is so desirable, but rather the merit which should precede it. "The predisposing conditions are, so to speak, the substance, while glory itself is but the accident, which works on its possessor as an exterior symptom, and confirms his own high opinion of himself. But this symptom is yet not infallible, for is there not glory without merit and merit without fame?"

As glory is incontestably but the echo, the image, the shadow, the simulachre of merit, and as in any case that which is admirable should be more highly valued than the admiration that it excites, it follows that that which causes happiness does not consist in glory, but rather in the attracting force of merit; or, to put it more exactly, in the possession of such character and faculties as predispose thereto.

To be deserving of fame is, then, its own exceeding great reward. There all the honor lies, and necessarily this must be true, "for, as a rule, the reverberation of a glory that is to echo through future ages rarely reaches the ears of him who is the object; and though certain instances to the contrary may be objected, yet they have usually been due to fortuitous circumstances which are otherwise without great importance. Men lack ordinarily the proper balance of judgment which is necessary for the appreciation of superior productions; and in these matters they usually take the opinion of others, and that, too, in such wise that ninety-nine admirers out of a hundred accord their praise at the nod of one." It is for this reason that the approbation of one's contemporaries, however numerous their voices may be, has so slight a value for the thinker, for at best he can hearken to the voices of the few, which in themselves may be but the effect of the moment. "Would a virtuoso be greatly flattered by the applause of his public if he learned that, with but two or three exceptions, the auditorium was filled with deaf mutes who, to conceal their infirmity, clapped a loud approval so soon as they saw a real listener move his hands? And how would it be if he knew the leaders of the clique were often paid to procure a great success to the most insignificant scraper of cat-gut?"

It is with reflections of this description that Schopenhauer explains why it is that sudden celebrity so rarely passes into immortal glory, and points—

> ..."how hard it is to climb
> The heights where Fame's proud temple shines afar,"

and even, the summit gained, the uselessness of it all.

This same conclusion has been reached by several other writers, notably by Leopardi, whose views have been already explained, and by Von Hartmann, whose theories are mentioned in the next chapter; but the main idea has perhaps been best expressed by D'Alembert, who, in speaking of the temple of fame, says, "Its interior is inhabited only by the dead who were not there in their life-time, and by certain aspirants who are shown the door as soon as they die."

To sum up what Schopenhauer has set forth, and of which the foregoing detached ideas can give at best but a lame conception, we find that to his mind, as perhaps to that of every serious thinker, the first and most essential condition of contentment is the quality of character; and this would be essential if only because it is always in action, but it is so, even to a greater extent, because it is the only possession which cannot in some manner be taken from us. In this sense he considers its value as absolute when opposed to the relative value of mere possessions and the opinion of others. In brief, man is not so susceptible to the influence of the exterior world as it is generally supposed, for only Time can exercise his sovereign rights upon him. Beneath this force the physical and intellectual qualities wane and gradually succumb, the moral character alone remaining invulnerable.

Considered in this connection, actual possessions and the opinions which others hold concerning us have this advantage over character: they need not necessarily be affected by time;

moreover, being accessible in their nature they both may be acquired, while, on the other hand, character once established remains invariable for life. Schopenhauer evidently does not hold with him who sings—

"That men may rise on stepping-stones
Of their dead selves, to higher things."

All that can be done, he has explained, is to employ the individuality, such as it is, to the greatest profit; or, in other words, a man should pursue only those aspirations which correspond to his disposition, and only choose in consequence that occupation and walk of life which is best suited to it.

From the preponderance thus given to the first of these three divisions over the two others, it follows that it is far better to watch over health and the development of the intellect than it is to attend to the acquisition of wealth. Schopenhauer, of course, does not mean that the acquisition of that which is necessary to one's proper maintenance should be in any wise neglected; far from it. His idea is simply that a superfluity of riches, instead of contributing to well-being, brings with it an inevitable vexation in the constant care which the management of a large fortune demands.

Briefly, then, the essential element of contentment is that which one is in himself, and it is simply because the dose is ordinarily so small that the majority of those who have been conquerors in the struggle with want feel themselves to be as thoroughly unhappy as those who are still in the thick of the fight. But still, whatever the issue of the conflict may be, each one among us is enjoined to aspire to a good repute. Honor is an inappreciable belonging, and glory, the most exquisite of all that is within the reach of man, is the Golden Fleece of the elect.

The second and third divisions have upon each other a reciprocal effect: wealth brings with it the good opinion of others, and the good opinion of others has aided many a man on the road to fortune; taken together they represent over again the *habes, haberis* of Petronius, yet the factors that reside within us contribute more liberally to contentment than those which are born of things.

It is somewhat in this manner, but with a conciseness of deduction and a felicity of diction which the foregoing summary is inadequate even to suggest, that Schopenhauer, without any noticeable effort, points quietly and with a certain suavity of self-confidence to the fact that there is, in spite of all our bluster and hurrying about, very little in life that is of much consequence. There is, of course, little that is terrifying in what he has written; there is no incentive and no stimulus, as the phrase goes, to be up and doing; indeed, to the reflective mind his logic will have somewhat the effect of a sedative, and to many he will seem to hold that the best use life can be put to is to pass it in a sort of dilettante quietism. Such in the main is his idea, but it is an idea which, to be acted upon, necessitates a refinement of the senses and a burnish of the intellect such as is possessed but by the few, and consequently the fear of its general adoption need cause but small alarm. It may be remembered that, beyond the surface of things here examined, he pointed, in another essay, to the influence of morality on general happiness, and recommended the practice of charity, forbearance, and good will to all men, as one of the first conditions of mental content.

Against all this, naturally, many objections might be raised, and several ameliorations could be suggested, but in the main the teaching has a certain sound value which it would be difficult to talk away. Champfort has said, "Happiness is no easy matter; it is hard to find it within us, and impossible to find it elsewhere," and this aphorism, with which Schopenhauer decked his title-page, served pretty much as keynote to the whole essay. All the way through he has insisted that the prime essential is what one *is* in one's self, that is, in character and disposition, but not wealth nor yet the esteem of others; these, it is true, are pleasing additions, but not the *sine qua non*.

Wealth, however, is too greatly prized to suffer from a theoretic treatment any appreciable diminution in general esteem, and there are necessarily few who will object to it because they are told it is an extra burden. Perhaps Schopenhauer would not have turned his back upon it either had he been put to the test, but as he escaped that, the conjecture is comparatively useless; still, few men can eat two dinners, and those who have that capacity are seldom objects of envy, even to the disciples of Baron Brisse. The dinners may stand, of course, for figurative repasts, and, according to Schopenhauer, if a man has enough, a superfluity is not only unnecessary, but may readily resolve itself into a cause of vexation.

Certainly, as Schiller said, we are all born in Arcadia: that is, we enter life fully persuaded that happiness exists, and that it is most easy to make acquaintance with it; but, generally speaking, experience soon lets us know that happiness is a will o' the wisp, which is only visible from afar, while on the other hand, suffering and pain have a reality so insistent that they present themselves not only at once and unexpectedly, but without any of the flimsiness of illusion. In Schopenhauer's view, the best the world has to offer is an existence of painless tranquillity; pleasures are and always will be negative, and to consider them otherwise is a mistake which brings its own punishment with it. Pain, on the contrary, is positive, and it is in its absence that the ladder to possible contentment may be found. If, then, from a condition of this description, viz.: one which is devoid of pain, boredom be also subtracted, then the reader may be sure that this is the pinnacle of earthly happiness, and that anything that lies beyond belongs to the domain of pure chimera.

In the chapter succeeding the one just considered Schopenhauer added certain reflections on the proper conduct of life which, though loose and unsystematic, are yet peculiarly fertile in suggestion, and entirely free from the more or less accentuated platitudes with which other writers have dulled the subject.

In this essay he holds that the supreme rule of earthly wisdom is contained in Aristotle's dictum that the sage will seek to dwell where pain is not, and not where pleasure is. The truth of this axiom he establishes by a constant reiteration of his favorite theory that pleasure as well as happiness is negative, and only pain is real. Now other writers, particularly Mr. James Sully and Herr von Hartmann, have rebelled against this statement, but the force of their arguments has not been strong enough to confute it. Indeed, mere logic can make no man contented, and in any event, if a philosopher considers pleasure as a negative condition, and the critic prefers to look upon it in a different light, the student is no more bound to agree with the one than with the other; he will, if properly advised, draw his conclusions from his own sensations. In accordance with the best views, however, Schopenhauer is right and his critics wrong. A homely example which he suggests may perhaps serve to set the matter straight: when we are in perfect health, and there is but one little painful spot somewhere—for instance, an aching tooth or a swollen finger—our otherwise perfect health is unnoticed, and our attention is directed entirely to the pain we are experiencing, while pleasure, determined, as always, by the totality of the sensations, is entirely effaced. In the same manner, when everything in which we are interested is going as we wish, save one thing which is going the wrong way, it is this particular thing that is constantly in our mind, and not the other and more important matters, which are giving us no concern.

Schopenhauer's advice, therefore, is that attention should not be directed to the pleasures of life, but to the means by which its innumerable evils may best be escaped. If this recommendation is not sound, then Voltaire's aphorism—happiness is but a dream and only pain is real—is as false in appearance as it is correct in reality. Whoever, then, would draw up a balance sheet of pleasure and pain should not base the sum total on the amount of pleasures which he has enjoyed, but rather in accordance with the pains which he has avoided. For as it has been pointed out, life at best is not given to us to be enjoyed, but to be endured, and the happiest man is, therefore, he who has wandered through life with the smallest burden of physical and mental suffering, and not he to whom the most vivid delights and intensest joys have been accorded.

In any case, the greatest piece of stupidity of which man can be guilty is to wish to transform his theatre of misery into a pleasure-ground, and to attempt to seek happiness therein, instead of trying, as he should, to avert as many pains as possible. There are, of course, many who are foolish enough not to take this view of life; but, according to Schopenhauer, those who do not do so are much more at fault than those who, with excess of precaution, look upon the world as a burning pit, and occupy themselves to the best of their ability in procuring a fire-proof dwelling.

The simpleton will always run after pleasure, and the pessimist will do all he can to give pain a wide berth; if, in spite of his efforts, the success of the latter is small, the fault is not so much his as that of fate; and if, in pursuance of this idea, he has taken a very roundabout way and uselessly sacrificed any amount of possible pleasures without any appreciable benefit, he can at least take heart again in the knowledge that he has in reality lost nothing at all, for the possible pleasures are such pure chimeras that it is simply childish to grieve about them.

It is, Schopenhauer says, because this mistake is so frequently made in favor of optimism that such a number of misfortunes occur, for in those moments that we are free from discomfort "disquieting desires dazzle our eyes with the illusions of an unreal yet seductive happiness, and lure us on to a suffering which is neither the one nor the other; then indeed do we grieve over the lost estate, which was exempt from pain, as over a paradise on which we have wittingly turned the key. In this way it seems as though some evil spirit was constantly working a deceptive mirage to draw us from that freedom from pain, which is the supreme and only real happiness."

Now, the average young man is usually possessed of some vague conviction that the world, stretching out before him to unseen limits, is the seat of a tangible happiness, which only escapes those who are not clever enough to grasp it. This conviction, moreover, is strengthened by romance and verse, and by that hypocrisy which leads the world always by the thread of exterior appearance. Ever after, his life is a more or less prudently conducted hunt, a chase for a fictitious game, until at last with a round turn he is pulled up face to face with disenchantment, and finds that the infinite vistas narrow down to a dark alley, with a dead wall at the end.

On the other hand, the careful observer of men and things will mark a protest on his own existence; he will have no great hopes, and but few regrets; Plato long ago said there is nothing in life worth a struggle, and to this maxim Schopenhauer's ideal reader will attune his days and, in any variations he may attempt, keep always to the minor key.

The chief difficulty, however, which the candidate in pessimism will encounter in his first attempt to practice the foregoing recommendations is that which is raised by the hypocrisy of the world, to which allusion has been already made; and yet, in Schopenhauer's teaching, the most practical lesson that can be given to youth is the showing up of the whole thing for the sham that it is. "The splendors are merest tinsel," he says; "the essence of the thing is lacking; the fêtes, the balls, the illuminations, the music, are but the banners, the indications, the hieroglyphics of joy; yet, as a rule, joy is absent, it alone has sent a regret. When it does present itself, it comes ordinarily without invitation and unannounced; it enters, *sans façon*, in the simplest manner, often for the most trivial reason, and under circumstances that are well-nigh insignificant. Like the gold in Australia, it is spread about here and there according to the whim of hazard, without law or rule, generally in small particles, and but seldom in an appreciable quantity."

This certainly cannot be termed an enthusiastic view of life, nor, for that matter, is it intended to be so considered. There was too much unreasoning enthusiasm, Schopenhauer thought, and too much unwary skating over thin surfaces, and it was precisely for this reason that he set about painting Danger in the biggest and blackest-looking characters. If his advice, therefore, is not always cheerful, it is at least practical, and in any event no one can go far astray in following the monitory finger-posts which he was the first to erect; the wayfarer who takes them for guidance may perhaps stand still, but at least he will not stumble into any artificial pitfalls, or happen upon unexpected quagmires.

In treating of our conduct to ourselves, Schopenhauer lays much stress on the recommendation that such proportion be preserved between the attention which we give to the present and that which we grant to the future, that the one will in nowise interfere with the other. As there are many who live for the hour and many who live for the future, the right measure is seldom attained; but, as Schopenhauer points out, the future, like the past, has a value which is more apparent than real. It is the present that is actual, it is the present that is certain, while the future, on the contrary, usually turns out in a manner totally different from our expectation. The distance which "robes the mountains" expands them in our thoughts, but the present alone is true and effective; and as it is therein that our existence exclusively rests, it should not only be hospitably received, but every hour that is free from vexation or pain should be enjoyed to the fullest extent, and not saddened with the memory of irrecoverable hopes, or darkened by apprehensions of the morrow. In other words, let the dead past bury its dead, and for the moment take Seneca for model, and agree with him that each day separately is a separate life. As for the future, it rests in the lap of the gods.

"The only misfortunes concerning which we should alarm ourselves are those that are inevitable; but then, after all, how many are there of this nature? Misfortunes, broadly considered, are either possible and probable, or else certain, though in the indefinite future; and if we bother ourselves over all that *might* come to pass, we would never enjoy a moment's repose." In order, therefore, that tranquillity may not be unnecessarily disturbed, Schopenhauer advises that possible misfortunes be looked upon as though they would never occur, and inevitable misfortunes as though they were still far distant.

It is a curious fact that the blind, who of all people are usually pitied as the most unfortunate, possess, as a class, the calmest and most contented expression. This phenomenon may serve as some corroboration of a theory, which Schopenhauer expands at great length, that the narrower the circle of vision the greater the happiness; and conversely, the wider it is the greater the inquietude and torment. It is, then, in the simplicity and uniformity of life—so long, of course, as it does not engender weariness of mind—that the greatest measure of happiness is to be found. Under conditions of this description, which every poet from Horace to Joaquin Miller has more or less praised, the burden from which life is inseparable is borne most lightly, and existence flows like a rivulet, without tides or waves.

The claims of society, the effort to keep in the swim, *dans le mouvement*, as the French say, is not, of course, very conducive to the tranquil contentment which is here so earnestly commended. Schopenhauer has much to say on the subject. As a self-constituted recluse he necessarily judged the world, and as necessarily found it wanting. Indeed, it may fairly be said that he held in utter contempt the entire machinery of fashion, and looked upon the whole thing as a toy for imbeciles. To say that he hated it would be unjust, for, like most sensible people, he held hatred to be an elixir far too precious to be wasted on trivial matters. He simply took up society and then let it drop, and he did so not because it soiled his gloves, but because it did not seem worth the holding.

Such views as he cared to express on this subject are unmarked by any striking vividness of originality; for the most part they are simple, every-day observations, as pertinent to Europe half a century ago as to contemporary London and New York, and imply, briefly, that society is a mill of the conventional which grinds individualities into a tiresome sameness of sample. Individuality was like a strong-box into which Schopenhauer placed all his valuables, and to which, we are led to believe, he clung with all his might and main. Rather than have it tampered with he carried it off to a hermitage and kept it there, one might say, in cotton. It may be, however, that the underlying reason of the sombre obliqueness with which he viewed the world at large sprang from a cause which was natural, if commonplace; it did not appreciate him. Nor is this very surprising; society, as a rule, has an immense fund of appreciation, which it lavishes liberally on every merit, save alone that of intellectual ability; on this it looks askant, or, as Schopenhauer says, "as if it were smuggled." "Furthermore," he goes on to say, "good society, so called, not only brings one in contact with a lot of people whom he can neither approve of nor like, but it will not permit us to be ourselves, to be such as our nature demands; on the contrary, it compels us, that we may remain on the same diapason with the rest, to shrivel up completely, and even at times to appear deformed."

Wit and repartee are admittedly out of place save among one's peers; in ordinary society such manifestations are either not understood, or looked upon as dreadfully bad form. For that matter, it is only the novice who thinks that brilliant conversational powers will serve as passport; as a rule, it does nothing of the sort; rather does it excite among the majority a feeling nearly akin to hatred, and which is all the more bitter because it must be concealed.

"Ordinarily," Schopenhauer says, "when two people are talking together, so soon as one of them notices a great superiority on the part of the other he tacitly concludes, and without definite reason for so doing, that his own inferiority has been noticed by his companion, for whom he immediately conceives a blind resentment, even a violent dislike; nor in this is he much to be blamed, for what is a display of wit and judgment but an accusation to others of their own commonplace stupidity and dullness? To please in society, therefore, one needs to be scatter-brained or ignorant; and it is precisely those who are the one or the other, or even both, who are welcome and well received."

From Schopenhauer's standpoint, then, the society that is worth the trouble of cultivating is not such as is told of in the morning papers. The ball-goers, the dinner-givers, the pleasure-seekers of every class and denomination, were to him mentally insolvent, and unable to offer any indemnity for the boredom and fatigue which their reunions and conversation created. To be socially inclined was to him irrefutable evidence of a vacuous mind; and with some of that grim humor which characterized much of his work, he compared the modern assembly to that Russian orchestra which, composed of horns that have but one note apiece, is harmonious only through the exact coincidence of each instrument; taken separately, each one is appallingly monotonous, and it is only in conjunction with others that they amount to anything at all. So it is, he finds, with the majority of people; individually, they seem to have but one thought, and are in consequence both tiresome and sociable.

There is a tolerably familiar anecdote of Louis XIII., which represents that feeble monarch as hailing one of his officers with the bland suggestion that they should wile away the hour in common boredom: *"Venez, monsieur,"* run the historic words, *"allons nous ennuyer ensemble;"* and it is perhaps this self-same, but unanalyzed motive which leads so many to ease their weariness in the companionship of their fellows, for, after all, it cannot but be admitted that the most gregarious seek the presence of others, and even of those for whom they care nothing, not so much for the sake of society as to get away from themselves and the dull monotone of an empty head.

Such, at any rate, is Schopenhauer's idea; and he is careful, in pointing to the retired existence of all really distinguished thinkers, to note that the desire for companionship is not derived from a love of society, but from a fear of solitude, and that so soon as the latter is mastered there is no further desire to mingle with the crowd. The only society, therefore, that is worth the trouble of cultivation is that of one's own self; in this Schopenhauer apparently makes no exception; however closely the bonds of love or friendship may be woven, there is always some clash of temperament; an echoless shock it may be, but to nerves properly attuned none the less unpleasant. In regard to the society of the distinguished thinkers, of whose conspicuous solitude he makes constant parade, nothing is said; but it is perhaps allowable to suppose that genius, when it does descend from its lofty seclusion, quickly tires of giving, giving always, without return, and on its summits fraternizes as seldom with its peers as kings do with their equals. In brief, then, the sociability of man is in an inverse ratio to his intellectual value, and to say of some one "he is not at all sociable," may be generally taken to mean "he is a man of great ability."

The praises of solitude have been written over and over again; almost all the essayists, and most of the poets, have expatiated more or less volubly on its charms, but no one has entered so thoroughly into the core of the subject as did this spectacled misanthrope. Emerson has told a quaint little story of a friend who took an exquisite delight in thinking of the incalculable number of places where he was not, and whose idea of felicity was to dwell far off somewhere among the back stars, "there to wear out ages in solitude, and forget memory itself." Had Schopenhauer known this gentleman he would have loved him, though perhaps at a distance; as it was, he expressed an approval that was well-nigh rapturous of La Bruyère's well-known axiom: "All our misfortunes come from an inability to be alone," and at measured intervals repeated Voltaire's maxim that "the world is full of people who are not worth speaking to." His own ideas on the subject savor highly of the epigrammatic. "Solitude," he says, "offers a double advantage to the thinker: the first in being with himself, the second in not being with others."

The love of solitude, however, cannot be considered otherwise than as an acquired taste; it must come as the result of experience and reflection, and advance with the development of the intellect as well as with the progress of age. A child will cry with fright if it be left alone even for a moment; in boyhood, solitude is a severe penance; young men are eminently sociable, and it is only the more elevated among them who from time to time wander off by themselves; but even so, a day passed in strict seclusion is no easy matter. In middle age, it is not so difficult, while to the aged, solitude seems the natural element. But in each individual, separately considered, the growth of the inclination for solitude is always in proportion to the strength of the intellect, and, according to Schopenhauer, it is never thoroughly matured until the individual becomes firmly convinced that society is the most disagreeable of all the unpleasant things in the world.

To this conclusion both Petrarch and Zimmerman came in their respective works on solitude. Chamfort says somewhere, very wittily, "It is sometimes said of a man that he lives alone and does not care for society; this is very much the same as saying that he does not care for exercise, because he does not make excursions at night in the forest of Bondy." In short, all those whom Prometheus has fashioned from his finer clay have brought testimony of like purport. To Schopenhauer a desire for solitude was a sure indication of aristocratic tastes. "Every blackguard," he says, "is pitiably sociable, but true nobility is detected in the man who finds no pleasure in the companionship of others, and who, in preferring solitude to society, gradually acquires the conviction that, save in rare exceptions, there is little choice between isolation and vulgarity." Angelus Silesius, whose name has descended to us in a halo of Christian tenderness, bears witness to the truth of this theory,

> "Though solitude is hard, yet the refined
> Will still in ev'ry place a desert find."

It is especially in old age, when one has ceased to expect anything in particular from the generality of mankind, when one has become pretty well satisfied that in the long run men do not improve on acquaintance, and when one is usually divested of those illusions which make the companionship of others seem desirable,—it is at this period that the taste for solitude, which heretofore has demanded a succession of struggles, becomes at once natural and matter of fact. One feels, then, as much at ease therein as the fish does at high water.

But in spite of the advantages of solitude there is a hackneyed proverb about the rose and the thorn which has here a most direct application. In the same manner that every breath of frosty air injuriously affects any one who constantly keeps to his own room, so does a man's disposition become so sensitive in solitude that he is vexed and annoyed at the most trivial incident, at a word, or even at an expression of the countenance. It is hard, however, to catch Schopenhauer napping, and for this he has a remedy which, if not within the reach of all, is none the less efficacious. His recipe is simply that every aspirant should accustom himself to carry a part of his solitude into society, and learn to be alone even in a crowd; in other words, not to tell others at once what he thinks, and not to pay much attention to what others may say; in this way he will in a measure keep himself unaffected by the stupidities which must necessarily surge about him, and harden himself to exterior influences.

As has been noted, it was far from Schopenhauer's intention to recommend an idle folding of the hands. Solitude is all very well, but to be habitable it must be peopled with thoughts and deeds; the essence of life is movement, and in inaction it is a most difficult thing to be tranquil. Indeed, the most thoughtless must do something, even if that something consist but in a tattoo beaten on the window-pane. Schopenhauer's words, however, are presumably not addressed to thoughtless people. To struggle and cope is, he says, as much of a necessity to man as burrowing is to the mole. To conquer resistance constitutes the fullness of human delight, and whether the obstacles are of a material nature, as in action and exercise, or purely mental, as in study and research, it is the combat and the victory that bring happiness with them.

In treating of our conduct to others, Schopenhauer seems always to be peering down and sounding bottom in unfathomed depths of the human heart, and to be taking measure of those crevices and sinuosities for which Balzac and La Rochefoucauld, with all their equipment of bitterness, possessed no adequate compass. The result of his soundings and measurements is a lesson of circumspection and indulgence, of which the first stands as guarantee against prejudice, and the second as shelter from quarrels and disputes. Machiavelli warned every one to as carefully avoid an injury to the self-esteem of an inferior as one would the commission of a crime. Schopenhauer goes even further; his theory is that whoever is obliged to live among his fellows should never repulse any one, however pitiful, wicked, or ridiculous his character may be; on the contrary, he should accept him as something immutable, and consider that there must necessarily be some one of that class too. If he does otherwise he commits not only an imprudence, but provokes a life-long enmity, for, after all, no one can modify his own character, and if a man is condemned unreservedly there is, of necessity, nothing left for him to do but to declare war to the knife. It is for this reason that when one wishes, or is obliged to live among his fellow-creatures, it becomes necessary to let each one work out his own nature and accept each individual as he stands; the most that can be done is to attempt to utilize the qualities and dispositions of each, so far as they may be adaptable, but in no case is a man to be condemned purely and simply for what he is. This is the true signification of the dictum, "Live and let live."

Meanwhile, in learning how to treat others it will not come amiss, Schopenhauer goes on to say, to exercise a little patience on any of the inanimate objects which in virtue of some physical or mechanical necessity obstinately annoy and thwart us every day; for in so doing we learn to bestow on our fellows the patience already acquired, and in this manner become accustomed to the thought that they, too, whenever they form an obstacle to our wishes, do so because they cannot help it, in virtue of a natural law which is as rigorous as that which acts on inanimate things, and because it is as absurd to get angry with them as to be annoyed at the stone which slips between our feet.

But in all this Schopenhauer is far from recommending any

over-indulgence or excess of amiability, for he readily recognizes that the majority of people are like children, who become pert as soon as they are spoiled. Refuse a loan to a friend, he says, and you will not lose him as readily as you would if you had advanced the money; in the same manner a trace of haughtiness and indifference on your part will generally quell any of those preliminary symptoms of arrogance that follow upon too much kindness. Indeed, it is the idea that one has need of them that few men can bear,—they become presumptuous at once; and it is for this reason that there are so few with whom one can be really intimate.

Most especially should we avoid any familiarity with vulgar natures. "If by chance an inferior imagines for a moment that I have more need of him than he has of me, he will suddenly act as though I had stolen something from him, and hurry to re-venge himself and get his property back." In brief, the only way in which superiority can be maintained is in letting others see that we have no need of them at all. Moreover, Schopenhauer notes, it is a good plan to appear a trifle disdainful from time to time; such an attitude has a strengthening effect on friendship: "*Chi non istima, vien stimato*" (he who shows no respect is re-spected himself) runs the sagacious Italian proverb. But above all, if any one does possess a high value in our eyes it should be hidden from him as a sin. This advice is not particularly exhila-rating, but it is sound. Too much kindness disagrees with dogs, to say nothing of men.

It is a curious fact that the more intellectual a man is the more easily he is deceived. There seems to be something almost incompatible between a high degree of culture and an extended knowledge of men and things, whereas, in the case of people of ordinary calibre, a lack of experience will not necessarily hinder them from properly conducting their affairs; they possess, as it were, an *a priori* knowledge which is furnished to them by their own nature, and it is precisely the absence of this knowledge that causes the mistakes of the more refined. Even when a man has learned from the teaching of others and through his own experience just what he may expect from men in general, even when he is thoroughly convinced that five sixths of them are so constituted that it is better for him to have nothing at all to do with them, even then, his knowledge is insufficient to preserve him from many false calculations. A presumable wiseacre, for instance, may accidentally be drawn into the society of people with whom he is unacquainted, and be astonished to find that in conversation and manners they are sensible, loyal, and sincere, and, perhaps, intelligent and witty. In that case, Schopenhauer warns him to keep well on his guard, for the reason that Nature is entirely unlike the dramaturge who, when he wishes to create a scoundrel or a simpleton, sets about it so awkwardly that he seems to be standing behind each character in turn, and in disavowing their gestures and words to be warning the audience that one is a ruffian and the other a fool, and that no one is to believe a word that they say. It is not at all in this way that Nature acts: her method is that of Shakespeare and Goethe, in whose plays each person, be he the Devil himself, speaks as he ought to, and is conceived so realistically that he attracts and commands attention. To think, then, that the Devil goes about with horns, and the fool with bells, is to lay one's self open to a continual deception, for, as a rule, our moralist says, men behave very much like the moon or like the hunchback; they show only one side, and even then they have a peculiar talent for making up their faces into a species of mask, which exactly represents *what they ought to be*, and this they assume whenever they wish to be well received. Put not your trust in princes, say some; Schopenhauer's advice is, Put not your trust in masks; and to substantiate his warning he quotes an old proverb, which holds that no matter how vicious a dog may be he can still wag his tail.

To all these rules and suggestions there are, of course, exceptions; there are even exceptions that are incommensurably great, for the difference between individuals is gigantic, but taken as a whole, Schopenhauer condemns the world as irreclaimably bad, and it may be added that one does not need to be a professional pessimist to arrive at very nearly the same conclusion. But beyond these broad recommendations a few others are given on our proper bearing and attitude to the world at large, and which, summed up in his own words, amount, in brief, to the teaching that one half of all wisdom consists in neither loving nor hating, and the other half in saying nothing and believing nothing.

Lamennais exclaimed one day, "My soul was born with a sore," and to some it may perhaps seem that on Schopenhauer's heart an ulcer had battened during each of the seventy years that formed his life. Certainly he has appeared to force the note many times, but it is permissible to doubt that he prepared a single paragraph in which he expressed himself otherwise than as he really thought. In his pessimism there is no pose and as little affectation; he wrote only what he felt to be true, and he did so with a cheerful indifference to approval or dislike; his position was simply that of a notary drawing up provisos and conditions in strict accord with the statutes of life of which he stood as witness. His mother, who had little cause to come forward as an eulogist, paid him—years after their separation—this one sincere tribute: "With all his vagaries," she said, "I have never known my son to tell a lie." Other encomiums have, of course, been passed upon him, but it is impossible to imagine one more glorious than this. Over and above his disregard of sham and falsehood, beyond his theory of force and the seductions of his ethics, Schopenhauer is chiefly remarkable in this: that he was the first to detect and logically explain that universal nausea which, circulating from one end of Europe to the other, presents those symptoms of melancholy and disillusion which, patent to every observer, are indubitably born of the insufficiencies of modern civilization.

Where, then, it may be asked, for this malady of the refined, are the borderlands of happiness to be found? From the standpoint of this teacher the answer is that they are discoverable simply and solely in an unobtrusive culture of self, in a withdrawal from every aggressive influence, and above all in a supreme indifference which, culpable though alluring, permits the neophyte to declaim with Baudelaire,—

"*Résigne-toi, mon cœur, dors ton sommeil de brute.*"

The foregoing attempt to winnow some of the finer fibres of thought from the six volumes which form the complete edition of Schopenhauer's works leaves admittedly much to be desired. There has been, as the phrase goes, an *embarras des richesses*, and in consequence much attendant indecision as to the choice to be made of different yet equally interesting topics. The passages that have been selected and annotated in this and in the preceding chapter have been, it may be explained, so selected, because they seemed, when arranged with some attempt at orderly sequence, to present in the fewest possible words the essence of the main idea which runs through the entire philosophy, and which in the absence of some such arrangement demands a concentration more prolonged than is usually at the disposal of the ordinary reader. Those who are already acquainted with Schopenhauer's works, and who may do the present writer the honor of reading this exposition, will perhaps object to it on the ground that it does not enter sufficiently into the scientific side of the doctrine, and through this neglect leaves the reader in the dark as to its true value. To this presumable objection the writer begs leave to make answer that the scientific aspect of the doctrine has been so exhaustively treated by others that it has seemed to him a waste of time to enter into any further consideration of a subject whose true value, in spite of the numberless controversies and arguments which it continues to create, still remains undetermined. Moreover, as will have been readily seen, the foregoing pages have in no sense been addressed to the scientist, and that for the reason that exact information is only obtainable from the philosophy itself, or from such a complete and, therefore, voluminous analysis as would be out of place in a treatise of this description. The aim of these chapters is but to draw in outline the principal features of this doctrine, and in so doing to present in the absence of complete translations a little of that vigor and color which has raised the original to the prominent position it holds among the foremost works of modern thought. No attempt at the polemical has been made, and this for the reason that it is seldom advisable to attack the truth; the notations and criticisms which have been offered have been prepared, not with the wish to controvert, but rather with the hope that they might serve to a clearer understanding of the whole philosophy.

CHAPTER FIVE.

The Great Quietus.

It is related of Schopenhauer that he was in the habit of putting down a gold piece on the *table d'hôte* where he dined, and of taking it up again when the dinner was ended. This gold piece, he explained to his Boswell, was for the waiter the first time that any one of the different officers, who frequented the dining-room, was heard discussing a loftier topic than that which is circled in wine, woman, and song. As the story runs, no occasion ever presented itself in which he could in this manner express his pleasure and contentment; but had he lived long enough to meet Lieutenant Von Hartmann there is little doubt that the gold piece would have formed an immediate and rightful part of the waiter's perquisites.

This gentleman, who is now no longer an officer, but simply a thinker and a man of letters, may, in many respects, be regarded as Schopenhauer's direct descendant. To the world at large very little concerning him is known, and that little is contained in a modest autobiography which appeared a few years ago, and to which his publisher has since added a supplement.

The meagre details that are furnished therein amount, in brief, to this: Eduard von Hartmann was born in 1842, in Berlin, in which city he passed an uneventful boyhood. The school which he attended, and which like most other schools forced the pupils to master a quantity of subjects whose usefulness may be questioned, brought him into an almost open revolt against a system of education which, in nine cases out of ten, is nothing more than a pure waste of time. On leaving the gymnasium he decided, for reasons which to the average German must seem fantastic, to enter the military service at once instead of passing the usual semesters at a university. To this budding pessimist student life seemed to offer but dull variations between commonplaceness and vulgarity: to listen or not to listen to sundry poorly expressed lectures by day, to engulf at night a certain quantity of beer in stone measures, and to diversify these occupations in receiving slashes on the cheek-bone, or in affording amusement to the Hebes of Prussian restaurants, was not to him the life that was called ideal. Very wisely, then, and in accordance with the example which his father had already given, he chose in a military career a profession most apt to satisfy those inclinations of the scientist and of the artist which had already begun to exert an influence upon him.

In the year 1858 Herr von Hartmann entered the crack artillery regiment of Berlin as volunteer. He then passed three years at the artillery school, intermingling the scientific studies of his profession with artistic and philosophic researches, and frequenting meanwhile the refined society to which his family belonged. About this time a rheumatic affection, which had first declared itself toward the close of his school-days, became complicated with a fracture of some of the delicate machinery of the knee. The injury was both painful and incurable, and in 1864 he was obliged to resign his position, and thereupon left the army with the grade of first lieutenant. These latter details are given by way of counterbalance to the calumnies of his enemies, who, in explaining his pessimism by the state of his health,—which they insinuate was brought about by excessive and unusual debauchery,—have in one way and another managed to vituperate his chief work into nine editions.

On leaving the army he sought a career first as painter and then as musician; it did not take him long, however, to discover that his vocation was not such as is found in purely artistic pursuits; "the bankruptcy of all my ambitions," he says, "was complete; there remained to me but one thing, and that was thought." It was from thought, then, that he demanded a consolation and an employment, and turning to metaphysics he began at once to plan his *Philosophy of the Unconscious*. Meanwhile, for his own distraction and instruction he had written a few essays, of which but one was destined to see the light of day. This monograph, *Die dialektische Methode*, was so favorably viewed at Rostock, that he received therefrom the degree and title of Doctor of Philosophy.

The Philosophy of the Unconscious, when completed, remained a year in his closet, and was only published in 1868, owing to an accidental meeting with an intelligent publisher. Before, as since, the appearance and success of this work, which is very generally considered as the chief philosophical event of the last two decades, Dr. von Hartmann has lived at Berlin, where he endeavors in every-day life to prove the practical value of evolutionary pessimism, which it is his wish to substitute for the indifferentism and quietist doctrines of Schopenhauer.

Personally, Dr. von Hartmann is a very attractive individual, and his attractiveness is increased by the fact that there is nothing commonplace, and at the same time nothing affected about him. When I called at his house, I found him coiled up in a rug on one of those long chairs that are familiar to every ocean traveler. My first impression was that I was in the presence of a giant; and as the Berlinese as a race are notoriously tall, I was only surprised at the great size of his head, which differed singularly from that of the ordinary Prussian. His hair was brushed back from his forehead in the manner popularly termed *à la Russe*, but which is more noticeable in Vienna than in St. Petersburg; his eyes, which were large and luminous, possessed an expression of such indulgence as would put the most timid visitor at ease. Owing partly to the arrangement of his hair, his forehead seemed to me to be the most expansive that I had ever seen; the lower part of his face was hidden in a beard which descended very nearly to his waist, while as for his mustache, it is, I think, the longest in metaphysics. In some way or another I had gotten to believe that it was part of the professional philosopher to be both self-contained and absent-minded; I always pictured him as a class as wearing spectacles far down on the nose, as being somewhat snuffy, and carelessly tired in loose and shabby dressing-gown. I can give no reason for this fancy of mine other than that it is one of those pictures which we all draw of people and places that we have not seen. If I remember rightly, Mr. Sala said that he imagined Leipzig to be a city of very squat houses, in which dwelt little girls in blue skirts, and this until he got there and found that it was precisely like any other of its kind.

As a child, and indeed until very lately, I invariably thought of Hungary as having red roads, bordered by crimson houses and bluffs of green, while all about I saw in fancy splendid horses prancing in rich caparisons; but, as any traveler will admit, Hungary, in point of natural effects, is as humdrum as Connecticut; for real color, I suppose one must go to Japan, and yet there are many who have done so and then returned utterly disillusioned. Dr. von Hartmann took away my illusion about the philosopher; he had a rug, it is true, but no dressing-gown, or at least not one which was visible, and there was nothing of the careless mien and abstracted attitudes which I had expected; to use a current phrase, he was very wide awake, and I may add that to one who has lived among Germans he seemed refreshingly hospitable and graciously courteous.

Even in its most pleasant season, Berlin is not a pleasant city; a lounge of but half an hour on the Unter den Linden results through unconscious imitation in an enforced quickstep; to begin with, there are too many big houses, and then there are too many big soldiers; and while the soldiers present to the stranger an appearance of arrogant hostility, the houses, not to be outdone, try to look as much like the soldiers as possible, and loom up in alert unbending aggressiveness; indeed, I have now in my mind a certain street which, when I looked down it, almost got up and threatened me. I experienced, therefore, a subtle pleasure on discovering that out of the whole of rigid Berlin Dr. von Hartmann had chosen his residence in the most unsoldierly, and for that reason the most attractive part; and it was to this quarter of the city that I went to visit the man who, in spite of certain vagaries of thought, may be considered as Germany's first thinker. When he had disentangled himself from the folds of his rug, the impression which had been produced by the size of his head and the breadth of his shoulders vanished entirely. I thought for the moment of the quaint myths of the earlier Teutons, of the gnomes and kobolds, for Dr. von Hartmann, while massive in head and shoulders, is yet short and undersized, and the suggestion of the Rhine legends which his appearance caused was heightened by the strange effect produced by the luxuriance of his beard and mustache.

He had barely spoken, however, before I recognized in him not only the man of the world, which goes without the telling, but the gentleman, and, in a moment, the thinker. Stendhal says somewhere, in speaking of German, that it took him "two whole years to forget the beastly language." Stendhal was what is termed nowadays an impressionist, and his expression may perhaps on that account be excused; in any event German is decidedly an unpleasant tongue; it is very rich, rich even to exuberance, and when it is well handled it is to the initiate delightful in many respects; but to the Latin, and the average Anglo-Saxon, it is terribly tortuous, and most easy to lose one's way in. I had hoped, therefore, that I might be allowed to talk with Dr. von Hartmann in some more flowing form of speech, but as he preferred German, it was not, of course, my place to rebel, and I soon found that I had nothing to regret. I have had in the Fatherland the privilege of hearing some very accomplished actors, and I have also sat beneath some very eloquent speakers, but the amplitude and resources of the German language were first made clear to me by this gentleman. When he spoke, I may say, without exaggeration, that his words seemed less like figures of speech than evocations of pictures. I had puzzled for some time over a particular point in his teaching, and when I told him of my difficulty he drew down before me a series of illustrations and examples, which were as well defined as though they formed a panorama on the wall; and therewithal was such a fluency of verb, such a precision of adjective, and such a nicety of accent, that for the first and only time I loved the German language.

Dr. von Hartmann is in no sense a misanthrope. He leads a quiet and easy life, demonstrating by his own example that pessimism is not a gospel of desolation. Personally, he has had many grave misfortunes; he has suffered in health, in name, and in purse, he has lost many who were most dear to him, but his laugh is as prompt and as frank as a boy's. At the head of his table sits a gracious and charming woman, his children are rich in strength and spirits, and an observer lately said of him and his family, "If you wish to see happy and contented faces, go call on the Hartmanns."

Beyond writing a dozen or more monographs, and dissertations on philosophical subjects, Dr. von Hartmann has also charmed the public with two elaborate and well-conceived poems. His chief claim to recognition, however, and the one which has placed him at the head of contemporary metaphysics, is the work already mentioned, in which, somewhat after the manner of his predecessor, and yet with a diffuseness of argument which had no part in Schopenhauer's system, he reduces the motor forces of the universe to a dual principle which he terms the *Unbewussten*, or the Unconscious.

It is unnecessary to enter into any minute examination of this theory of his, in which, with a juggle of fancies and facts, he tries to reconcile the teaching of Hegel with that of Schopenhauer, for, however it may be considered, it is in any event but loosely connected with that part of his philosophy which treats of the matter in hand.

It will be sufficient for the understanding of what is to follow, to note simply that after examining the forms of phenomenal existence, matter, life organic and inorganic, humanity, and so on, he presents the Unconscious as the One-in-all, the Universal soul, from which, through determined laws, the multiplicity of individuals and characters is derived. This one-in-all is sovereignly wise, and the world is admirable in every respect; but while he argues in this way that the world is the best one possible, he has no difficulty in showing that life itself is irreclaimably miserable.

The originality of his system consists in a theory of optimistic evolution as counterbalanced by a pessimistic analysis of life, and also in the manner in which, with a glut of curious argument, he concludes that as the world's *progressus* does not tend to either universal or even individual happiness, the great aim of science should be to emancipate man from the love of life, and in this wise lead the world back to chaos.

The main idea runs somewhat as follows. The interest of the Unconscious is opposed to our own; it would be to our advantage not to live, it is to the advantage of the Unconscious that we should do so, and that others should be brought into existence through us. The Unconscious, therefore, in the furtherment of its aims, has surrounded man with such illusions as are capable of deluding him into the belief that life is a pleasant thing, well worth the living. The instincts that are within us are but the different forms beneath which this unreasoning desire to live is at work, and with which the Unconscious inspires man and molds him to its profit. Hence the energy so foolishly expended for the protection of an existence which is but the right to suffer, hence the erroneous idea which is formed of the pain and pleasure derivable from life, and hence the modification of past disenchantments through the influence of fresh and newer hopes.

With regard to happiness, there are, according to Hartmann, three periods or forms of illusion, from all of which the world must be thoroughly freed before the great aim of science can be attained. The first of these illusions consists in the idea that under certain circumstances happiness is now obtainable on earth; the second, in the belief that happiness is realizable in a future state; and the third, in the opinion that happiness will be discovered in the march of progress through the coming centuries.

Of these three ideas, the first has for some time past been recognized by many as a chimera. In certain quarters the decomposition of the second has already begun, but the belief in the reality of the third is unquestionably the paramount conviction of the present century. When each of these three illusions has been utterly routed and universally done away with, then, Hartmann considers, the world will be ripe for its great quietus.

The first of these three forms is, of course, the most tenacious; indeed, it is an incontestible fact that man, even when miserable, clings to life, and loves it not only when there is some vague hope of a brighter future, but even under its most distressing conditions. It is, therefore, against this illusion that pessimism, to be successful, must rain the hardest blows.

The views of many eminent writers on this subject have already been expressed in the course of these pages, but their views, while in a measure important, should nevertheless be received with a certain amount of caution, for they emanate from superior minds, in which melancholy as the attribute of genius constantly presides.

Let us imagine, then, with Hartmann, a man who is not a genius, but simply a man of ordinary culture, enjoying the advantages of an enviable position; a man who is neither wearied by pleasure nor oppressed by exceptional misfortunes; in brief, a man capable of comparing the advantages which he enjoys with the disadvantages of inferior members of society; let us suppose that Death comes to this man and speaks somewhat as follows: "Your hour is at hand; it remains with you, however, to live at once a new life, with the past entirely effaced, or to accept the grave as it is."

There can be little doubt, if this hypothetical individual has not lived carelessly and thoughtlessly, and does not permit his judgment to be biased by the desire for life at any price, that he would choose death in preference to another existence, in which he would be assured of none of the favorable conditions which he had hitherto enjoyed. He will recommence his own life, perhaps, but no other of an inferior grade.

This choice, however, would be that of an intelligent man, and might be objected to on a ground not dissimilar to the one already advanced against the judgments of genius. But let us follow Hartmann still further, and in descending the spiral of humanity put the same question to every one we meet; let us take, for instance, a woodcutter, a Hottentot, or an orangutan, and ask of each which he prefers, death, or a new existence in the body of a hippopotamus or a flea. Each will answer, "death," but none of them will hesitate between their own lives and death; and if a like question be put to the hippopotamus and the flea, their answers will be precisely similar.

The difference in the comparative judgment that each would bring to bear on his own life, and on that of life in an inferior degree, results evidently from the fact that on being questioned each enters imaginatively into the existence of the lower creation, and at once judges its condition to be insupportable. The difference between the opinion which the flea holds on the value of its own existence and our own private judgment on this insect is derived simply from the fact that the flea has a quantity of absurd illusions which we do not share, and these illusions cause it such an excess of imaginary happiness that in consequence it prefers its own life to death. In this the flea is not wrong; on the contrary, it is quite right, for the value of an existence can only be measured in accordance with its natural limitations. In this sense illusion is as serviceable as truth.

From this introduction it follows quite of itself that each and every creature is capable of weighing the discomforts of an existence inferior to that in which it dwells, and yet is unable to rightly judge its own. Each can discern the illusions with which its inferior is surrounded, but is always defenseless against its own, save under exceptional circumstances, as in the case of genius. Hartmann concludes, therefore, very logically that an intelligence which is capable of embracing every form of life would condemn existence in its totality in the same manner that an intelligence relatively restricted condemns it in part.

In drawing up the balance-sheet of life, Hartmann differs from Schopenhauer on the question of the purely negative character of pleasure. That pleasure is at times a negative condition, as in the cessation of pain, he willingly admits, but from his standpoint it is something else besides; it may be either positive, although derived from an illusion, as in love, or real, as in art and science. Nevertheless, the predominance of pain over pleasure seems to be firmly established, and his examination of this subject is not without a repellant interest.

The four greatest blessings of life are admittedly health, youth, liberty, and well-being; but from their nature, Hartmann points out, these things are incapable of raising man out of indifference into pleasure save only as they may help to diminish an anterior pain, or guard him from a possible discomfort. Take the case of health, for instance; no man thinks of his nerves until they are affected, nor yet of his eyes until they ache; indeed, it may fairly be said that a man who is in perfect condition only knows that he has a body because he sees and touches it. Liberty may be regarded in much the same manner: it is unnoticed until it is in some way interfered with; while youth, which is the most propitious condition of life, is in itself but capability and possibility, and not possession, nor yet delight.

Well-being, the certainty of shelter from need and privation, Hartmann very rightly considers merely as the *sine qua non* of life in its baldest aspect, for, he argues, were it otherwise, the simple fact of living would satisfy and content us; but we all know that an assured existence is a torment if nothing fills the gap.

In the menagerie of beasts that torture life there is one, Baudelaire says in his easy metre, that is more hideous than all the rest; it is:—

> ..."*l'ennui! L'œil chargé d'un pleur involontaire*
> *Il rêve d'échafauds en fumant son houka—*
> *Tu le connais, lecteur, ce monstre délicat,*
> *—Hypocrite lecteur,—mon semblable,—mon frère!*"

This insupportable companion of inaction is usually banished by work; but then, to him who is obliged to labor, is not work often distasteful, and even a species of misfortune? Indeed, there are few, if any, who ever work save under compulsion; and whether the compulsion is caused by the attracting force of fame, the desire to escape from want, or comes simply as a promise of relief from boredom, the incentive and necessity are one and the same. It is true that man when at work is consoled by the thought of rest, but then work and rest merely serve to change his position, and they do so very much in the same manner as that uneasiness which forces the invalid to turn in bed, and then to turn back again, when it has shown him that the second position is no better than the first.

The great blessings of life, therefore, reduce themselves, in brief, to this: they represent but that affranchisement from pain which is equivalent to a state of pure indifference; but as no one reaches this condition save momentarily and by accident, it seems to follow that life has less charm than non-existence, which represents indifference in its most absolute and unquestioned form.

This state of beatitude is yet to be acquired; meanwhile, as Schiller says, so long as philosophy does not govern the world, hunger and love will suffice to keep it in motion. After the four causes of contentment, Hartmann's views on the two incentives to activity remain to be examined.

In regard to the first, it may be said without extravagance that the sufferings of hunger rule the greater portion of the 1300 millions of the earth's inhabitants. Europe not long since averaged a famine every seven years; now, the facilities of communication have replaced famine with an increased valuation of food. Death is the rarest and the least important evil that hunger occasions; what is most to be regarded is the physical and intellectual impoverishment, the mortality among children, and the particular maladies which it engenders.

According to Hartmann, the analysis of hunger shows that

in satisfying its demands the individual does not raise his sensibility above a state of pure indifference. He may, it is true, under favorable circumstances, cause a certain pleasure to predominate over suffering by means of taste and digestion; but in the animal kingdom, as in humanity, taken as a whole, the tortures caused by hunger are greatly in excess of any pleasures that may attach to it. In fact, from Hartmann's standpoint, the necessity of eating is in itself a misfortune.

After all that has been said through centuries of literature on the subject of love, it is certainly difficult to be original; but Hartmann has at least the merit of presenting it in a more abstract light, and from a less alluring standpoint than any other writer who has handled the subject. For love, according to his views, is either contrary to the laws of society, and as such environed by perils and pains, vice and degradation, or it is perfectly legal, and, in that case, quickly extinguished. "In the majority of cases," he says, "insurmountable obstacles arise between the two lovers and cause a consequent and immense despair, while in the rarer and more fortunate instances the expected happiness turns out to be purely illusory."

It is, however, as hard to love as it is not to love; but he (Hartmann) says, "Who once recognizes that the happiness which it offers is but a chimera, and that its pains are greater than its pleasures, will, while unable perhaps to escape entirely from its allurements, be none the less able to judge it differently from the novice, and therefore capable of diminishing some of its suffering, and some of the disproportion between its joys and its sorrows." According to this savage moralist, then, love is either an illusory and quickly vanishing happiness, or an actual suffering, and resembles hunger precisely in that it is in itself and to the individual a veritable curse.

Hartmann judges marriage with an epigram borrowed from Lessing: "There is, at most, but one disagreeable woman in the world; it is only a pity that every man gets her for himself." In very much the same manner are the ties of family and friendship weighed and judged. Scattered here and there is some reflection of Schopenhauer's wit and wisdom, but generally the discussion is defective, and lacks the grace of style and purity of diction which characterized the latter writer. The sentiments of honor, public esteem, ambition, and glory depend, he says, on the opinion of others, and are therefore merely toys of the imagination, "for my joys and troubles exist in my mind, and not in the minds of other people. Their opinion concerning me has merely a conventional value, and not one which is effective for me."

But to him who journeys through the desert called life, there is still one suave and green oasis. Hartmann is not utterly relentless, and though perhaps on all other subjects he may seem skeptical as a ragpicker, he has yet a word or two of cheer for art and science. These pleasant lands, however, are only traversable by rare and privileged natures, for if from the pleasure which attaches to music, painting, poetry, philosophy, and science, a deduction be made of all that which is but sham, dilettanteism, and vanity, the more considerable part of this supreme resource will be found to have disappeared. That which remains over is the compensation which nature preserves as recompense to the extreme sensibility of the artist and thinker, to whom the miseries of life are far more poignant than to other men, whose sensibilities are duller and less impressionable. Now, if the ubiquity of suffering is admitted, the temperament of this latter class is, in the long run, undoubtedly preferable to the more refined organization of the artist; for, after all, a state of comparative insensibility is evidently not too dearly bought, when the price is merely the lack of a delight, whose absence is not a privation, and which, to those able to appreciate it, is as rare as it is limited in duration. Moreover, even the real and ineffaceable pleasures which the thinker and artist enjoy are obtainable only after much trouble and discomfort.

Genius does not fall from the skies ready-made and complete in armor and equipment; the study which is to develop it is a task painful and tiresome, whose pleasures are rare, and, generally speaking, but those of anticipation and vanquished obstacles. Each art has its mechanical side, which demands a long apprenticeship; and even then, after the preliminary preparation, the only pleasant moments are those of conception, which, in turn, are directly succeeded by the long hours of technical execution.

In the case of the amateur, the pleasure of listening to good music, of seeing a fine actor, or of looking at works of art, is undoubtedly the one that causes the least amount of inconvenience, and yet Hartmann is not to be blamed for noting that even this pleasure is seldom unalloyed. In the first place, there is the bother of going to the picture-gallery; then there is the bad air and hubbub in the theatre; after this come the dangers of catching cold, of being run into, or annoyed in a dozen different ways, and especially the fatigue of watching and listening.

In the case of the artist there are the inevitable deceptions; the struggles with envy, the indifference and disdain of the public. Chamfort was wont to exclaim, "The public indeed! how many idiots does it take to make a public?" The public, nevertheless, has the ability to make itself very disagreeable, and not every one courts its smile with success. If, in addition to all these things, the nervous organization of the thinker, more vibrant a thousandfold than that of other men, is taken into consideration, it will be seen that Hartmann is not wrong in stating that the pleasures to which this class is privileged are expiated by a greater sensibility to pain.

But while art is not without its disadvantages, Hartmann declares that life still holds one solace that is supreme and unalloyed. "Unconscious sleep," he says, "is relatively the happiest condition, for it is the only one from which pain is completely banished. With dreams, however, all the miseries of life return; and happiness, when it then appears, does so only in the vague form of an agreeable sensation, such as that of being freed from the body, or flying through the air. The pleasures of art and science, the only ones which could reconcile a sensible man to life, are intangible herein, while suffering, on the other hand, appears in its most positive form."

Among the different factors which are generally supposed to be more or less productive of happiness, wealth or its symbol, money, usually represents the enchanted wand that opens the gate to every joy of life. It is true that we have seen that all these joys were illusions, and that their pursuit was more painful than pleasing, but Hartmann here makes an exception in favor of the delights which art and science procure, and also, like a true Berlinois, of those which the table affords.

"Wealth," he says, "makes me lord and master. With it I can purchase the pleasures of the table, and even those of love." It is unnecessary to contend with him on this point: our tastes all differ; still there are few, it is to be imagined, who will envy him in an affection which is purchasable with coin of the realm. Moreover, wealth does not make one lord and master; there is a certain charm in original and brilliant conversation which neither Hartmann nor any one else could buy, even though all the wealth of Ormus and the Ind stood to his credit on the ledgers of the Landesbank. Wealth, however, he hastens to explain, should be valued not for the commodities which it can procure, but rather because we are enabled therewith to shield ourselves from inconveniences which would otherwise disturb that zero of the sensibility which the pessimist holds to be the nearest approach to reality in happiness.

It is said that the drowning man will clutch at a straw, and it is possible that the reader who has seen his illusions dispersed and slaughtered one by one has perhaps deluded himself with the fancy that hope at least might yet survive; if he has done so, he may be sure that he has reckoned without his host. Hartmann guillotines the blue goddess in the most off-hand manner; she is the last on the list, and he does the job with a hand which is, so to speak, well in. Of course hope is a great delight; who thinks of denying it? Certainly not the headsman, who even drops a sort of half tear over her mangled wings. But if we come to look over the warrant which has legalized the execution, the question naturally arises who and what is hope? It is of little use to ask the poets, for they are all astray; what they see in hope is a fair sky girt with laurels,—in other words, the rape of happiness; but has it not been repeated even to satiety that happiness does not exist, that pain outbalances pleasure? What is hope, then, but an illusion? and an illusion, too, that plays all manner of tricks with us, and amuses itself at our expense; one, in fact, which makes use of us until our task is accomplished, and we understand that all things are different from that which we desired. "He, then," Hartmann says, "who is once convinced that hope is as vain and illusory as its object will see its influence gradually wane beneath the power of the understanding, and the one thing to which he will then look forward will be, not the greatest amount of happiness, but the easiest burden of pain."

In all that has gone before, Hartmann has endeavored to show that suffering increases with the development of the intellect, or rather, that happiness exists only in the mineral kingdom, which represents that zero of the senses above which man struggles in vain. It has been seen that they whose nervous systems are most impressionable have a larger share of suffering than their less sensitive brethren; furthermore, experience teaches that the lower classes are more contented than the cultivated and the rich, for while they are more exposed to want, yet they are thicker-skinned and more obtuse. In descending the scale of life, therefore, it is easy to show that such weight of pain as burdens animal existence is less than that which man supports. The horse, whose sensibility is most delicate, leads a more painful existence than the swine, or even the fish, whose happiness at high tide is proverbial. The life of the fish is happier than that of the horse, the oyster is happier than the fish, the life of the plant is happier yet, and so on down to the last degrees of organic life, where consciousness expires and suffering ends.

The balance sheet of human pleasure and pain may therefore be summed up somewhat as follows: in the first column stand those conditions which correspond to a state of pure indifference, and merely represent the absence of certain sufferings; these are health, youth, liberty, and well-being; in the second are those which stand as illusory incentives, such as the desire for wealth, power, esteem, and general regard; in the third are those which, as a rule, cause more pain than pleasure, such as hunger and love; in the fourth are those which rest on illusions, such as hope, etc.; in the fifth are those which, recognized as misfortunes, are only accepted to escape still greater ones: these are work and marriage; in the sixth are those which afford more pleasure than pain, but whose joys must be paid for by suffering, and in any event can be shared but by the few: this is the column of art and science.

Let a line be drawn and the columns added up, the sum total amounts to the inevitable conclusion that pain is greatly in excess of pleasure; and this not alone in the average, but in the particular existence of each individual, and even in the case of him who seems exceptionally favored. Hartmann has taken great care to point out that experience demonstrates the vanity of each of the opulent aspirations of youth, and that on the subject of individual happiness intelligent old age preserves but few illusions.

Such is the schedule of pleasure and pain which each one is

free to verify by his own experience, or, better still, to disregard altogether; for, from what has gone before, it is easy to see that man is most happy when he is the unconscious dupe of his own illusions. In Koheleth it is written: "To add to knowledge is to add to pain." He, then, whose judgment is obscured by illusions is less sensible to the undeniable miseries of life; he is always prepared to welcome hope, and each deception is forgotten in the expectation of better things. Mr. Micawber, whose acquaintance we have all made, is not alone a type, but a lesson, the moral of which is sometimes overlooked.

In brief, Hartmann's teaching resolves itself into the doctrine that the idea that happiness is obtainable in this life is the first and foremost of illusions. This conclusion, in spite of certain eccentricities of statement, is none the less one which will be found singularly difficult to refute. But every question has two different sides, and this one is no exception. The devil, whom Schopenhauer painted in a good grim gray, Hartmann has daubed all over with a depth of black of which he is certainly undeserving; and not only that, but he has taken an evident pleasure in so doing. It is not, therefore, unfair to use his own weapon, and tell him that he, too, is the dupe of an illusion, or, to borrow a simile from the prince of wits, to insist that while he may not carry any unnecessary quantity of motes in his eye, some dust has assuredly settled on his monocle.

As is the case with others who have treated the subject, Hartmann confounds the value of the existence of the unit with the worth of life in the aggregate. Taken as a whole, it is undeniably and without doubt unfortunate, but that does not prevent many people from being superlatively, and, to the pessimist, even insultingly happy; and though the joy of a lifetime be circumscribed in a single second, yet it is not rash to say that that second of joy may be so vividly intense as to compensate its recipient for all miseries past and to come. It may be noted, further, that the balance-sheet which has just been reviewed is simply a resultant of Hartmann's individual opinion. Sometimes, it is true, he deals with unquestioned facts, and sometimes with unanswerable figures; but it has been wittily said that nothing is so fallacious as facts except figures; and certain of these figures and facts, which seem to bear out his statements, are found at times to be merely assertions, and exaggerated at that.

The second great illusion from which Hartmann would deliver us is the belief that happiness is realizable in a future life. As has been seen, he has already contended that earthly felicity is unobtainable, and his arguments against a higher state are, in a word, that unless the condition which follows life is compared to the anterior state of being, chaos, the successor of life, can bring to man neither happiness nor unhappiness; but as the belief in the regeneration of the body is no longer tenable, it follows that this contrast cannot be appreciated by the non-existent, who are necessarily without thought or consciousness.

This doctrine, which is very nearly akin to Buddhism, has, of course, but little in common with Christianity. Christianity does not, it is true, recognize in us any fee simple to happiness, but it recommends the renunciation of such as may be held, that the value of the transcendent felicity which it promises may be heightened to a still greater extent. It was this regenerating hope, this association of a disdain for life to a promise of eternal well-being, that saved antiquity from the despair and distaste for life in which it was being slowly consumed. But, according to the tendency of modern thought, every effort to demonstrate the reality of ultramundane happiness only results in a more or less disguised and fantastic representation of Nirvana, while the idea which each forms of such a condition varies naturally with the degree of his culture. It is certainly not at all astonishing that all those who are more or less attached to the Christian conception of life should, as Hartmann says, indignantly repulse any and every suggestion of this description. For such ideas to be accepted, a long and worldly civilizing preparation is needed.

A period of this nature is found in his analysis of the third and last great illusion, which holds that happiness will be realizable in the progressing evolution of the world. The chapter in which this subject is treated is one of the most masterly in his entire work, and as such is well deserving of careful examination.

First, it may be explained that to the student of modern science the history of the world is that of a continuous and immense development. The union of photometry and spectral analysis enables him to follow the evolution of other planets, while chemistry and mineralogy teach him something of the earth's own story before it cooled its outer crust. Biology discloses the evolution of the vegetable and animal kingdom; archæology, with some assistance from other sources, throws an intelligible light over the prehistoric development of man, while history brings with it the reverberation of the ordered march of civilization, and points at the same time to larger and grander perspectives. It is not hard, then, to be convinced of the reality of progress; the difficulty lies in the inability to present it to one's self in a thoroughly unselfish manner. From an egoist point of view, man—and by man is meant he who has succeeded in divesting himself of the two illusions just considered—would condemn life not only as a useless possession, but as an affliction. He has, however, Hartmann tells him, a *rôle* to fill under the providential direction of the Unconscious, which, in conformity with the plan of absolute wisdom, draws the world on to a beneficent end, and this *rôle* exacts that he shall take interest in, and joyously sacrifice himself to life. If he does otherwise, his loss prevents no suffering to society, on the contrary, it augments the general discomfort by the length of time which is needed to replace a useful member. Man may not, then, as

Schopenhauer recommended, assist as a passive spectator of life; on the contrary, he must ceaselessly act, work, and produce, and associate himself without regret in the economic and intellectual development of society; or, in other words, he must lend his aid to the attainment of the supreme goal of the evolution of the universe, for that there is a goal it is as impossible to doubt as it is unreasonable to suppose that the world's one end and aim is to turn on its orbit and enjoy the varied spectacle of pain. And yet, what is this goal to which all nature tends? According to a theory which nowadays is very frequently expressed, it is the attainment of universal happiness through gradual advancement and progress.

But, whatever progress humanity may realize, it will never be able, Hartmann affirms, to do away with, nor yet diminish those most painful of evils, illness, old age, poverty, and discontent. So, no matter to how great an extent remedies may be multiplied, disorders, and especially those which are light but chronic, will spread with a progression far more rapid than the knowledge of therapeutics. The gayety of youth, moreover, will never be but the privilege of a fraction of mankind, while the greater part will continue to be devoured by the melancholy of old age. The poverty of the masses, too, as the world advances, becomes more and more formidable, for all the while the masses are gaining a clearer perception of their misery. The happiest races, it has been said over and over again, are those which live nearest to nature, as do the savage tribes; and after them come necessarily the civilized nations, which are the least cultivated. Historically speaking, therefore, the progress of civilization corresponds with the spread of general nausea.

May it not be, then, as Kant maintained, that the practice of universal morality is the great aim of evolution? Hartmann considers the question at great length, and decides in the negative; for, were it such, it would necessarily expand with time, gain ground, so to speak, and take a firm hold on the different classes of society. These feats, of course, it has not performed, for immorality in descending the centuries has changed only in form. Indeed, putting aside the fluctuations of the character of every race, it will be found that everywhere the same connection is maintained between egotism and sympathy. If one is shocked at the cruelty and brutality of former days, it should nevertheless be remembered that uprightness, sincerity, and justice were the characteristics of earlier nations. Who shall say, however, that today we do not live in a reign of falsehood, perfidy, and the coarsest crimes; and that were it not for the assured execution of the repressive enactments of the state and society, we should see the naked brutality of the barbarians surge up again among us? For that matter, it may be noted that at times it does reappear in all its human bestiality, and invariably so the moment that law and order are in any way weakened or destroyed. What happened in the draft riots in New York, and in Paris under the Commune?

Since morality cannot be the great aim of evolution, perhaps it may be art and science; but the further back one looks, the more does scientific progress appear to be the exclusive work of certain rare and gifted minds, while the nearer one approaches the present epoch, the more collective does the work become. Hartmann points out that the first thinkers were not unlike the magicians who made a monument rise out of nothing, whereas the laborers who work at the intellectual edifice of the present day are but corporations of intelligent builders who each, according to their strength, aid in the construction of a gigantic tower. "The work of science hereafter will," he says, "be broader and less profound; it will become exclusively inductive, and hence the demand for genius will grow gradually less. Similarity of dress has already blended the different ranks of society; meanwhile we are advancing to an analogous leveling of the intelligence, which will result in a common but solid mediocrity. The delight in scientific production will gradually wane, and the world will end in knowing only the pleasures of passive understanding. But the pleasure of knowledge is tasteless when truth is presented like a cake already prepared: to be enjoyed it must cost an effort and a struggle."

Art will be handicapped in much the same manner. It is no longer now what it was for the youth of humanity, a god august dispensing happiness with open hands; it is simply a matter of amusement, a remedy for ennui, and a distraction from the fatigues of the day. Hence the increase of dilettantism and the neglect of serious study. The future of art is to Hartmann self-evident. "Age has no ideal, or rather, it has lost what it had, and art is condemned in the increasing years of humanity to hold the same position as the nightly ballets and farces now do to the bankers and brokers of large cities."

This consistent treatment of the subject Hartmann cleverly founds on the analogy of the different ages of the life of the individual with the development of humanity. It is, of course, merely a series of affirmations, but not for that reason necessarily untrue. The great thinkers have disappeared, as have also the great artists; and they have done so, Hartmann would say, because we no longer need them. Indeed, there can be little doubt that could the Greeks come back, they would tell us our art was barbarous; even to the casual observer it has retrograded, nor is it alone in painting and sculpture that symptoms of decadence are noticeable; if we look at the tendencies in literature, nothing very commendable is to be found, save in isolated instances, where the technicalities of style have been raised very near to perfection; but, apart from a few purists who can in no sense be called popular, the majority of the manufacturers of fiction have nothing to offer but froth and rubbish.

The modern stage, too, brings evidence that a palpitant tableau is more appreciated than a polished comedy, and the concert-hall tells a story which is not dissimilar. Music, which with Mozart changed its sex, has been turned into a harlot by Offenbach and his successors; and there are but few nowadays who would hesitate between Don Juan and the last inanity of Strauss. One composer, however, of incontestable genius, has been slowly fighting his way into the hearts of cultivated people, and, curiously enough, has sought to translate with an orchestra some part of the philosophy of pessimism. Schopenhauer, it is said, shook his head at Wagner, and would have none of him; yet if Schopenhauer was ever wrong, he was certainly wrong in that; for Wagner has expressed, as no one will do again, the flooding rush of Will, and the unspiritual but harmonious voice of Nature.

But whatever may become of art, science is not to be dismissed so abruptly. Practically considered, the political, social, and industrial advance of the world depends entirely on its progress; and yet, from Hartmann's standpoint, all that has been accomplished hitherto, by the aid of manufactories, steamships, railways and telegraphs, has merely served to lessen the embarrassments which compressed the activity of man; and the sole advantage which society has reaped by their aid is that the force heretofore expended in actual labor is now free for the play of the intellect, and serves to hasten the evolution of the world. This result, Hartmann remarks, while of importance to general progress, in no wise affects the happiness of the individual.

This last statement of his will perhaps be better understood if it be taken into consideration that the increased production of food which will necessarily follow on a more intelligent culture of the soil will greatly augment the population. An increase of population will multiply the number of those who are always on the verge of starvation, of which there are already millions. But an advance of this kind, while a step backward one way, must yet be a step forward in another; for the wealth which it will bring in its train will necessarily aid in diminishing suffering.

Politically considered, the outlook does not seem to be much more assured. An ideal government can do nothing more than permit man to live without fear of unjust aggressions, and enable him to prepare the ground on which he may construct, if he can, the edifice of his own happiness. Socially, the result will be about the same: through solidarity, association, and other means, men will learn how to make the struggle of the individual with want less severe; yet, in all this, his burdens will be merely lightened, and positive happiness will remain unobtained.

Such are the outlines of Hartmann's conception of what future progress will amount to. If the ideal is realized, man will be gradually raised out of the misery in which he is plunged, and little by little approach a state of indifference in every sphere of his activity. But it should be remembered that the ideal is ever intangible; man may approach, but he can never reach it, and consequently will remain always in a state of suffering.

In this manner, but with a profusion of argument, which, if not always convincing, is yet highly instructive, Hartmann has shown in brief that the people that dwell nearest to nature are happier than the civilized nations, that the poor are more contented than the rich, the poor in spirit more blessed than the intelligent, and that in general that man is the happiest whose sensibilities are the most obtuse, because pleasure is then less dominated by pain, and illusions are more steadfast and complete; moreover, that the progress of humanity develops not only wealth and its needs, and consequently discontent, but also the aptitudes and culture of the intellect, which in turn awaken man to the consciousness of the misery of life, and in so doing heighten the sentiment of general misfortune.

The dream that another golden age is to visit the earth is, therefore, puerile in the extreme. As the wayfarer's burden grows heavier with the miles, so do humanity's suffering and the consciousness of its misery continually increase. The child lives in the moment, the adolescent dreams of a transcendent ideal; man aspires to glory, then to wealth or practical wisdom; lastly, old age, recognizing the vanity of all things, holds but to peace, and bends a tired head to rest. "And so it is with civilization,—nations rise, strengthen, and disappear. Humanity, by unmistakable signs, shows that it is on the wane, and that having employed its strength in maturity, age is now overtaking it. In time it will be content to live on the accumulated wisdom of the centuries, and, inured to thought, it will review the collective agitations of its past life, and recognize the vanity of the goal hitherto pursued.... Humanity, in its decline, will leave no heir to profit by its accumulated wealth. It will have neither children nor grandchildren to trouble the rigor of its judgment through the illusions of parental love. It will sink finally into that melancholy which is the appanage of great minds; it will in a measure float above its own body like a spirit freed from matter; or, as Œdipus at Colonna, it will in anticipation taste the calm of chaos, and assist with compassionate self-pity at the spectacle of its own suffering. Passions that have vanished into the depths of reason will be resolved into ideas by the white light of thought. Illusions will have faded and hope be done with, for what is there left to hope? Its highest aim can be but the absence of pain, for it can no longer dream of happiness; still weak and fragile, working to live, and yet not knowing why it does so, it will ask but one gift, the rest of an endless sleep that shall calm its weariness and immense ennui. It is then that humanity will have passed through the three periods of illusion, and in recognizing the nothingness of its former hopes will aspire only to absolute insensibility and the chaos of Nirvana."

It remains but to inquire what is to become of disillusionized humanity, and to what goal evolution is tending. The foregoing account of Hartmann's theory should have shown that this goal cannot be happiness, for at no period has it ever been reached, and, moreover, that with the progress of the world man is gaining a clearer perception of his misery. On the other hand, it would be illogical to suppose that evolution is to continue with no other aim than that of the discharge of the successive moments that compose it; for if each of these moments is valueless, evolution itself would be meaningless; but Hartmann, it may be remembered, has recognized in the Unconscious a principle of absolute wisdom, and the answer must be looked for elsewhere, but preferably in that direction which most noticeably points to some determined and progressive perfection. No such sign, however, is to be met with anywhere save in the development of consciousness; here progress has been clearly and uninterruptedly at work, from the appearance of the first globule to contemporaneous humanity, and in all probability will continue to advance so long as the world subsists. All things aid in its production and development, while to its assistance there come not only the perfecting of the nervous system, but also such personal incentives as the desire for wealth, which in increasing general welfare disfranchises the intellect; then, too, there are the stimulants to intellectual activity, vanity and ambition, and also sexual love, which heightens its aptitudes; in short, every instinct which is valuable to the species, and which costs the individual more pain than pleasure, is converted into an unalloyed and increasing gain for consciousness.

In spite of all this, however, the development of consciousness is but the means to an end, and cannot therefore be considered as an absolute goal; "for consciousness," Hartmann says, "is born of pain, and exists and expands with suffering, and yet what manner of consolation does it offer? Merely a vain self-mirroring. Of course, if the world were good and beautiful, this would not be without its advantage; but a world which is absolutely miserable, a world which must curse its own existence the moment it is able to judge it, can never regard its apparent and purely ideal reflection as a reasonable goal and termination of its existence. Is there not suffering enough in reality? Is it necessary to reproduce it in a magic lantern? No; consciousness cannot be the supreme goal of a world whose evolution is directed by supreme wisdom.... Some other end must be sought for, then, to which the development of consciousness shall be but the means."

But, however the question is regarded, from whatever standpoint the matter is viewed, there seems to be but one possible goal, and that is happiness. Everything that exists tends thereto, and it is the principle on which rests each of the diverse forms of practical philosophy; moreover, the pursuit of happiness is the essence of Will seeking its own pacification. But happiness has been shown to be an illusion; still there must be some key to the riddle. The solution is at once simple and unexpected. There can be no positive happiness, and yet happiness of some kind is necessary; the supreme aim of universal progress, of which consciousness is but the instrument, is then the realization of the highest possible felicity, which is nothing else than the freedom from all pain, and, in consequence, the cessation of all life; or, in other words, total annihilation.

This climax is the only one which Hartmann will consent to consider; from any other point of view evolution would be a tireless *progressus* which some day might be blindly arrested by chance, while life in the mean time would remain in the utter desolation of an issueless purgatory.

The path, however, through which the great deliverance is to be effected is as tortuously perplexing as the irrational duality of the Unconscious. Many generations of pessimists are needed before the world will be fully ripe for its great leap into the night of time; even then, though Hartmann does not appear to suspect it, there will probably be quite a number of pantheists who, drunk on Nature, will stupidly refuse the great bare bodkin, which will have thus been carefully prepared for their viaticum.

It should not be supposed that in all this there is any question of the suicide of the individual: Hartmann is far too dramatic to suggest a final tableau so tame and humdrum as that; besides, it has been seen that the death of the individual does not drag with it the disappearance of the species, and in no wise disturbs the heedless calm of Nature. It is not the momentary and ephemeral existence that is to be destroyed, for, after its destruction, the repairing and reproducing force would still survive; it is the principle of existence itself which must be extinguished; the suicide, to be effectual, must be that of the cosmos. This proceeding, which will shortly be explained, "will be the act of the last moment, after which there will be neither will nor activity; after which, to quote Saint John, 'time will have ceased to be.'"

But here it may be pertinently asked whether humanity, such as it now is, will be capable of this grandiose development of consciousness which is to prepare the absolute renunciation of the will to live, or whether some superior race is to appear on earth which will continue the work and attain the goal. May it not be that the globe will be but the theatre of an abortive effort of this description, and long after it has gone to increase the number of frozen spheres, some other planet, which is to us invisible, may, under more favorable circumstances, realize the self-same aim and end? To this the answer is made that if humanity is ever destined to conduct the world's evolution to its coronation, it will assuredly not complete its task until the culminating point of its progress has been reached, nor yet until it has united the most favorable conditions of existence. We need not, however, bother about the perspective which science has disclosed, and which points to a future period of congelation and complete inertia; long before that time, Hartmann says, evolution will have ended, and this world of ours, with its continents and archipelagos, will have vanished.

The manner in which this great and final annihilation is to be accomplished is of a threefold nature; the first condition necessary to success is that humanity at some future time shall concentrate such a mass of Will that the balance, spread about elsewhere over the world, will be insignificant in proportion. This, Hartmann explains, is in no wise impossible, "for the manifestation of Will in atomic forces is greatly inferior to that which is exercised in the vegetable and animal kingdom, and hence much less than that which irrupts in man. The supposition, therefore, that the greater part may be capitalized in man is not necessarily an idle dream. When that day arrives, it will suffice for humanity to no longer will to live to annihilate the entire fabric; for humanity will at that time represent more Will than all the rest of Nature collectively considered."

The second condition necessary to success is that mankind shall be so thoroughly alive to the folly of life, so imperiously in need of peace, and shall have so completely disentangled every effort from its aimlessness, that the yearning for an end to existence will be the prime motive of every act. A condition such as this, Hartmann thinks, will probably be realized in the old age of humanity. The theory that life is an evil is already admitted by thinkers; the supposition, therefore, that it may some day triumph over the prejudices of the multitude is neither absurd nor preposterous. As is shown in the history of other creeds, an idea may penetrate so deeply into the minds of its adherents as to breed an entire race of fanatics; and it is the opinion, not of Hartmann alone, but of many serious and cultivated scholars, that if ever an idea was destined to triumph without recourse to either passion or violence, and to exercise at the same time an action purely pacific, yet so profound and durable as to assure its success beforehand, that idea, or rather that sentiment, is the compassion which the pessimist feels not only for himself, but for everything that is. Its gradual adoption these gentlemen consider not as problematical, but merely as a question of time. Indeed, the difficulty is not so great as might be supposed; every day the will of the individual suffices to triumph over the instinctive love of life, and, Hartmann logically argues, may not the mass of humanity do the same thing? The denial of the will to live on the part of the individual is, it is true, barren of any benefit to the species, but, on the other hand, a universal denial would result in complete deliverance.

Mankind, however, has yet a long journey before it, and many generations are needed to overcome, and to dissipate little by little, through the influence of heredity, those passions which are opposed to the desire for eternal peace. In time, Hartmann thinks, all this will be brought about; and he holds, moreover, that the development of consciousness will correspond with the weakening of passion, which is to be one of the characteristics of the decline of humanity, as it is now one of the signs of the day.

The third condition necessary for the perfect consummation of this gigantic suicide is that communication between the inhabitants of the world be so facilitated that they may simultaneously execute a common resolution. Full play is allowed the imagination in picturing the manner in which all this is to be accomplished. Hartmann has a contempt for details, and contents himself with asserting that it is necessary and possible, and that in the abdication of humanity every form of existence will cease.

Such, in brief, is this vehement conception of the ordering of the world, and the plan for its precipitate destruction. With a soldierly disregard of objection, but with a prodigality of argument and digression which, if not always substantial, is unusually vivid, Hartmann explains the Unconscious and its reacting dualism of Will and Idea. One principle is, as has been seen, constantly irrupting into life, and it is through the revolt of the second that the first is to be thwarted and extinguished. Nothing, indeed, could be more simple; and it would be a graceless and pedantic task to laboriously clamber to the same vague altitudes to which Hartmann has so lightly soared, and there contradict his description of the perspective.

To any one who has cared to follow the writer thus far, the outlines given of Hartmann's conspiracy against pain must have seemed aggressively novel. Schopenhauer's ideas on the same subject were seemingly more practical, if less lurid, but then Schopenhauer hugged a fact and flouted chimeras. It may be that Schopenhauer was a little behind the age, for Hartmann has criticized him very much as a collegian on a holiday might jeer at the old-world manners of his grandfather. As they cannot both be right, each may be wrong; and it may be that the key to the whole great puzzle is contained in that one word, resignation, which the poet-philosopher pronounced so long ago. As a remedy this certainly has the advantage of being a more immediate and serviceable palliative to the sufferer than either of those suggested in the foregoing systems. It is admitted that—

"Man cannot feed and be fed on the faith of to-morrow's baked meat;"

and it is in the same manner difficult for any one to hypnotize himself and his suffering with the assurance that in the decline of humanity all pain will cease; on the other hand, whether we have in regard to future generations an after-me-the-deluge feeling, and practically care very little whether or no they annihilate themselves and pain too, still the more intelligent will readily recognize the ubiquity of sorrow, and consider resignation at present as its most available salve.

But in spite of its vagaries, pessimism, as expounded by Schopenhauer and Hartmann, possesses a real and enduring value which it is difficult to talk away; it is naturally most easy to laugh, in the heyday of youth and health, at its fantastic misanthropy; indeed, it is in no sense perfect; it has halted and tripped many times; it has points that even to the haphazard and indifferent spectator are weak and faulty, and yet what creed is logically perfect, and what creed is impregnable to criticism? That there is none such can be truly admitted. The reader, then, may well afford to be a little patient with pessimism; theoretically, it is still in its infancy, but with increasing years its blunders will give way to strength; and though many of the theories that it now holds may alter, the cardinal, uncontrovertible tenet that life is a burden will remain firm and changeless to the end of time.

CHAPTER SIX.

Is Life an Affliction?

IN VERY STATELY WORDS, THAT WERE TYPICAL OF HIM WHO
uttered them, Emerson said, "I do not wish to be amused;" and
turned therewith a figurative back on the enticements of the
commonplace.

Broadly speaking, the sentiment that prompted this expression is common to all individual men. The so-called allurements
and charms of the world are attractive to the vulgar, but not to
the thinker, and whether the thinker be a Trappist or a comedian, he will, if called to account, express himself in a manner
equally frank.

For sentiments of this description neither orthodoxy nor
pessimism is to blame. They are merely the resultants of the obvious and the true; they leap into being in every intelligent mind.
The holiday crowd on its way to the Derby, to Coney Island, the
Lido, or to any one of the other thousand places of popular resort, causes even the ordinary observer to wonder why it is that
he cannot go too, and enjoy himself with the same boisterous

good humor which palpitates all about him; he thinks at first that he has some fibre lacking, some incapacity for that enjoyment which has in so large a measure been given to others; but little by little the conviction breaks upon him that he has a fibre more, and that it is the others who lack the finer perceptions with which he is burdened.

That the others are to be envied, and he to be pitied, there can be no manner of doubt, but all the same the fact that he is unable to take part in popular amusements steadfastly remains; and while the matter of the extra fibre is more or less reassuring, it is not always perfectly satisfactory, and he then begins to look about for the reason. If to his power of observation there be added also a receptive mind and an introspective eye, it will be unnecessary for him to have ever heard of M. Renan to become gradually aware that he is the victim of a gigantic swindle. In common with many others, he has somehow imagined that the world was a broad and fertile plain, with here and there a barren tract. It is impossible for him to give any reason for this fancy; "In the world ye shall have tribulation," is the explicit warning of the Founder of Christianity, and to this warning all creeds, save that of the early Hellenists, concur. It did not, therefore, come from any religious teaching, nor, for that matter, from any philosophy. Still the impression, however vague it may seem when analyzed, has none the less been with him, as with all others, the reason being simply that he grew up with it as he may have grown up with fairy tales, and it is not until his aspirations stumble over facts that he begins to see that life, instead of being the pleasant land flowing with milk and honey, which he had imagined, is in reality something entirely different.

These deductions, of course, need not follow because a man finds that he is more or less indifferent to every form of entertainment, from a king's revel to a walking-match; but they may follow of any man who has begun to dislike the propinquity of the average, and to feel that where the crowd find amusement there will be nothing but weariness and vexation of spirit for him. Under such circumstances he is an instinctive pessimist, and one who needs but little theoretic instruction to learn that he, as all others, has been made use of, and cheated to boot. The others, it is true, are, generally speaking, unaware of the deception that has been practiced on them; they have, it may be, a few faint suspicions that something has gone wrong somewhere, but even in uttermost depression the untutored look upon their misfortunes as purely individual, and unshared by the world at large. Of the universality of suffering, of the fact, as John Stuart Mill has put it, that there is no happiness for nineteen twentieths of the world's inhabitants, few have any conception or idea. They look, it may be, over their garden wall, and, hearing their neighbor grumble, they think that, being cross-grained and ill-tempered, his life is not one of unalloyed delight. But their vision extends no further. They do not see the sorrow that has no words, nor do they hear the silent knell of irrecoverable though unuttered hopes, "the toil of heart, and knees, and hands." Of all these things they know nothing; household worries, and those of their neighbor and his wife, circle their existence. If they are not contented themselves, then happiness is but a question of distance. Another street, or another town, or another country holds it, and if the change is made, the old story remains to be repeated.

There are those, too, who from dyspepsia, torpidity of the liver, or general crankiness of disposition, are inclined to take a gloomy view of all things; then there is a temperamental pessimism which displays itself in outbursts of indignation against the sorrows of life, and in frantic struggles with destiny and the meshes of personal existence; there is also the sullen pessimism of despair noticeable in the quiet folding of hands, and which with tearless eyes awaits death without complaint; then there are those who complain and sulk, who torment themselves and others, and who have neither the spunk to struggle nor the grace to be resigned, —this is the *"forme miserable;"* there is also a haphazard pessimism which comes of an unevenness of disposition, and which asserts itself on a rainy day, or when stocks are down; another is the accidental type, the man who, with loss of wife, child, or mistress, settles himself in a dreary misanthropy; finally, there is hypochondria, which belongs solely to pathology.

In none of these categories do the victims have any suspicion that a philosophical significance is attached to their suffering. Curiously enough, however, it is from one or from all of these different classes that the ordinary acceptation of pessimism is derived; it is these forms that are met with in every-day life and literature, and yet it is precisely with these types, that spring from the disposition and temperament of the individual who exhibits them, that scientific pessimism has nothing to do. It ignores them entirely.

Broadly stated, scientific pessimism in its most advanced form rests on a denial that happiness in any form ever has been or ever will be obtained, either by the individual as a unit or by the world as a whole; and this for the reason that life is not considered as a pleasant gift made to us for our pleasure; on the contrary, it is a duty which must be performed by sheer force of labor,—a task which in greater matters, as in small, brings in its train a misery which is general, an effort which is ceaseless, and a tension of mind and body which is extreme, and often unbearable. Work, torment, pain, and misery are held to be the unavoidable lot of nearly every one, and the work, torment, pain, and misery of life are considered as necessary to mankind as the keel to the ship. Indeed, were it otherwise, were wishes, when formed, fulfilled, in what manner would the time be employed? Imagine the earth to be a fairyland where all grows of itself, where birds fly roasted to the spit, and where each would find his heart's best love wreathed with orange flowers to greet his coming; what would the result be? Some would bore themselves to death, some would cut their throats, while others would quarrel, assassinate, and cause generally more suffering than is in the present state of affairs actually imposed upon them. Pain is not the accident, but the necessary and inevitable concomitant of life; and the attractiveness of the promise "that thy days may be long in the land which the Lord thy God giveth thee," is, in consequence, somewhat impaired.

Nor, according to scientific pessimism, is there any possibility that happiness will be obtained in a future life. In this there is no atheism, though the arguments that follow may seem to savor of the agnostic.

As has been seen, pleasures are, as a rule, indirect, being cessations or alleviations of pain. If it be taken for granted that in a future life there will be no pain, the difficulty is not overcome, but rather increased by the fact of the rapid exhaustion of nervous susceptibility to pleasure. Furthermore, as without brain there is no consciousness, it will not be illogical to suppose that every spirit must be provided with such an apparatus; in which case the psychological laws in the other life must be strictly analogous to those of early experience. The deduction follows of itself,—there, too, must be pain and sorrow.

To this it may be objected that in a future life there need be no question either of pain or pleasure, and that the ransomed soul will, in contemplation, or love, or the practice of morality, be too refined to be susceptible to any sensations of a grosser nature.

To all this advanced pessimism has a ready answer: first, there can be no morality, for where there is no body and no property it is impossible to injure another; second, there can be no love, for every form of love, from the highest to the lowest, rests on the basis of sensibility; when, therefore, after the abstraction of shape, voice, features, and all bodily actions that are manifested through the medium of the brain, nothing but an unsubstantial shadow remains, what is there left to love? third, there can be no contemplation, for in a state of clairvoyance contemplation is certainly useless.

In these arguments pessimism, it may be noted, does not deny the possibility of future existence; it denies merely the possibility of future happiness; and its logic, of course, can in no wise affect the position of those who hold that man is unable to conceive or imagine anything of that which is, or is not to be.

From a religious standpoint advanced pessimism teaches that the misery of life is immedicable, and strips away every illusion with which it has been hitherto enveloped; it offers, it is true, no hope that a future felicity will be the recompense of present suffering, and if in this way it ignores any question of reward and punishment, it does not for that reason necessarily open a gate to license and immorality; on the contrary, pessimism stands firmly to the first principle of the best ethics, and holds that men shall do good without the wish to be rewarded, and abstain from evil without the fear of being punished.

In regard to what follows death, it recognizes in the individual but the aspiration to be liberated from the task of coöperating in evolution, the desire to be replunged in the Universal Spirit, and the wish to disappear therein as the raindrop disappears in the ocean, or as the flame of the lamp is extinguished in the wind. In other words, it does not aim at mere happiness, but at peace and at rest; and meanwhile, until the hour of deliverance is at hand, it does not acquit the individual of any of the obligations that he owes to society, nor of one that is due to himself. In short, the creed as it stands is one of charity and good-will to all men; and, apart from its denial of future happiness, it does not in its ethics differ in any respect from the sublime teachings of the Christian faith.

It seems trite to say that we are passing through a transition period, for all things seem to point to a coming change; still, whatever alterations time may bring in its train, it is difficult to affirm that the belief here set forth is to be the religion of the future, *n'est pas prophète qui veut*; in any event, it is easy to prove that pessimism is not a religion of the past. Its very youth militates most against it; and while it may outgrow this defect, yet it has other objectionable features which to the average mind are equally unassuring: to begin with it is essentially iconoclastic; wherever it rears its head, it does so amid a swirl of vanishing illusions and a totter and crash of superstition. There are few, however, that part placidly with these possessions; illusions are relinquished grudgingly, and as for superstitions,—a wise man has said, Are they not hopes? It would seem, then, that in showing the futility of any quest of happiness here or hereafter, this doctrine, if received at all, will have performed a very thankless task. Indeed, it is this reason, if no other, that will cause it for some time to come to be regarded with distrust and dislike. The masses are conservative, and their conservatism usually holds them one or two centuries in arrears of advancing thought; and even putting the masses out of the question, one has to be very hospitable to receive truth at all times as a welcome guest, for truth is certainly very naked and uncompromising; we love to sigh for it, Béranger said, and, it may be added, most of us stop there.

Pessimism, moreover, seemingly takes, and gives nothing in return; but if it is examined more closely it will be found that its very melancholy transforms itself into a consolation which, if relatively restricted, is none the less valuable. Taubert, one of its most vigorous expounders, says, "Not only does it carry the imagination far beyond the actual suffering to which every one is condemned, and in this manner shield us from manifold deceptions, but it even increases such pleasures as life still holds, and doubles their intensity. For pessimism, while showing that each joy is an illusion, leaves pleasure where it found it, and simply incloses it in a black border, from which, in greater relief, it shines more brightly than before."

Another objection which has been advanced against pessimism is that it is a creed of quietist inactivity. Such, however, it can no longer be considered; for if it be viewed in the light of its recent developments, it will be found to be above all other beliefs the one most directly interested in the progress of evolution. Pessimism, it may be remembered, came into general notice not more than twenty-five years ago; at that time it aroused in certain quarters a horrified dislike, in others it was welcomed with passionate approval; books and articles were written for and against it in much the same manner that books and articles leaped into print in defense and abuse of the theory generally connected with Darwin's name. Since then the tumult has gradually calmed down; on the one hand pessimism is accepted as a fact; on the other new expositors, less dogmatic than their great predecessor, and with an equipment of a quarter of a century's advance in knowledge, prune the original doctrine, and strengthen it with fresh and vigorous thought. Among these, and directly after Hartmann, Taubert takes the highest rank. This writer recognizes the truth of Schopenhauer's theory that progress brings with it a clearer consciousness of the misery of existence and the illusion of happiness, but at the same time much emphasis is laid on the possibility of triumphing over this misery through a subjugation of the selfish propensities. It is in this way, Taubert considers, that peace may be attained, or at least the burden of life noticeably diminished.

The bleakness in which Hartmann lodged the Unconscious is through this treatment rendered, if not comfortable, at least inhabitable. But while in this manner Taubert plays the upholsterer, another exponent wanders through the shadowy terraces of thought, and in so doing looks about him with the grim suavity of a sheriff seeking a convenient spot on which to clap a bill of sale. This writer, Julius Bahnsen, is best known through his *Philosophy of History,* and a recent publication, *The Tragic as the World's First Law*, whose repulsively attractive title sent a fresh ripple eddying through the seas of literature. In these works the extreme of pessimism may be said to have been reached, for not only does their author vie with Schopenhauer in representing the world as a ceaseless torment which the Absolute has imposed on itself, but he goes a step further, and in denying that there is any finality even immanent in Nature, asserts that the order of phenomena is utterly illogical. It may be remembered that the one pure delight which Schopenhauer admitted was that of intellectual contemplation:—

> "That blessed mood,
> In which the burden of the mystery,
> In which the heavy and the weary weight
> Of all this unintelligible world
> Is lightened."

But from Bahnsen's standpoint, inasmuch as the universe is totally lacking in order or harmonious design, since it is but the dim cavernous abode of unrelated phenomena and forms, the pleasure which Schopenhauer admitted, so far from causing enjoyment, is simply a source of anguish to the intelligent and reflective mind. Even the hope of final annihilation, which Schopenhauer suggested and Hartmann planned, has brought to him but cold comfort. He puts it aside as a pleasant and idle dream. To him the misery of the world is permanent and unalterable, and the universe nothing but Will rending itself in eternal self-partition and unending torment.

---

*   *Zur Philosophie der Geschichte,* u. s. w. Carl Duncker, Berlin; also *Das Tragische als Weltgesetz,* u. s. w. Lauenburg.

Beyond this it is difficult to go; few have cared to go even so far, and the bravado and vagaries of this doctrine have not been such as to cause anything more than a success of curiosity. Indeed, Bahnsen's views have been mentioned here simply as being a part of the history, though not of the development of advanced pessimism, and they may now very properly be relegated to the night to which they belong.

To sum up, then, what has gone before, the modern pessimist is a Buddhist who has strayed from the Orient, and who in his exodus has left behind him all his fantastic shackles, and has brought with him, together with ethical laws, only the cardinal tenet, "Life is evil." Broadly considered, the difference between the two creeds is not important. The Buddhist aspires to a universal nothingness, and the pessimist to the moment when in the face of Nature he may cry:—

> *"Oh! quelle immense joie, après tant de souffrance!*
> *À travers les débris, par-dessus les charniers,*
> *Pouvoir enfin jeter ce cri de délivrance—*
> *'Plus d'hommes sous le ciel! Nous sommes les derniers!'"*

Beyond this difference, the main principles of the two beliefs vary only with the longitude. The old, yet still infant East demands a fable, to which the young yet practical West turns an inattentive ear. Eliminate palingenesis, and the steps by which Nirvana is attained, and the two creeds are to all intents and purposes precisely the same.

Of the two, Buddhism is, of course, the stronger; it appeals more to the imagination and less to facts; indeed, numerically speaking, its strength is greater than that of any other belief. According to the most recent statistics the world holds about 8,000,000 Jews, 100,000,000 Mohammedans, 130,000,000 Brahmins, 370,000,000 Christians, and 480,000,000 Buddhists, the remainder being pagans, positivists, agnostics and atheists. Within the last few years Buddhism has spread into Russia, and from there into Germany, England, and the United States, and wherever it spreads it paves in its passing the way for pessimism. The number of pessimists it is of course impossible to compute: instinctive pessimists abound everywhere, but however limited the number of theoretic pessimists may be, their literature at least is daily increasing. For the last twenty years, it may safely be said that not a month has gone by unmarked by some fresh contribution; and the most recent developments of French and German literature show that the countless arguments, pleas, and replies which the subject has called forth have brought, instead of exhaustion, a new and expanded vigor.

The most violent opposition that pessimism has had to face has come, curiously enough, from the Socialists. For the Socialists, while pessimists as to the present, have optimistic views for the future. Their cry is not against the misery of the world, but against the capital that produces it. The artisan, they say, is smothered by the produce of his own hands: the more he produces, the more he increases the capital that is choking him down. In time, Marx says, there will exist only a few magnates face to face with a huge enslaved population; and as wealth increases in geometric proportion so will poverty, and with it the exasperation of the multitude. Then the explosion is to come, and Socialism to begin its sway. Now Socialism does not, as is generally supposed, preach community of goods; it preaches simply community of profits, and the abolition of capital as a productive agent. When the explosion comes, therefore, the Socialists propose to turn the state into one vast and comprehensive guild, to which all productive capital, land, and factories shall appertain. The right of inheritance of personal property, it may be noted, will be retained; and this for a variety of reasons, of which the most satisfactory seems to be that such a right serves as an incentive to economy and activity. Money may be saved and descend, but it is not to be allowed the power of generation.

It will be readily understood, even from this brief summary, that such a doctrine as Hartmann's, which is chiefly concerned in disproving the value of every aspect of progress, was certain to call out many replies from those who see a vast area for the expansion of human comfort and happiness in the future developments of social life.

To these replies the pessimists have but one rejoinder, and that is that any hope of the expansion of happiness is an illusion. And is it an illusion? Simple Mrs. Winthrop said, "If us as knows so little can see a bit o' good and rights, we may be sure as there's a good and a rights better nor what we knows of." But then Mrs. Winthrop was admittedly simple, and her views in consequence are hardly those of the seer. From an endæmonist standpoint, the world does not seem to be much better off now than it was two or three thousand years ago; there are even some who think it has retrograded, and who turn to the civilization of Greece and Rome with longing regret; and this, notwithstanding the fact that from the peace and splendor of these nations cries of distress have descended to us which are fully as acute as any that have been uttered in recent years. Truly, to the student of history each epoch brings its own shudder. There have been ameliorations in one way and pacifications in another, but misery looms in tireless constancy through it all. Each year a fresh discovery seems to point to still better things in the future, but progress is as undeniably the chimera of the present century as the resurrection of the dead was that of the tenth; each age has its own, for no matter to what degree of perfection industry may arrive, and to whatever heights progress may ascend, it must yet touch some final goal, and meanwhile pessimism holds that with expanding intelligence there will come, little by little, the fixed and immutable knowledge that of all perfect things which the earth contains misery is the most complete.

To question whether life is an affliction seems, from the facts and arguments already presented, to be somewhat unnecessary. The answer appears in a measure to be a foregone conclusion. Yet, if the question be examined without bias and without prejudice the issue is not only doubtful, but difficult to ascertain. If in any intelligent community the matter were put to vote by acclamation, the decision would undoubtedly be in the negative; and that for a variety of reasons, first and foremost of which is that ninety and nine out of a hundred persons are led by the thread of external appearance, and whatever their private beliefs may be, they still wish their neighbors to think that they at least have no cause to complain.

It is this desire to appear well in the eyes of others that makes what is termed the shabby-genteel, and which prevents so many proud yet vulgar minds from avowing their true position. Indeed, there are few who, save to an intimate, have the courage to acknowledge that they are miserable; there is at work within them the same instinct that compels the wounded animal to seek the depths of the bushes in which to die. People generally are ashamed of grief, and turn to hide a tear as the sensitive turn from an accident in the street, and veil their eyes from deformity. Moreover, it is largely customary to mock at the melancholy; and in good society it is an unwritten law that every one shall bring a certain quota of contentment and gayety, or else remain in chambered solitude.

Added to this, and beyond the insatiable desire to appear serene and successful in the eyes of others, there is the terrible dread of seeming to be cheated and outwitted of that which is apparently a universal birthright; and, according to a general conception, there is the same sort of moral baseness evidenced in an unuttered yet visible appeal for sympathy, as that which is at work in the beggar's outstretched palm. Many, it is true, there are who drop the furtive coin, but the world at large passes with averted stare. "There is work for all," is a common saying, and for the infirm there are hospitals and institutions; "What, then, is the use of giving?" it is queried, and the answer follows, "They who ask for alms are frauds." If the alms be taken to stand for sympathy, the frauds will be found to be few and far between; for, if each man and woman who has arrived at the age of reason, at that age, in fact, which is not such as is set by the statute, but which each individual case makes for itself; if each one should have his heart first wrung dry and then dissected, there would be such an expanse and prodigality of sorrow discovered as would defy an index and put a library to shame.

If the tendency of current literature is examined, it will be found to point very nearly the same way. In earlier days the novel ended with the union of two young people, and the curtain fell on a tableau of awaited happiness. Nowadays, however, as the French phrase goes, we have changed all that. Realistic fiction is a picture of life as it is, and not, as was formerly the case, a picture of life as we want it. Probably the strongest and most typical romance of recent American authors is *The Portrait of a Lady*; and this picture of a thoroughbred girl, awake to the highest possibilities of life, ends not only in her entire disenchantment, but also, if I have understood Mr. James aright, in her utter degradation. In that very elaborate novel, *Daniel Deronda*, the moral drawn is not dissimilar, and yet its author stood at the head of English fiction.

In French literature, the same influence is even more noticeably at work. It is the fashion to abuse Zola, and to say that his works are obscene; so they are, and so is the life that he depicts, but his descriptions are true to the letter; and the gaunt and wanton misery which he described in *l'Assommoir* is not, to my thinking, such as one need blush over, but rather such as might well cause tears. The work which those princes of literature, the

Goncourts and Daudet, have performed, has been prepared, as one may say, with pens pricked in sorrow. *Germanie Lacerteux, la Fille Eliza, Chérie, Jack,* the *Nabab,* and the *Évangéliste,* are but one long-drawn-out cry of variegated yet self-same agony. In this respect Tourguénieff was well up to the age, as is also Spielhagen, who is very generally considered to be the best of German novelists.

The splendid wickedness of mediæval Italy has done little to inspire her modern authors. The romances most abundant there are cheap translations from the French. De Amicis, the most popular native writer, and one whose name is familiar to every one as a traveler in Gautier's footsteps, has written but few stories, of which the best, however, *Manuel Menendez,* is the incarnation of the soul of tragedy.[*]

Less recently, Stendhal, Balzac and Flaubert have harped the same note of accentuated despair; Musset has sung songs that would make a statue weep, and Baudelaire seems to have supped sorrow with a long spoon. In brief, the testimony of all purely modern writers amounts pretty much to the same thing; life to them seems an affliction.

This, of course, it may do without altering its value to others; let any one, for instance, go to a well-nurtured and refined girl of eighteen and tell her that life is an affliction, and she will look upon her informant as a retailer of trumpery paradox. And at eighteen what a festival is life! To one splendid in beauty and rich in hope how magnificent it all seems; what unexplored yet inviting countries extend about the horizon! winter is a kiss that tingles, and summer a warm caress; everything, even to death, holds its promise. And then picture her as she will be at eighty, without an illusion left, and turning her tired eyes each way in search of rest.

---

[*] An admirable translation (the work of Professor Charles Carroll, of New York) of this romance appeared a few years ago in *Harper's Monthly.*

Life is not an affliction to those who are, and who can remain young; there are some who, without any waters of youth, remain so until age has sapped the foundation of their being; and it is from such as they that the greatest cheer is obtained. But to those who live, so to speak, in the thick of the fight, who see hope after hope fall with a crash, and illusion after illusion vanish into still air; to the intelligent, to the observer, and especially to him who is forced against his will to struggle in the van, life is an affliction, a mishap, a calamity, and sometimes a curse.

That there are many such is proven by the statistics which the daily papers afford; and could one play Asmodeus, and look into the secret lives of all men, the evidence obtainable would in its baldness seem hideously undesirable. The degrees of sensitiveness, however, and the ability or inability to support suffering, vary admittedly with the individual. There are men who rise from an insult refreshed; there are many to whom an injury is a tonic and pain a stimulant; and there is even a greater number whose sensibilities are so dull that what is torture to another is barely a twinge to them.

It was the melancholy privilege of the writer to assist, a short time since, at an operation performed in a German hospital. A common soldier had been thrown from a horse with such force that his elbow was dislocated; in the *Klinik* he put his uninjured arm around a post, and then let the surgeon pull on a strap which had been fastened to the other, until the joint was once more in position. His arm was then bandaged, and he was told to return in a fortnight. On his second visit the bandage was removed, and the surgeon, after a violent effort, moved the stiffened joint backwards and forwards. During both operations, the only noticeable evidence of pain was a slight contraction of the upper lip, while the general expression of his face was that of a calm as stolid as is required of the soldier when in the presence of his superior. To such an one as he life is no more an affliction than it is to the turtle.

Then, there are those to whom life is the amusing dream of an hour, who flit through existence in loops of yellow light, who find pleasure in all things, and are careless of the morrow; and these, perhaps, above all others, are the most to be envied. It is such natures as theirs that are usually met with in ordinary fiction, and which are so singularly infrequent in real life. In fancy they are evoked with ease, and yet somehow they do not seem to bear the stamp which experience has set upon the real. That there are such natures it is, of course, absurd to deny, but to affirm that they are persistent types is scarcely in accordance with facts. There are, for instance, many young people who enter life with a prodigality of supposition which is certainly lavish; they see that others are smiling, and that life, even to its outskirts, presents an appearance of pleasing serenity. The supposition which they foster, that a percentage of happiness will be allotted to them, is then not unreasonable; on the contrary, it is very natural; but as far as the expectation goes, we are, most of us, very well aware that it holds its own but for a short space of time.

This fact, while self-evident, is not always satisfactorily explained; indeed, the reason why so many become disappointed with life is, perhaps, explainable only on psychological grounds. By all means the most important *rôle* throughout the entire length and breadth of humanity is that which is played by thought. Its influence is as noticeable in a bakeshop as in the overthrow of an empire; yet, in spite of the results which are constantly springing from it, it was Rousseau's opinion that "*l'homme qui pense est un animal dépravé.*" Balzac caught at this theme, and wrung from it its most severe deductions. To him it was a dissolvent of greater or less activity, according to the nature of the individual in whom it worked. Others have considered it to be the corrosive acid of existence, and the mainspring of every misfortune; all this it may or may not be, but that at least it is the prime factor of disenchantment is evidenced by such an every-day instance as that man, as a rule, and with but few exceptions, pictures in advance the pleasures and sensations which the future seems to hold, and yet when the pictured future becomes the actual present the disproportion between fact and fancy is so great that it results, in nine cases out of ten, in a complete insolvency. After one or more bankruptcies of this description the individual very generally finds that he has had enough, so to speak, and lets hope ever after alone, whereupon disillusionment steps in and takes its place.

It is thought, then, that does the mischief; or to be more exact, it is the inability to maintain an equilibrium between the real and the ideal; that is, in the majority of cases, the cause of disenchantment. To this it may be also added that it is because every one is so well organized for misfortune that such a small amount of open revolt is encountered. When it does appear, it is, as a rule, presented by such thinkers as have been mentioned in the course of these pages, who, through their assertion of the undeniable awake the dislike and animosity of those who have not yet had their fill of proceedings in bankruptcy, and still hope to find life a pleasant thing well worth the living.

It may be said in conclusion, and without any attempt at the discursive, that the moral atmosphere of the present century is charged with three distinct disturbances,—the waning of religious belief, the insatiable demand for intense sensations, and the increasing number of those who live uncompanied, and walk abroad in solitude. That each of these three effects is due to one and the self-same cause is well-nigh unquestionable. The immense nausea that is spreading through all lands and literature is at work on the simple faith, the contented lives, and joyous good-fellowship of earlier days, and in its results it brings with it the signs and portents of a forthcoming though undetermined upheaval. Jean Paul said that we care for life, not because it is beautiful, but because we should care for it; whence follows the oft repeated yet hollow reasoning,—since we love life it must be beautiful; and it is from a series of deductions not dissimilar that the majority of those who are as yet unaffected by that which after all may be but a passing change still cling resolutely to the possibility of earthly happiness.

Out of a hundred intelligent Anglo-Saxons there are seldom two who think precisely alike on any given subject, be that subject what it may,—art, politics, literature, or religion. Indeed, there is but one faith common to all, and that is custom. It is not, however, customary to discuss a subject such as that which is treated in these pages; and it is, as a rule, considered just as bad form to question the value of life as it is to touch upon matters of an indelicate or repulsive nature.

It is, perhaps, for this latter reason, as also in view of the great difference of expressed opinion on all topics, that in England, and especially in America, so little is said on this subject, which for many years past has been of interest to the rest of the thinking world, and which each year is gaining in strength and significance. What its final solution will be is, of course, uncertain. Schopenhauer recommended absolute chastity as the means to the great goal, and Hartmann has vaguely suggested a universal denial of the will to live; more recently, M. Renan has hazarded the supposition that in the advance of science some one might discover a force capable of blowing the planet to atoms, and which, if successfully handled, would, of course, annihilate pain. But these ideas, however practicable or impracticable they may be in the future, are for the moment merely theories; the world is not yet ripe for a supreme quietus, and in the mean time the worth of life may still be questioned.

The question, then, as to whether life is valuable, valueless, or an affliction can, with regard to the individual, be answered only after a consideration of the different circumstances attendant on each particular case; but, broadly speaking, and disregarding its necessary exceptions, life may be said to be always valuable to the obtuse, often valueless to the sensitive; while to him who commiserates with all mankind, and sympathizes with everything that is, life never appears otherwise than as an immense and terrible affliction.

The Anatomy
of Negation.

"Lost at nightfall in a forest, I have but a feeble light to guide me. A stranger happens along: 'Blow out your candle,' he says, 'and you will see your way the better.' That stranger is a theologian."

-Diderot

CHAPTER ONE.

The Revolt of the Orient.

MAN, AS DESCRIBED BY QUATREFAGES, IS A RELIGIOUS ANIMAL. The early naturalists said the same thing of the elephant; but while this statement, which contains all the elements of a libel, has fallen into disrepute, the former, little by little, has assumed the purple among accepted facts.

Man's belief in the supernatural antedates chronology. It was unfathered and without a mother. It was spontaneous, natural, and unassisted by revelation. It sprang into being with the first flight of fancy.

The characteristic trait of primitive man seems to have been that of intellectual passivity. He was never astonished: if he noticed anything, it was his own weakness; the power of the elements he accepted as a matter of course. The phenomena that he witnessed, the sufferings that he endured, were to him living enemies whose violence could be conjured by prayers and donations. Everything had its spectre; phantoms were as common as leaves. There was not a corner of the earth unpeopled by vindictive demons. In sleep he was visited by them all, and as his dreams were mainly nightmares, his dominant sensation was that of fright.

As his mind developed, frontiers were outlined between the imaginary and the real; the animate and the inanimate ceased to be identical. Instead of attributing a particular spirit to every object, advancing theology conceived a number of aggrandized forces. The earth, sea and sky were laid under contribution, and the phenomena of nature were timidly adored. In the course of time these open-air deities were found smitten by a grave defect—they were visible. The fear of the unseen demanded something more mysterious, a hierarchy of invisible divinities of whom much might be suspected and but little known. It was presumably at this point that the high-road to polytheism was discovered; and when man grew to believe that the phenomena which his ancestors had worshiped were but the unconscious agents of higher powers, the gods were born.

Consecutive stages of development such as these have evidently been far from universal. There are races whose belief in the supernatural is so accidental that any classification is impossible. There are others in whose creeds the transition from animism to broader views is still unmarked. In the equatorial regions of Africa, in Madagascar, Polynesia, and among certain Tartar tribes, animism and its attendant fetishism is reported to be still observable. The distinction between the palpable and the impalpable, the separation between what is known to be material and that which is conceived to be divine, does not necessarily exist even in countries that have reached a high degree of civilization. In India, the dance of the bayaderes before the gilded statues, and the top-playing that is to amuse a stone Krishna, are cases in point. But these instances are exceptions to the general rule. It seems well established that man, in proportion to his intelligence, passed out of animism, loitered in polytheism, and drifted therefrom into monotheistic or pantheistic beliefs.

The race whose beliefs have held most steadfast from their incipiency to the present day is the Hindu. In their long journey these beliefs have encountered many vicissitudes; they have been curtailed, elaborated and degraded, but in the main they are still intact. At the contact with fresher faiths, the primitive religions of other lands have either disappeared abruptly or gradually faded away. It is India alone that has witnessed an autonomous development of first theories, and it is in India that the first denying voice was raised. To appreciate the denial it is necessary to understand what was affirmed. For this purpose a momentary digression may be permitted.

In the beginning of the Vedic period, Nature in her entirety was held divine. To the delicate imagination of the early Aryan, the gods were in all things, and all things were gods. In no other land have myths been more fluid and transparent. Mountains, rivers and landscapes were regarded with veneration; the skies, the stars, the sun, the dawn and dusk were adored, but particularly Agni, the personification of creative heat. Through lapses of time of which there is no chronology, this charming naturalism drifted down the currents of thought into the serenest forms of pantheistic beliefs.

The restless and undetermined divinities, omnipresent and yet impalpable, the wayward and changing phenomena, contributed one and all to suggest the idea of a continuous transformation, and with it, by implication, something that is transformed. Gradually the early conception of Agni expanded into a broader thought. From the spectacle of fire arose the theory of a deva, one who shines; and to this deva a name was given which signified both a suppliant and a supplication—Brahma. In this metamorphosis all vagueness was lost. Brahma became not only a substantial reality, but the creator of all that is. Later, the labor of producing and creating was regarded as an imperfection, a blemish on the splendor of the Supreme. It was thought a part of his dignity to be majestically inert, and above him was conceived the existence of a still higher being, a being who was also called Brahma; yet this time the name was no longer masculine, but neuter and indeclinable—neuter as having no part in life, and indeclinable because unique.[*]

This conception of a neuter principle, eternal, inactive, and a trifle pale perhaps, was not reached during the period assigned to the Vedas. It was the work of time and of fancy, but it was unassisted. The religion of India is strictly its own; its systems were founded and its problems solved before the thinkers of other lands were old enough to reflect. In Greece, which was then in swaddling clothes, Anaxagoras was the first who thought of a pure Intelligence, and this thought he contented himself with stating; its development was left to other minds, and even then it remained unadorned until Athens heard the exultant words of Paul. Nor could the Hindus have gathered their ideas from other countries. Their brothers, the Persians, were watching the combat between Ahura-Mazda and Ahriman. With the Hebrews there was no chance nor rumor of contact: Elohim had not given way to Jehovah. Chaldea was celebrating the nuptials of Nature and the Sun; while far beyond was Egypt, and on her heart the Sphinx.

It seems, then, not unsafe to say that the Vedas and the theories that were their after-growth have no connection with any foreign civilization. Beyond this particular, Brahmanism enjoys over all other religions the peculiar distinction of being without a founder. Its germ, as has been hinted, was in the Vedas; but it was a germ merely that the priests planted and tended, and watched develop into a great tree, which they then disfigured with engraftments.

Emerson recommended us to treat people as though they were real, and added, "Perhaps they are," But the doubt that lin-

_____

[*]   Burnouf: Essai sur le Veda. Taine: Essais.

gered in the mind of the stately pantheist never entered into that of the Hindu. In its purest manifestation the creed of the latter was a negation of the actuality of the visible world. The forms of matter were held to be illusive, and the semblance of reality possessed by them was considered due to Māyā. Māyā originally signified Brahma's longing for something other than himself; something that might contrast with his eternal quietude; something that should occupy the voids of space; something that should lull the languors of his infinite ennui. From this longing sprang whatever is, and it was through Māyā, which afterwards became synonymous with illusion, that a phantom universe surged before the god's delighted eyes, the mirage of his own desire.

This ghostly world is the semblance of reality in which man dwells: mountains, rivers, landscapes, the earth itself, the universe and all humanity, are but the infinite evolutions of his fancy. The ringing lines that occur in Mr. Swinburne's "Hertha" may not improperly be referred to him:

> "I am that which began;
>   Out of me the years roll;
> Out of me, God and man;
>   I am equal and whole.
> God changes, and man, and the form of them bodily;
>   I am the soul."

Familiarly, Brahma is the spider drawing from his breast the threads of existence: emblematically, a triangle inscribed in a circle; poetically, the self-existing supremacy that is enthroned on a lotus of azure and gold; and theologically, the one really existing essence, the eternal germ from which all things issue and to which all things at last return.

From man to Brahma, a series of higher forms of existence are traceable in an ascending scale till three principal divinities are reached. These, the highest manifestations of the First Cause, Brahma the Creator, Vishnu the Preserver, and Siva the Destroyer, constitute the Tri-murti, the Trinity, typified in the magically mystic syllable Om. To these were added a host of inferior deities and even local gods similar to those which the Romans recognized in later years. Such was and still is the celestial hierarchy. In the eyes of the Hindu, none of these gods are eternal. At the end of cycles of incommensurable duration, the universe will cease to be, the heavens will be rolled up like a garment, the Tri-murti dissolved; while in space shall rest but the great First Cause, through whose instrumentality, after indefinite kalpas, life will be re-beckoned out of chaos and the leash of miseries unloosed.

This delicious commingling of the real and the ideal degenerated with the years. Like Olympus, it was too fair to last. Brahma, Vishnu and Siva, once regarded as various manifestations of the primal essence, became in lapses of time concrete. Female counterparts were found for them, and the most poetic of the creeds of man was lowered into a sensuous idolatry. Today there is nothing, however monstrous or grotesque, that is deemed unfit for worship. In Benares there is a shrine to small-pox; in Gaya there is one to the police; and it may be that somewhere between Cape Comorin and the Himalayas an altar has been raised to those who dull digestion with the after-dinner speech.

This, however, is the work of the priest. In earlier days the higher castes of man, the younger brothers of the gods, were thought capable of understanding the perfection that resides in Brahm. It was held that they might ascend to the rank of their elders, and with them at last be absorbed in the universal spirit. The one pathway to this goal was worship, and over it the priests constituted themselves the lawful guides.

The laws which they codified were numberless, and an infraction of any one of them was severely visited on the transgressor. For each fault, whether of omission or commission, there was an expiation to be undergone, and it was taught that the unatoned violation of a precept precipitated the offender into one of twenty-eight hells which their inflammable imaginations had created.

In the face of absurdities such as these, it is permissible to suppose that, like the Roman augurs, the educated Brahmans could not look at each other without laughing; yet, however this may be, it seems certain that many of the laity laughed at them. Already in the Rig-Veda mention was made of those who jeered at Agni. The question as to whether there is really another life seems to have been often raised, and that too in the Brahmanas. Yaska, a venerable sage, found himself obliged to refute the opinions of sages older and more venerable than himself, who had declared the Vedas to be a tissue of nonsense. This skepticism had found many adherents. The name given to these early disbelievers was Nastikas—They who deny. Like other sects, they had aphorisms and slokas of their own, which with quaint derision they attributed to the tutor of the gods. The aphorisms appear to have been markedly anti-theistic, while the slokas were captivating invitations to the pleasures of life.

> "*Vivons, ouvrons nos cœurs aux ivresses nouvelles:*
> *Dormir et boire en paix, voila l'unique bien.*
> *Buvons! Notre sang brule et nos femmes sont belles:*
> *Demain n'est pas encore, et le passe n'est rien!*"

Among those who laughed the loudest was Kapila. His life is shrouded in the dim magnificence of legends. There let it rest; yet if little can be said of the man, his work at least is not unfamiliar to students. The Sānkhya Kārika, which bears his name, is one of the most important and independent relics of Indian thought. In its broadest sense, Sānkhya means rationalism or system of rational philosophy. In India it is known as the philosophy Niriswara, the philosophy without a god.

Kapila was the first serious thinker who looked into the archaic skies and declared them to be void. In this there was none of the moderation of skepticism, and less of the fluctuations of doubt. Kapila saw that the idea of a Supreme Being was posterior to man; that Nature, anterior to her demiurge, had created him; and he resolutely turned his back on the Tri-murti, and denied that a deity existed, or that the existence of one was necessary to the order and management of the world. The motor-power he held to be a blind, unconscious force, and of this force, life was the melancholy development. If he had disbelieved in transmigration, Schopenhauer would not have startled the world with a new theory.

Kapila's purpose was to relieve man from suffering. There were no rites to be observed. Knowledge and meditation were alone required. He recognized but three things—the soul, matter and pain. Freedom from pain was obtainable, he taught, by the liberation of the soul, from the bondage of matter. According to his teaching, the heavens, the earth and all that in them is, are made up of twenty-five principles, and of these principles matter is the first and the soul the last. Matter is the primordial element of universal life, the element that animates and sustains all things. The principles that succeed it are simply its developments. Of these, the soul is the chief. It is for matter to act and for the soul to observe. When its observations are perfect and complete, when it has obtained a discriminative knowledge of the forms of matter, of primeval matter and of itself, then is it prepared to enter into eternal beatitude.

On the subject of eternal beatitude, each one of the systems of Eastern thought has had its say. That which Kapila had in view is not entirely clear. He gave no description of it otherwise than in hinting that it was a state of abstract and unconscious impassibility, and he appears to have been much more occupied in devising means by which man might be delivered from the evils of life than in mapping charts of a fantastic paradise.

The sentiment of the immedicable misery of life is as prominent in the preface of history as on its latest and uncompleted page. The problem of pain agitated the minds of the earliest thinkers as turbulently as it has those of the latest comers. In attempting to solve it, in endeavoring to find some rule for a law of error, the Hindu accepted an unfathered idea that he is expiating the sins of anterior and unremembered existences, and that he will continue to expiate them until all past transgressions are absolved and the soul is released from the chain of its migrations. According to the popular theory, the chain of migrations consists in twenty-four lakhs of birth, a lakh being one hundred thousand.

Apparently such beatitude as lay beyond the tomb consisted to Kapila in relief from transmigration, and this relief was obtainable by the ransomed soul, only, as has been hinted, through a knowledge acquired of matter and of itself. Garmented in the flesh of him that constitutes its individuality, the soul was to apply itself to an understanding of Nature, who, with the coquetry of a bayadere, at first resists and then unveils her beauties to the eyes of the persistent wooer. This knowledge once obtained, the soul is free. It may yet linger awhile on earth, as the wheel of the spinner turns for a moment after the impulse which puts it in motion has ceased to act; but from that time the soul has fulfilled all the conditions of its deliverance, and is forever affranchised from the successive migrations which the unransomed soul must still undergo.

In his attack on official theology, Kapila paid little attention to its rites and observances. He probably fancied that if the groundwork was undermined, the superstructure would soon totter. In this he was partially correct, though the result of his revolt was entirely different from what he had expected. The climax of his philosophy is a metaphysical paradox: "Neither I am, nor is aught mine, nor is there any I"—a climax which must have delighted Hegel, but one which it is difficult to reconcile with the report of the philosophy's present popularity. And that it is popular there seems to be no doubt. There is even a common saying in India that no knowledge is equal to the Sankhya, and no power equal to the Yoga, which latter, a combination of mnemonics and gymnastics, is a contrivance for concentrating the mind intently on nothing.

But whatever popularity the Sankhya may now enjoy, it is evident that, like other systems of Eastern thought, it was understood only by adepts; and even had the science which it taught been offered to the people, it was not of a nature to appeal to them. The masses today are as ignorant as carps, and at that time they were not a whit more intelligent. Besides, it was easier to understand the Tri-murti than twenty-five abstract principles. Brahma was very neighborly, and his attendant gods were known to tread the aisles of night. The languid noons and sudden dawns were sacred with their presence. What could be more reasonable? If life was an affliction, that very affliction carried the sufferer into realms of enchantment, where Brahma was enthroned on a lotus of azure and gold.

It is small wonder then that Kapila's lessons left the established religion practically unharmed. Kant's *Kritik* did not prevent the Konigsbergians from listening to the Pfarrer with the same faith with which their fathers had listened before them. And Kant, it may be remembered, was not only a popular teacher, he was one that was revered. But aside from any influence that Kapila's philosophy may have exerted, it was evidently smitten by a grave defect. Concerning the soul's ultimate abiding-place it was silent. This silence enveloped the entire system in an obscurity which another and a greater thinker undertook to dissipate.

It has been said before, and with such wisdom that the

saying will bear repetition, that revolutions are created, not by the strength of an idea, but by the intensity of a sentiment. In great crises there is a formula that all await; so soon as it is pronounced, it is accepted and repeated; it is the answer to an universal demand. Toward the close of the sixth century before the present era, at Kapilavastu, a city and kingdom situated at the foot of the mountains of Nepal, a prince of the blood, after prolonged meditations on the misfortunes of life, pronounced a watchword of this description.

The name of this early Muhammad was Siddartha. He was the heir of the royal house of Sakya, and in later years, in remembrance of his origin, he was called Sakya-Muni, Sakya the Anchorite, to which was added the title of Buddha, the Sage. The accounts of his life are contained in the *Lalita Vistâra*, a collection of fabulous episodes in which the supernatural joins hands with the matter-of-fact. It is said, for instance, that he was born of an immaculate conception, and died of an indigestion of pork. Apart from the mythical element, his life does not appear to have been different from that of other religious reformers, save only that he is supposed to have been born in a palace instead of a hovel. To his twenty-ninth year Siddartha is represented as living at court, surrounded by all the barbaric ease and gorgeousness of the Ind. Yet even in his youth his mind appears to have been haunted by great thoughts. He took no part in the sports of his companions, and was accustomed, it is said, to wander away into the solitudes of bamboo, and there to linger, lost in meditation.

In the course of time he was married to a beautiful girl, but even in her fair arms his thoughts were occupied with the destinies of the world. During the succeeding festivals and revels, amid the luxury of the palace and the enticements of love, he meditated on the miseries of life. In Brahmanism he found no consolation. At its grotesqueness he too smiled, but his smile was nearer to tears than to laughter. The melancholy residue of his reflections was with him even in dream, and one night—so runs the legend—he was encouraged in a vision to teach mankind a law which should save the world and establish the foundation of an eternal and universal rest.

A combination of fortuitous circumstances, the play of the merest hazard, appears to have strengthened the effect of this vision. On the high-roads about Kapilavastu he encountered a man bent double with age, another stricken by fever, and lastly a corpse. "A curse," he cried, "on youth that age must overcome; a curse on health that illness destroys; a curse on life which death interrupts! Age, illness, death, could they but be forever enchained!" Soon after, he disappeared, and seeking the jungles, which at that time were peopled with thinkers of ken, he devoted himself to the elaboration of his thoughts. It was there that he seems to have acquired some acquaintance with the philosophy of Kapila. He divined its significance and saw its insufficiency. Thereafter for six years he gave himself up to austerities so severe that, in the naïve language of the legend, they startled even the gods. These six years are said to have been passed at Ouruvilva, a place as famous in Buddhist annals as Kapilavastu. In this retreat he arranged the principles of his system, and perfected the laws and ethics which were to be its accompaniment. Yet still the immutable truth that was to save the world escaped him. A little longer he waited and struggled. The Spirit of Sin, with all his seductive cohorts, appeared before him. The cohorts were routed and the Spirit overcome; the struggle was ended; and under a Bodhi-tree which is still shown to the pilgrim, Siddartha caught the immutable truth, and thereupon presented himself as a saviour to his fellows.

Such is the popular legend. Its main incidents have been recently and most felicitously conveyed in *The Light of Asia*. As a literary contribution, Mr. Arnold's poem is simply charming; as a page of history, it has the value of a zero from which the formative circle has been eliminated. The kingdom of Kapilavastu, or rather Kapilavatthu, was an insignificant hamlet. The Buddah's father was a petty chieftain, the raja of a handful of ignorant savages. Palaces he had none; his wealth was his strength; and could his concubine be recalled to life, she would, had she any sense of humor, which is doubtful, be vastly amused at finding that she had been given a rôle in the solar myth.

There can, however, be no doubt that the Buddha really lived. His existence is as well established as that of the Christ. To precisely what an extent he was a visionary is necessarily difficult of conjecture. Yet unless all belief in him be refused, it seems almost obligatory to assume that after years of reflection he considered himself in possession of absolute knowledge. The truth which he then began to preach was not doctrine that he held as personal and peculiar to himself, but rather an eternal and changeless law which had been proclaimed from age to age by other Buddhas, of whom he fancied himself the successor.

To speak comparatively, it is only with recent years that the attention of Western students has been attracted to Buddhist literature. Today, however, thanks to translations from the Pali and kindred tongues, it is possible for any one to study the doctrine from the sacred books themselves. There are verses in the Vedas which when recited are said to charm the birds and beasts. Compared with them, the Buddhist Gospels are often lacking in beauty. To be the better understood, the priests, who addressed themselves not to initiates but to the masses, employed a language that was simple and familiar. There are in consequence many repetitions and trivial digressions, but there are also parables of such exquisite color, that in them one may feel the influence of a bluer sky than ours, the odor of groves of sandal, the green abysses of the Himalayas, and the gem-like splendor of white Thibetian stars.

The Buddha believed neither in a personal nor an impersonal God. The world he compared to a wheel turning ceaselessly on itself. Of Brahman tenets he preserved but one, that of the immedicable misery of life. But the doctrine which he taught may perhaps best be summarized as resting on three great principles—Karma, Arahatship and Nirvana. When these principles are understood, the mysteries of the creed are dissolved, and the need of esoteric teaching diminished.

It may be noted, by way of proem, that the theory of the transmigration of souls is not advanced in the Vedas. It is a part of Brahman teaching, but Brahmanism and Vedaism are not the same. The Vedas are claimed as the outcome of direct revelation, while all that part of post-Vedic literature in which Brahmanism is enveloped is held to be purely traditional. The origin of the theory of the transmigration is indiscoverable, but it is one which has been shared by many apparently unrelated races. It was a part of the creed of the Druids; the Australian savage, as well as some of the American aborigines, held to the same idea; thinkers in Egypt and in Greece advanced identical tenets; it is alluded to in the Talmud, and hinted at in the Gospel which bears the name of St. John. Possibly it was held by the pre-Aryan inhabitants of India, and in that case it is equally possible that it was through them that the doctrine descended into Brahmanism. But whether or not its engraftment came about in this way is relatively a matter of small moment. The important point to be observed is that it was not received by the Buddhists. The popular idea to the contrary is erroneous.

Spinoza noted that there is in every man a feeling that he has been what he is from all eternity, and this feeling has not left the Buddhist unaffected. But between such a sentiment and a belief in transmigration the margin is wide. The popular error in which the two are confused has presumably risen from a misunderstanding of the laws of Karma and Vipaka, the laws of cause and affect. The difference therein discoverable amounts in brief to this: in the theory of transmigration the soul is held to be eternal; in Buddhism the existence of the soul is denied. In the one, the ego resurrects through cycles of unremembered lives: in the other, nothing survives save the fruit of its actions. In the one, every man is his own heir and his own ancestor; in the other, the deeds of the ancestor are concentrated in a new individual. In each there is a chain of existences, but in the one they are material, in the other they are moral. One maintains the migration of an essence, the other the results of causality; one has no evidence to support it, the other accords with the law of the indistructibility of force. One is metempsychosis, the other palingenesis; one is beautiful, and the other awkward; but one is a theory, and the other a fact.

From this chain the Hindu knew no mode of relief. Prior to the Buddha's advent, there was an unquestioned belief that man and all that encompasses him rolled through an eternal circle of transformation; that he passed through all the forms of life, from the most elementary to the most perfect; that the place which he occupied depended on his merits or demerits; that the virtuous revived in a divine sphere, while the wicked descended to a yet darker purgatory; that the recompense of the blessed and the punishment of the damned were of a duration which was limited; that time effaced the merit of virtue as well as the demerit of sin; and that the law of transmigration brought back again to earth both the just and the unjust, and threw them anew into a fresh cycle of terrestrial existences, from which they could fight free as best they might.

When the Buddha began to teach, he endeavored to bring his new theories into harmony with old doctrines. Throughout life, man, he taught, is enmeshed in a web whose woof was woven in preceding ages. The misfortunes that he endured are not the consequences of his immediate actions; they are drafts which have been drawn upon him in earlier days—drafts which he still must honor, and against which he can plead no statute of limitations. Karma pursues him in this life, and unless he learns its relentless code by heart, the fruit of his years is caught up by revolving chains, and tossed back into the life of another. How this occurred, or why it occurred, is explainable only by a cumbersome process from which the reader may well be spared; and it may for the moment suffice to note that while the Buddha agreed with the Brahmans that life formed a chain of existences, it was the former who brought the hope that the chain might be severed.

The means to the accomplishment of this end consist in a victory over the lusts of the flesh, the desire for life and the veils of illusion. When these have been vanquished, the Arahat, the victor, attains Nirvana.

Nirvana, or Nibbana as it stands in the Pali, is not a paradise, nor yet a state of post-mortem trance. It is the extinction of all desire, the triple victory of the Arahat, which precedes the great goal, eternal death. The fruits of earlier sins remain, but they are impermanent and soon pass away. Nothing is left from which another sentient being can be called into existence. The Arahat no longer lives; he has reached Para Nirvana, the complete absence of anything, that can be likened only to the flame of a lamp which a gust of wind has extinguished.

The Buddha wrote nothing. It was his disciples who, in councils that occurred after his death, collected and arranged the lessons of their master. In these synods the canon of sacred scripture was determined. It consisted of three divisions, called the Tri-pitaka, or Three Baskets, and contained the Suttas, the discourses, of the Buddha—the Dharmas, the duties enjoined on the masses—and lastly the Vinayas, the rules of discipline.

The Dharmas contain the four truths whose discovery is credited to the Buddha. The first is that suffering is the concomitant of life. The second, that suffering is the resultant of desire. The third, that relief from suffering is obtained in the suppression of desire. And fourth, that Nirvana, which succeeds the suppression of desire, is attainable only through certain paths. These paths are eight in number; four of which—correctness in deed, word, thought and sight—were recommended to all men; the remainder—the paths of application, memory, meditation and proper life—being reserved for the eremites.

For the use of the faithful, the four truths have been condensed in a phrase: "Abstain from sin, practice virtue, dominate the flesh—such is the law of the Buddha." The recognition of the four truths and the observance of the eight virtues are obligatory to all who wish to reach Nirvana. The neophyte renounces the world and lives a mendicant. Yet inasmuch as a society of saints is difficult to perpetuate, members are admitted from whom the usual vows of continence and poverty are not exacted.

The charm of primitive Buddhism was in its simplicity. The faithful assembled for meditation and not for parade. The practice of morality needed no forms and fewer ceremonies. But with time it was thought well to make some concession to popular superstitions; and although the Buddha had no idea of representing himself as a divinity, every moral and physical perfection was attributed to him. The rest was easy. Idolatry had begun. To the right and left of a saint elevated to the rank of God Supreme, a glowing Pantheon was formed of the Buddhas that had preceded him. A meaningless worship was established; virtues were subordinated to ceremonies; and today before a gilded statue a wheel of prayers is turned, while through the dim temples, domed like a vase, the initiates murmur, "Life is evil."

In attempting to convert the multitude, the Buddha made no use of vulgar seductions. From him came no flattery to the passions. The recompense that He promised was not of the earth nor material in its nature. To his believers he offered neither wealth nor power. The psychic force, the seemingly supernatural faculties, that knowledge and virtue brought to those who had reached superior degrees of sanctity, were shared by the Brahmans as well; they were an appanage, not a bait. The one reward of untiring efforts was an eternal ransom from the successive horrors of Karma. The paradise which he disclosed was the death of Death. In it all things ceased to be. It was the ultimate annihilation from which life was never to be re-beckoned.

It is not surprising that the captivating quiet of a goal such as this should forcibly appeal to the inclinations of the ascetic; the wonder of it is that It could be regarded for a moment as attractive to the coarse appetites of the crowd. Nor does it seem that the Christ of Chaos made this mistake. It was the after-comers who undertook to lift the commonplace out of the humdrum. The Buddha's hope of the salvation of all mankind was a dream extending into the indefinite future; the theory of immediate emancipation was never shared by him. For the plain man, he laid down a law which was a law of grace for all, that of universal brotherhood. If its practice was insufficient to lead him to Nirvana, it was still a preparation thereto, a paving of the way for the travelers that were yet to come.

The method which he employed to convert his hearers seems to have been a tender persuasion, in which there was no trace of the dogmatic. He did not contend against strength, he appealed to weakness, varying the insinuations of his parables according to the nature of the listener, and charming even the recalcitrant by the simplicity and flavor of his words. In these lessons there were no warnings, no detached maledictions; but there were exhortations to virtue, and pictures of the sweet and sudden silence of eternal rest. His struggle was never with creeds, but with man, with the flesh and its appetites; and from the memory of his victorious combat with himself there came to him precepts and maxims of incomparable delicacy and beauty.

These were his weapons. His teaching was a lesson of infinite tenderness and compassion; it was a lesson of patience and resignation and abnegation of self, and especially of humility, which in its renouncement of temporal splendors opens the path to the magnificence of death.

In the ears of not a few modern thinkers, this promise of annihilation has sounded like a gigantic paradox. It has seemed inconceivable that men could be found who would strive unremittingly their whole lives through to reach a goal where nothing was. And yet there were many such, and, what is more to the point, their number is constantly increasing. On the other hand, it has been argued that to those who knew no prospect of supernal happiness and who had never heard of an eternity of bliss, the horror of life might be of such intensity that they would be glad of any release whatever. But the value of this argument is slight. The spectacle of a Buddhist converted to Christianity is the most infrequent that has ever gladdened the heart of a missionary. Per contra, the number of those who turn from other creeds to that of Buddhism is notoriously large. The number of its converts, however, is not a proof of its perfections. And Buddhism is far from perfect: its fantastic shackles may be alluring to the mystic, but they are meaningless to the mathematician. It may be charming to hold a faith which has put pessimism into verse, and raised that verse into something more than literature; but it is useless. The pleasure of utter extinction is one which we will probably all enjoy, and that too without first becoming Arahats; and yet, again, we may not. The veil of Māyā is still unraised. The most we can do to lift it is to finger feebly at the edges. Sakya-Muni taught many an admirable lesson, but in his flights of fancy, like many another since, he transcended the limits of experience. Let those who love him follow.

Charity is the New Testament told in a word. When it was preached on the Mount of Olives it must have brought with it the freshness and aroma of a new conception. Before that time, the Galileans had heard but of Justice and Jehovah; then at once they knew of Christ and Compassion; and ever since the name and the virtue have gone hand-in-hand. And yet five hundred years before, a sermon on charity was preached in Nepal.

The charity which Sakya-Muni taught was not the ordinary liberality which varies from a furtive coin to a public bequest. It was a boundless sympathy, a prodigality of abandonment in which each creature, however humble, could find a share, and which, once entered in the heart of man, extinguished every spark of egotism. This sentiment of universal compassion was one which the two greatest of the world's reformers sought alike to instil. Between the Prince of Kapilavastu and Jesus of Nazareth there are many resemblances, but none, it may be taken, more striking than this. Beyond the common legend of their birth, both were supposed to have been tempted by the devil; and by the Buddha, as the Christ, the devil was vanquished. Their lessons in ethics were nearly the same; both were nihilists; both held that the highest duty is to be at variance with self; both struck a blow at the virility of man, and neither of them wrote. About the lives of each the myth-makers have been at work; both were deified; and if today the believers in the Buddha largely outnumber those of the Christ, it is only fair to note that the former have enjoyed advantages which the latter have never possessed. Through none of their wide leisures have they ever held it a blasphemy to think.

Another religion without a God, and one which is a twin-sister to Buddhism, is that of the Gainas. Explanatory documents concerning it are infrequent, and in search of information the student is usually obliged to turn to Brahman sources. The Gainas are the believers in Gina, the Victorious, as the Buddhists are believers in Buddha, the Sage. A Gina—in Buddhism this term is one of the many synonyms of

Sakya-Muni—is a prophet who, having attained omniscience, comes to re-establish the law of salvation when it has become corrupted through the march of time. There are said to have been twenty-four Ginas, including the most recent; and as the Gainas maintain that the Buddha was a disciple of the founder of their creed, the number corresponds to that of Siddartha and his twenty-three predecessors. The Gainas, like the Buddhists, deny the authority of the Vedas; they consider them apocryphal, and oppose in their stead a collection of Angas of their own. No sect has been more rigorous than they in the respect of everything that lives. They eat no flesh; and it is reported that the stricter devotees filter their water, breathe through a veil, and as they walk sweep the ground before them, that no insect, however insignificant, may be destroyed. Among the customs in which they differ from Buddhism, suicide is the one worth noting. For a long period this rite seems to have been decorously observed. On most other points the two beliefs are in apparent agreement. The Gainas, too, are atheists. They admit of no Creator, and deny the existence of a perfect and eternal Being. The Gina, like the Buddha, has become perfect, but it is not thought that he has always been so. This negation has not prevented a particular division of the faith from affecting a kind of heretical and schismatic deism, Like the Nepalese, who have imagined an Adibuddha, a supreme Buddha, they also have invented a Ginapati, a perfect Gina, whom, in opposition to their canonical Angas, they regard as primordial creator. The Angas teach that man possesses a soul, and that his soul, although a pure and an immortal intelligence, is yet the prey of illusion, and for that reason condemned to bear the yoke of matter through an indefinite series of existences. In Gainism it is not existence that is an affliction, it is life; and the Nirvana is less an annihilation than an entrance into eternal beatitude. To distinguish between the two faiths, the Brahmans called the Buddhists, "They who affirm," and the Gainas, "They who say, Perhaps."*

The Chinese, who are our elders in little else than corruption, feel as much need for a religion as a civilian does for a military uniform. From the threshold of history to the present day, the inhabitants of the celestial Empire have had no term wherewith to designate a deity. The name of God has not entered into their philosophy. As a rule, then, when an educated Chinese is asked what his creed is, he answers, that not being a priest, he has none at all. The clergy have three: the official religion—originated by Confucius—Buddhism and Tauism. The latter faith was founded by Laou-tze.

The life of this early thinker has been as liberally interwoven with legends as that of the Buddha. The Orient seems to have had a mania for attributing the birth of reformers to immaculate conceptions; and one learns with the weariness that comes of a thrice-told tale, that the mother of Laou-tze, finding herself one day alone, conceived suddenly through the vivifying influence of Nature. But though the conception was abrupt, the gestation was prolonged, lasting, it is said, eighty-four years; and when at last the miraculous child was born, his hair was white—whence his name, Laou-tze, the Aged Baby. This occurred six hundred years before the present era.

The philosophy of this prodigy, contained in the *Taou-teh-king*, the *Book of Supreme Knowledge and Virtue*, is regarded by Orientalists as the most profound and authentic relic of early Chinese literature. The most profound, as rivaling the works of Confucius and Mencius; and the most authentic, in that it was the only one said to have been exempt from the different edicts commanding the destruction of manuscripts.

Laou-tze was probably the first thinker who established the fact that it is not in the power of man to conceive an adequate idea of a First Cause, and the first to show that any efforts in

---

*   Dictionnaire de sciences religieuses, art. Jainisme.

that direction result merely in demonstrating human incompetence and the utter vainness of the endeavor. When, therefore, he was obliged to mention the primordial essence in such a manner as to be understood by his hearers, the figurative term which he employed was Tau. "Tau," he said, "is empty, in operation exhaustless. It is the formless mother of all things." And to this description Spinoza found little to add.

Laou-tze appears to have dipped into all the philosophies then in vogue, and after taking a little eclectic sip from each, elaborated a system so cleverly that he may safely be regarded as the earliest moralist. His doctrine was thoroughly pantheistic. Man, he taught, is a passing and inferior phase of the Great Unity which is the beginning and end of all things, and into which the soul is absorbed. Happiness, he added, is like paradise, an imaginary Utopia, a fiction of the non-existent extending beyond the borderlands of the known. And on the chart which he drew of life, he set up a monitory finger-post, warning men that the only real delights were those that consist in the absence of pain. Enterprise, effort and ambition, were so many good, old-fashioned words which to this early pessimist represented merely a forethought for a future generation. And of a future generation he saw little need. The one laudable aim was in the avoidance of suffering. After all, what was there in life? Nothing save a past as painful as the present, with hope to breed chimeras and the future for a dream.

Like Buddhism, the doctrine of Laou-tze degenerated with the years. Their common simplicity was too subtle for the canaille, and to each gaudy superstitions have been added. Yet in their primal significance they are as ushers of negation, the initial revolt at the supernatural, the first reasoned attempts to route the spectres from the mind of man.

In earlier Hinduism, life was a nightmare, and the universe a phantasm that vaunted itself real. In an effort to escape, Kapila lost himself in abstractions, the Buddha ordered Death to stand a lackey at the door of Peace, while Laou-tze turned his almond eyes within and descended the stair of Thought. To the first, salvation lay in metaphysics; to the second, in virtue; to the third, in indifference. Had their theories been fused, the revolt might not have been so vain.

CHAPTER TWO

The Negations of Antiquity.

THE CLAMOR OF LIFE AND THOUGHT ENTERED GREECE through Asia Minor. Quinet has called the itinerary of the tribes that took possession of her hills and vales, an itinerary of the gods. That somnambulist of history has seen, as in a vision, their passage marked, here by a temple, there by a shrine. While the tribes dispersed, the gods advanced. Orpheus has told the story of their youth; but now Orpheus is indiscoverable, and the days of which he sang are as vague as the future. When the gods entered folk-lore, they had already ascended Olympus, and the divinity of Jupiter was attested in traditions out of which Homer formed another Pentateuch. The name of the Ionian Moses is as unsubstantial as that of Orpheus; but if his personality is uncertain, it is yet a matter of common knowledge that his epics formed the articles of an indulgent creed, and that from them the infant Greece first learned the pleasures that belong to dream. At this time the mysteries of the archaic skies were dissolved. Dread had vanished; in its place was the Ideal. Throughout the mellow morns and languid dusks there was an unbroken procession of the gayest, the most alluring divinities; their fare was ambrosia, their laughter was inextinguishable. Virtue was rewarded on earth, and Nemesis pursued the wrong-doer. The dower of men and maidens was beauty; love was too near to nature to know of shame; religion was more aesthetic than moral, more gracious than austere. The theologians were poets: first Orpheus, Musaeus and Linus, then Homer and Hesiod; mirth, magnificence and melancholy they gave in fee.

Homer was not only a poet, he was an historian as well; and it is a fact amply demonstrated that he believed as little in the sacerdotal legends as Tennyson in the phantom idyls of Arthur. At that time no semblance of revealed religion was affected: the people, however, like all others before and since, would have gods, and gods they got; yet in displaying them to the infant race, Homer laughed at the divinities, and predicted that their reign would some day cease.

This prescience of the incredulity that was to come is significant. The history of Greece is one of freedom in art, in action, but particularly in thought. The death of Socrates, the flight of Aristotle, are among the exceptions that make the rule. In its broad outlines, the attitude of Hellenic thought was one of aggressive skepticism. This attitude may have been due to the fact that there was nothing which in any way resembled a national faith; each town, each hamlet, each upland and valley, possessed myths of its own, and such uniformity as existed appears to have been ritualistic rather than doctrinal. But perhaps the primal cause is best attributable to that nimble spirit of investigation which is at once a characteristic of the Greek intellect and a contrast to the cataleptic reveries of the Hindu.

It goes without the need of telling that the philosophers put Jupiter aside much as one does an illusion of childhood, and possibly with something of the same regret. But this leniency on their part was not universally imitated. The story of Prometheus, the most ancient of fables, traces of which have been discovered in the Vedas, became in the hands of Æschylus a semi-historical, semi-cosmological legend, in which the Titan, as representative of humanity, mouths from the escarpolated summits of Caucasus his hatred and defiance of Jove. Euripides, too, was well in the movement. There was not an article of Hellenic faith that he did not scoff at. Then came the farce. Aristophanes found nothing too sacred for his wit; with the impartiality of genius he joked at gods and men alike.

While the poets and dramatists were pulling down, the philosophers were building up. If the belief in an eternal fancy ball on Olympus was untenable, something, they felt, should be suggested in its place. In lieu, therefore, of the theory that Jupiter was the first link in the chain of the universe, Thales announced that the beginning of things was water; Anaximenes said air; Heraclitus preferred fire. Anaximinder held to an abstraction, the Infinite. Pythagoras, who, like all his countrymen, dearly loved a quibble, declared that the First Cause was One. This One, Xenophanes asserted, was a self-existent Mind. Empedocles gave as definition a sphere whose centre was everywhere and circumference nowhere, a definition which Pascal revived as an attribute of the Deity. Anaxagoras, who was banished for his pains, believed in a pure Intelligence. This pure Intelligence was not a deity, except perhaps in the sense of a *deus ex machina*; it was an explanation, not a god. But even so, it looked like one; there were already too many unknown gods, and the idea was not received with enthusiasm. Among those who opposed it with particular vehemence was Diagoras, he who first among the Greeks received the name of atheist. This logician chanced one day to be at sea during a heavy storm. The sailors attributed the storm to him. All that they were enduring was a punishment for conveying such an impious wretch as he. "Look at those other ships over there," said Diagoras. "They are in the same storm, aren't they? Do you suppose that I am in each of them?"

Diagoras had learned his lessons from Democritus, a thinker who in certain schools of thought holds today a position which, if not superior, is at least equal to that of Plato. The reason of this admiration is not far to seek. Democritus is the grandsire of materialism. Materialism is out of fashion today, but to-morrow it may come in again. During a long and continually rejuvenated career, it has been a veritable hydra. Every time its head seemed severed for all eternity, there has sprouted a new one, and one more sagacious than the last.

The theory of atoms announced in the remote past and repeated in recent years underwent a baptism of fire at the beginning of the present century. Dalton applied it to the interpretation of chemical laws, and a little later a band of German erudites embellished it with the garlands of new discoveries. Contemporary science treats it with scant respect; but all who are of a liberal mind admit that its conclusions have been useful implements of progress. Its originator, Democritus, was a contemporary of Sakya-Muni. It is even possible that he sat at the Buddha's feet; he is said to have wandered far into the East; and it is also recorded that he visited Egypt, whither he had been preceded by Pythagoras, and where his questioning eyes must have met the returning stare of the Sphinx.

At that time traveling was not necessarily expensive, yet in his journeys Democritus squandered his substance with great correctness; and when after years of absence he returned to his home, he found himself amenable to a law of the land which deprived of the honors of burial those who had dissipated their patrimony. A statute of this description was not of a nature to alarm such a man as Democritus. He invited all who cared to do so, to meet him in the public square, and there, through the wide leisures of Thracian days, he recited passages from Diakosmos, his principal work. This procedure, together with the novelty of the ideas which he announced, so impressed his hearers, that they made for him a purse of five hundred talents, and after his death erected statues in his honor. Those indeed were the good old days.

In the system which Democritus suggested to his countrymen, matter was pictured as the union of an infinite number of indivisible elements, which in the diversity of their forms represent the phenomena of nature. Beyond these indivisible elements, space held but voids. Atoms and emptiness is the theory in a phrase. The voids are the absence of obstacles, and the atoms continually passing through them are the constituents of all that is. In their eternal voyage through space, these atoms meet, unite and separate, unruled save by the laws of unconscious and mechanical necessity. To their chance clash is due the world; the universe is one of their fortuitous combinations, and the hazard which presided at its formation will some day see it again dissolved. The word hazard, it may be noted, is used from lack of a better term. In exact speech there seems to be nothing which at all resembles it. The accident that occurs in the street, the rambles of the ball on the roulette-table, may seem the play of chance; but were the predisposing causes understood, the accident would be recognized as the result of a cause in which chance had no part, and in the rambles of the ball the operations of consistent laws would be discerned. Dubois Reymond has noted that if, during a short though determined space of time, an intelligent man were able to mark the exact position and movement of every molecule, he could, in accordance with the laws of mechanics, foresee the whole future of the world. In the same manner that an astronomer can foretell the date on which a comet, after years of remote wanderings, will re-visit our heavens, so in his equations could this imaginary individual read the precise day when England shall burn her last bit of coal, and Germany brew her last keg of beer.

Beyond this theory, which as a matter of course includes the denial that man is a free agent, Democritus was accustomed to assert that out of nothing, nothing comes—an axiom which one does not need to be a mathematician to agree with, though it is one that somewhat impairs the scientific value of the first chapter of Genesis. And were it otherwise, if things sprang from nothing, the producing cause would be limitless; men might issue from the sea, and fish from the earth. In the fecundity of chaos, everything, even to the impossible, would be possible. But in a system such as this, in which the operations of nature are represented as effected by invisible corpuscles which possess in themselves the laws of all their possible combinations, there is room only for the actual; the universe explains itself more or less clearly, and that too without recourse to a First Cause or an over-watching Providence.[*]

Democritus was one of the first quietists, but he was quietist without leanings to mysticism. He was among the earliest to note that it is the unexpected that occurs; and he barricaded himself as best he might against avoidable misfortune by shunning everything that was apt to be a source of suffering or annoyance. Beyond mental tranquility, he appears to have praised nothing except knowledge; and it is stated that he hunted truth not so much for the pleasure of the chase as for the delight which the quarry afforded.

The negations of Democritus had been well ventilated when the stage of history was abruptly occupied by a band of charlatan nihilists, who personified the spirit of doubt with ingenious effrontery. These were the sophists. To be called a sophist was originally a compliment. It meant one who was a master in wisdom and eloquence. But when Greece found herself imposed upon by a company of mental gymnasts, who in any argument maintained the pros and cons with equal ease, who made the

---

[*]   Nolen: *La philosophie de Lange.* Wurtz: *La théorie atomique.*

worst appear the best, who denied all things even to evidence, and affirmed everything even to the absurd, and who took sides with the just and the unjust with equal indifference—then the title lost its lustre and degenerated into a slur. This possibly was a mistake. A disapproval of the paradoxes of these dialecticians is almost a praise of the commonplace. Yet the sophists deserve small approbation. Their efforts to show that all is true and all is false, and, above all, the brilliancy of their depravity, undermined thought and morals to such an extent that philosophy, which had taken wings, might have flown forever away, had it not been re-beckoned to earth by the familiar reform instituted by Socrates.

Socrates was as ungainly as a satyr, but the suppleness of his tongue was that of a witch. At the hands of this insidious Attic, the sophists fared badly. He brought their versatilities into discredit; and in reviewing and enlarging a forgotten theory of Anaxagoras, purified thought with new lessons in virtue. This reaction seems to have been of advantage to moral philosophy, but detrimental to metaphysics; so much so, in fact, that his hearers turned their backs on theory, and devoted themselves to ethics. "Give me wisdom or a rope," cried Antisthenes, presumably to appreciative ears; and when Diogenes lit his dark lantern in broad daylight, he found every one eager to aid him in the ostentatious bizarrerie of that immortal farce.

In the midst of these pre-occupations there appeared a thinker named Pyrrho, to whom every skeptic is more or less indebted. Pyrrho was born at Elis. His people were poor, and doubtless worthy; but their poverty compelled him to seek a livelihood, which for a time he seems to have found, with his brush. By nature he was sensitive, nervous, as are all artists, and passionately in love with solitude. From some reason or another, but most probably from lack of success, he gave up painting, and wandered from one school to another, until at last a sudden introduction to Democritus turned the whole current of his restless thought. For this introduction he was indebted to Anaxarchus, a philosopher who went about asserting that all is relative, and confessing that he did not even know that he knew nothing. But in this there was possibly some little professional exaggeration. He was a thorough atomist, and very dogmatic on the subject of happiness, which, with broad good sense, he insisted was found only in the peace and tranquillity of the mind.

In Alexander's triumphal suite, Pyrrho went with this scholar to Asia, and together they visited the magi and the reflective gymnosophists. The abstracted impassibility of these visionaries caused him, it is said, an admiration so intense that he made from it a rule of daily conduct; and one day when his master, with whom he was walking, fell into a treacherous bog, Pyrrho continued calmly on his way, leaving Anaxarchus to the mud and his own devices. It may be that in this there was some prescience of the modern aphorism that any one is strong enough to bear the misfortunes of another; but even so, Pyrrho, when it was necessary, could be brave in his own behalf, and one of the few anecdotes that are current represent his unmurmuring endurance of an agonizing operation. This occurred before any one was aware of the imperceptibility of pain; the stoics were yet unborn.

During his long journey, Pyrrho acquired all, or nearly all, that the East had to teach. He listened to Brahman and Buddhist, and took from each what best they had to give. The impassibility of the one appealed to him forcibly, the ethics of the other seemed to him most admirable; and with these for luggage, packed together with an original idea of his own, he returned to his early home, where his fellow-citizens, as a mark of their appreciation, elevated him to the rank of high priest, a dignity which may have caused him some slight, if silent, amusement.

At that time Greece was rent by wars and revolutions. In

the uncertainty of the morrow and the instability of all things, there was a general effort to enjoy life while enjoyment was yet to be had, and to make that enjoyment as thorough as possible. When, therefore, Pyrrho announced his intention to teach the science of happiness, he found his audience ready-made.

The doctrine which he then unfolded was received at first with surprise, but afterwards with sympathetic attention; it gained for him wide praise, and also fervent followers. These followers, to whom the thanks of posterity are due, took to themselves the duty of preserving his teaching; for, like Socrates, Pyrrho wrote nothing.

It has been hinted that Pyrrho accepted the materialism of Democritus, admired the hedonism of Anaxarchus, and practised the impassibility of the Hindus. These elements, which formed what may be termed the angles of his system, were rounded and completed by an original doctrine, which represented doubt as an instrument of wisdom, moderation and personal welfare. Before this time there had been much skepticism, but it had been of a vacillating and unordered kind, the indecision of the uncertain, and no one had thought of making it a stepping-stone to happiness. This Pyrrho did, and in it lies his chief originality.

The skepticism which Pyrrho instituted was an unyielding doubt, and one, paradox as it may seem, which was highly logical. In it Kant found the outlines of his *Criticism* traced in advance, and that too by a master-hand. Pyrrho admitted no difference between health and illness, life and death. He expected nothing, asked for nothing, believed in nothing. If he ever struggled with himself, the struggle was a silent combat, of which his heart was the one dumb witness. He was not simply a skeptic, nor yet merely a cynic; he was a stoic, with a leaven of both. To the eternal question, "What am I?" he answered, "It matters not." He had but one true successor—Montaigne. The everlasting refrain, *Que sçay ie?* is an echo, faint may be, but still an echo, of his own unperturbed indifference. The only refuge in the midst of the uncertainties to which man is ever a prey, lay, Pyrrho held, in an entire suspension of judgment. Between assertion and denial he did not so much as waver; he balanced his opinion in a perfect equipoise. As there is no criterion of truth, his position was impregnable.

"There is," he taught, "nothing that is inherently beautiful or ugly, right or wrong, and hence nothing that can be defined as an absolute truth. Things in themselves," he added, "are diverse, uncertain and undiscernable. Neither sensation nor thought is capable of teaching the difference between what is true and what is false. As a consequence, the verdict of mind and of senses should be equally distrusted; an opinionless impassibility should be observed; nothing should be denied, nothing should be affirmed; or if one of the two seems necessary, let the affirmation and the denial be concurrent."

And happiness? some one may ask. But that is happiness. Where there is indifference and apathy, there too is ataraxia, the perfect and unruffled serenity of the mind. If in act, word and thought, an entire suspension of judgment be maintained—if men, and women too, and events and results and causes, concerning all of which we may have our fancies and our theories, but whose reality escapes us, are treated with complete indifference—then do we possess an independent freedom, an unroutable calm. Once freed from beliefs and prejudices, an exterior influence is without effect; perfect impassibility is obtained; and with it comes the passionless serenity, the ataraxia, which is the goal of the sage.

Such in its broadest outlines was Pyrrho's doctrine. Confute it who may. For the details the reader must turn to back bookshelves where speculative spiders are the only hosts, and there thumb the mildewed pages of Sextus Empiricus, Aristocles and

Diogenes Laertius. It should be noted that Pyrrho's skepticism did not extend to virtue, which he was fond of saying is the one thing whose possession is worth the gift. At an advanced age he died, greatly esteemed by his townsmen, who to do him honor exempted all philosophers from taxation. But elsewhere he was forgotten, and at the time of his death his brilliancy was eclipsed by the rising glories of Epicurus.

When Epicurus addressed the public, he was no longer a young man. His early life had been an unbroken journey. No sooner was he settled in one place, than circumstances compelled him to seek another. These inconveniences did not prevent him from cultivating philosophy, for which from boyhood he evinced a marked predilection. "In the beginning was chaos," his first tutor announced. "And where did chaos come from?" asked Epicurus. But to this the tutor had no answer, and the boy turned to Democritus.

To this master much of his subsequent philosophy is attributable, but his personal success was due to the charm of his manner and the seduction of his words. Syrians and Egyptians flocked to Athens to hear him speak, and few among them went away dissatisfied.

At that time the riot of war had demoralized society. The echoes from a thousand battlefields had banished all sense of security. Greece, moreover, was as tired of speculations as of conflicts; the subtleties of the Lyceum had outwearied the most intrepid. In the midst of the general enervation, Epicurus came, like another Pyrrho, to tell the secret of Polichinelle, to paint pleasure and describe happiness. In the telling he made no mysteries; his hearers approached him without effort. Pleasure, he held, was too simple and unaffected to need logical demonstrations; and to make her acquaintance, commonsense was a better letter than mathematics. But pleasure should not be sought merely for pleasure's sake. It should be regarded as a means to an end. Between pleasure and pleasure there is always a choice. There are pleasures that should be shunned, and there are trials that should be endured. There is the pleasure that is found in the satisfaction of the flesh, and there is the pleasure which is found in the tranquillity of the mind. The one lasts but a moment, and wanes in repetition; the other endures through life, and increases with the years. All this Epicurus thoroughly understood. He had a maxim to the effect that wealth does not consist in the vastness of possessions, but in the limitation of desires. He did not restrict his hearers to scanty enjoyments; on the contrary, he preached their multiplication, but it was a multiplication which was both a lure and a prohibition. He wished men to live so simply that pleasure, when it came, might seem even more exquisite than it is. Of all the high-roads to happiness, he pointed to prudence as the surest and most expeditious. The prudent are temperate in all things, unambitious and of modest requirements, and through this very prudence maintain the health of mind and body which in itself is the true felicity of the wise.

The Epicurean doctrine was one long lesson in mental tranquillity. Anything that ministered to contentment was welcomed, and all things that disturbed it were condemned. Among the latter were the gods.

> "*Ces dieux que l'homme a fait, et qui n'ont pas fait l'homme.*"

The proper way to treat them was a difficult question. Epicurus had no taste for hemlock, and he found his garden very pleasant. He had no wish to flee, like Aristotle, in the night, nor mope, like Anaxagoras, in a dungeon. He was a teacher, not a martyr. His position, therefore, was one of extreme delicacy. On the one hand, he was obliged to consider his personal inconvenience; on the other, the superstitions of the masses. To respect the former and banish the latter, Epicurus took the gods and juggled with them, and in the legerdemain they mounted to such altitudes that from them the vulgar had nothing left to hope or to fear. Their existence was openly admitted, and their intervention as openly denied. In words of devout piety he took from them the reigns of government, and pictured their idleness as an ideal impassibility. After that, Olympus was to let.

The early legends say that the first created thing was fear. After routing the gods, Epicurus undertook to banish dread; *il timor delta paura*, as the Italians have it in their insidious tongue—the fear of fright, or at least that particular form with which hallucinated antiquity was accustomed to terrify itself into repentant spasms. Aided by the materialism of his master, Epicurus looked across the tomb, and announced that there no tormenting phantoms lurked in ambush. The dissolution of the atoms composing the body was also a dissolution of the atoms composing the soul. This affirmation of nothing divested life of a constant anxiety. It took from it one more care. It made the tranquillity of the mind easier, and assured it against an idle pre-occupation.

This doctrine, far from giving free play to the passions, held them well in check. Epicurus could see two sides to a question as well as another. Morality and temperance even to abstinence were praised. His hearers were enjoined to limit their desires, and at all times to be just and to be charitable. The virtues, too, were praised; and this not so much perhaps on account of their inherent beauty, as because they were safeguards against mental disturbance.

In disclosing his ideas, Epicurus necessarily refuted other theories; but his candor, his unalterable placidity and his luminous good faith, disconcerted his adversaries, whose infrequent reprisals he answered, if at all, with an epigram.

In disinteresting his adherents from all things and even from themselves, it was the wish of Epicurus to create, not a school of thought, but a something whose status should approach that of a general disbelief. It was to be a religion whose one dogma was repose. In this purpose he very nearly succeeded. By the terms of his will, his garden, his writings and authority descended from one disciple to another in perpetuity. There was then no statute of mortmain, and the terms of the testament remained in force for seven hundred years—in fact, down to the last gasp of classic antiquity.

The continuity which it enjoyed is perhaps less attributable to its dogmas than to a sentiment of great delicacy which pervaded it. Christianity teaches that all men are brothers, but Epicurism practiced the lesson before it was taught. Its bonds were those of friendship. Cicero has given it to history that the Epicureans had one to another the most unselfish sentiments. There was no community of goods. Friendship gave its own from a sense of pleasure and not from constraint.

During its long reign, Epicurism attracted many converts from other sects, but lost none of its own adherents. This singularity was explained by a wit of the baths, who, adjusting his toga, noted with the light banter of the day that it was easy enough to make a eunuch of a man, but another matter to make a man of a eunuch. It is possible that this *bel esprit* had grasped the doctrine better than his hearers. Certainly it has not always been thoroughly understood. Montesquieu accused it of corrupting Rome; but the accusation is groundless, for at its advent the Eternal City was one vast lupanar.

Seneca said of Epicurus that he was a hero disguised as a woman, and it is in this disguise that he is usually represented. The doctrine which he gave to the world seemed to praise sensuality where in reality it preached repose. Idlers in all times have halted at the appearance and omitted to go further. For this reason, if for none that is better, there has always been a false and a true Epicurism. Unhappily, the bastard has been best received, and in its reception it has managed to discredit both the philosopher and the philosophy.

Over the gateway to his olive-gardens Epicurus had written: "Enter, stranger; here all is fair; Pleasure lords the day." The sign was a bait, and of a flavor far different from the repellent severity of the notice which swung from the Academe. There admittance was refused to those who did not know geometry. But when the stranger, attracted by the proffered allurement, entered the gardens, he found that the lording of pleasure meant health of body and of mind.

There were some who entered, and who, delighted at the teaching, remained. There were others who entered at one gate and passed out discomfited at another; and there was also a third class, who, noting the tenor of the invitation, and knowing that the host was a philosopher, passed on charmed with the idea that the gratification of the senses possessed the sanction of metaphysics. These latter necessarily compromised Epicurus; and when his doctrine passed from Athens to Rome, it had been preceded by a bad reputation. For this the excuse is, seemingly, small. Epicurus was as voluminous a writer as Voltaire; and if the Romans misunderstood him, it is either because their knowledge of Greek was slight, or else because they were content to accept his teaching on hearsay. Toward the close of the republic, the system—such little at least as was generally known—became largely the fashion; and the elegance of Rome, like the indolence of Athens, cloaked its corruption with a mind-woven mantle of imaginary philosophy.

In descending the centuries, its reputation has not improved. Epicurism is not now synonymous, as it once was, with refined debauchery; yet at the dinner-tables of contemporary clubland there are many still unaware that he who is claimed as patron-saint had tastes so simple that his expense for food was less than an obolus a day, while Metrodorus, his nearest friend, expended barely a lepton more. Now and then, on high-days and festivals, a bit of cheese was eaten with sensual relish; but it is a matter of history that the ordinary fare of these voluptuaries was bread dipped in water.

The national divinity of the Romans is unknown. To all but the hierophants his name was a secret. Cicero has admitted that to him it was undisclosed. A tribune was even put to death for having pronounced it. If, in such a matter, conjectures were worth anything, it would not be irrational to fancy that the deity who ranked as Jupiter's superior was Pavor, Fright.

The hardiest and foremost conquerors in the world, the descendants of a she-wolf's nursling, were timid as children before the unintelligibility of the universe. Their earliest gods were revealed in the thunder; their belief was a panic; and when the panic subsided, it was succeeded by a dull, unreasoning dread.

No other land has seen a vaster Pantheon. There were so many divinities that Petronius said it was easier for the traveller to meet a god than a man. The more there were, the less insecure they felt. When they conquered a country, they took the gods as part of the spoils, but they treated them with great reverence; the temples were left standing and the altars unharmed. This moderation was probably due less to a sense of duty than to fear. They were afraid of their own gods; they were afraid of those of other nations; and those of whom they knew the least seem to have frightened them most.

In those days there was no iconoclasm, nor was there any attempt to make proselytes. The whole sentiment of Roman antiquity was opposed to the suppression of a creed, and such an idea as supplanting one religion by another was unknown. This liberality was particularly manifest during the latter part of the republic. At that time a statue to Isis was erected vis-a-vis to Jupiter. Sylla escorted a Syrian goddess to Rome, and Mithra, who had been lured from the East, became very popular among the lower classes. But all this occurred after triumphant campaigns. When Rome was young, her gods, if equally numerous, were less concrete.

The religion of the Sabines and the Latins was the naturalism of their Aryan ancestors. In it the gods, if emblematic, were unimaged; they were manifestations of the divine, but not actual divinities. Each new manifestation was a fresh revelation, to which the early Italiot was quick to give a name and found a worship; but in the worship there was more of dread than of hope, the dread of the unknown and the invisible.

Gradually the gods became less abstract, but as M. Boissier has hinted, they were probably as lack-lustre as the imagination of the laborers that conceived them, and so remained dully and dimly perceived until peddlers from Cumae and Rhegium came over with wares and legends. To their tales the Romans listened with marvelling surprise. Their gods, like themselves, were poor and prosaic; they had no history, no myths; and with a pleasant and liberal sense of duty, they robed them with the shreds and tatters of Ionian verse.

At precisely what epoch this occurred is uncertain; but as the art of writing was familiar to the Romans in very ancient times, and as it has been shown that the Roman alphabet was drawn from Eolo-Dorian characters, it is not unreasonable to infer that relations between the two races were established at a comparatively early date.

The gods to whom the freedom of the city was thus unwarily granted, grew and expanded with it, but their native charm had been lost in crossing the sea. The serene mythology in which they were nursed was supplanted by gloomy superstitions; the gay and gracious fictions were dulled with grave chronicles; and the gods, who at home were cordial and indulgent, developed under the heavy hand of their adopters into an inquisitive and irritable police.

Instead of being loved, they were feared, and the fear they inspired was the heartrending fright of a child pursued.

To the untrained minds of their supplicants they lurked everywhere, even in silence. They were cruel and vindictive; they tormented the Roman out of sheer wantonness, for the mere pleasure of seeing him writhe. Plutarch has confided to posterity that in those days a man could not so much as sneeze without exposing himself to their anger. In such circumstances, worship was not merely a moral obligation, it was a matter of business, a form of insurance against divine risks, in which the worshipper with naïve effrontery tried to bargain with the gods that they should hold him harmless. This effort was solemnized by a religious ceremony whose meaning had been forgotten, and during which the priests mumbled prayers in a jargon which they did not understand.

With a retrospect even of two thousand years, it is a little difficult to fancy that the Romans pinned their faith to these mummeries, yet such seems to have been the case. In Greece there was much incredulity, but it was the laughing incredulity of a boy who has disentangled himself from the illusions of the nursery. That of the Romans took a different form; it was an irritated skepticism which vacillated between defiant negation and fervent belief. Doubtless there were enlightened men who took it all easily and with several grains of Attic salt; but they were infrequent; incredulity seems to have been the exception and in no wise the rule.

When the Roman, angered to exasperation, braved the gods with a sacrilege, at the first sign of impending danger he was quick to implore their protection. Sylla, feeling in the humor, sacked Delphi and insulted Apollo; all of which, Plutarch says, did not prevent him, the first time he was frightened, from praying to the very god whose temple he had pillaged. And Sylla, it may be remembered, was the last one to harbor any unnecessary superstitions. If remorse was felt by such an accomplished ruffian as he, what could be expected of the mass of his compatriots, who, if equally ruffian, were far less accomplished?

In reading back through history, it seems as though the Romans hated their divinities and yet were afraid to show their hatred; and it seems too that had one of them met a god alone, that god would have fared badly. Indeed, it is probable that the majority were animated with a feeling of displeasure like to that of the Norse warrior who ardently wished to meet Odin that he might attack and slay him. Nevertheless, they attended to their religious ceremonies; though they did so, perhaps, very much as most people pay their taxes. Of two evils, they chose the least. But when it was found that Evemerus had announced that the gods were ordinary bullies, who had been deified because every one was afraid of them, it was very generally thought that the right nail had been struck full on the head. In any event the idea was highly relished; and when in a certain play an individual was introduced who denied that there was such a thing as a Providence, the applause of the audience was appreciatively eruptive. It was like the sight of a sail to shipwrecked sailors.

This, however, was all very well in comedy, where any little blasphemy brought with it the thrill and flavor of forbidden fruit; but tragedy was a different matter. There, it is said, when the hero announced his escape from the infernal regions, children screamed and women shuddered. And indeed the contemporary pictures of the land of shades seem well calculated to terrify even the valiant. In the imagination of the people, any life beyond the tomb was nearly synonymous with an eternal nightmare. Of actual and physical torture there was none, or at least none, they believed, for them. The vengeance of Jupiter descended only on Titans and insurgent kings; It disdained the insignificance of the vulgar.

Nor was there any hope of happiness. The beatitude of the

Elysian Fields was only for the anointed. The common mortal received neither reward nor punishment. The just and the unjust were plunged into the grotesque horrors of a fantastic night, from which, save on the stage, there was no escape.

The poets, admittedly, gave pictures of afterlife that were other and more alluring than this, but their pictures were discredited; and besides, between the conceptions of the dreamer and the opinions of the masses there is a chasm that is never bridged. To the general public the idea of immortality does not seem to have been a consolation. Probably it partook something of the character of an embarrassing dilemma. On the one hand was the liberty to accept it for what it was worth; on the other was the privilege to disbelieve in it entirely. There were doubtless not a few who took the latter course, and whose consequent freedom of thought must have been a cause of shuddering envy to the orthodox; but so inextinguishable is the love of life, that the majority seem to have preferred to believe that existence, however miserable, was continued beyond the tomb, to adopting any theory which savored of extinction. They were afraid, Seneca said, to go to Hades, and equally afraid not to go anywhere.

Toward the latter part of the republic, the credulity of the masses was somewhat impaired. Echoes of the *obita dicta* of the enlightened reached their ears. Besides, there was then little time for devotional exercises. Rome was in a ferment; the tramp of soldiery was continuous; cities were up at auction; nations were outlawed; institutions were falling; laws were laughed at; might was right, and magnificent vice triumphant. The field, then, was prepared for nothing if not a moralist, and Nature, who is often beneficent, produced one in the nick of time.

The annals of literature are harmonious with the name of Rome, yet Rome was the mother of but two men of letters—Cæsar and this moralist who was called Lucretius. Concerning the latter, history has been niggardly. It is said that he was born when Cæsar was a child, and died when Vergil was putting on the *toga virilis*; but beyond these dates history is dumb.

Lucretius is known to be the author of a poem, the most exquisite perhaps in the Latin tongue; but after that is recorded there are no anecdotes to help the sentence out. "Veil thy days," Epicurus had said, and the passionate Roman took the maxim for a motto. How he lived or why he lived, has been and now always will be purely conjectural. Yet if there is no diary to tell of the poet's incomings and outgoings, it is not a difficult matter to familiarize oneself with his train of thought and to picture the circumstances that directed it.

During his childhood, Sylla and Marius were playing fast-and-loose with their armies and with Rome. As a boy he could have witnessed a massacre beside which St. Bartholomew's was a street row—the massacre of fifty thousand allies at the gates of Rome—and on the morrow he may have heard the cries of eight thousand prisoners who were being butchered in the circus; while Sylla, with the air of one accounting for a trivial incident, explained to the startled Senate that the uproar came from a handful of insurgents bellowing at the whip. Later came the revolt of Spartacus, the conspiracy of Cataline, the flight of the coward Pompey, and finally the passing and apotheosis of Cæsar. If such things are not enough to give impressions to a poet, then one may well wonder what are.

In a monograph on this subject,[*] to which, it should be said in passing, the present writer is much indebted, M. Martha has noted that Lucretius believed in but one god. That god was Epicurus. "*Deus ille fuit, deus,*" he exclaimed; and if the words sound exuberant, they may perhaps find an excuse in the fact that the Romans were very ignorant and Epicurus very wise. How he became acquainted with the works of the grave Athenian is unrecorded. In Rome, as has been hinted, contemporary acquaintance with them was scant and consisted of hearsay. At

---

[*]   *Le Poème de Lucrèce.*

that time some fragmentary translations of Greek physics had been made, and it is possible that through them his attention was directed to materialism in general and Epicurism in particular. There is even a legend which represents him studying in Athens at the fountain-head. But however this may be, it is clear that Lucretius gave Rome her first real lesson in philosophy.

The doctrine which Lucretius preached to his compatriots was one of renunciation—renunciation of this world and renunciation of any hope of another. He was fanatical in his disbelief, and he expounded it with a vehemence and with an emphasis which, while convincing enough in its way, was yet in striking contrast to the apathy of Epicurus, who, serenely consistent to his principles, saw, as M. Martha says, no need to get excited when admonishing others to be quiet. But their tasks were dissimilar. Epicurus addressed himself to those who were already indifferent, while those who listened to Lucretius were still among the horrors of their original faith.

It was these horrors that Lucretius set about to dissipate. His imagination had caught fire on the dry materialism of Greece, and it was with the theory of atoms that he sought to rout the gods. The undertaking was not a simple matter. The abolition of the divine was an abolition of every tenet, political as well as devotional. The moment the atomistic theory was accepted, away went the idea that the phenomena of nature were dependent on the will of the gods; the whole phantasmagoria of religion faded, and with it the elaborate creed of centuries evaporated into still air. There was nothing left; even death was robbed of its grotesqueness.

To those who objected that in devastating the skies a highroad was opened to crime, Lucretius, pointing to the holocausts, the hecatombs and the sacrifices, answered, "It is religion that is the mother of sin."

"Religio peperit scelerosa atque impia facta."

Other teachers had tried to purify religion, but Lucretius wished nothing short of its entire suppression; it had been without pity for Rome, and he was without pity for it. He hacked and hewed it with all his strength, and with a strength that was heightened by irony and science. The irony was not new to Rome, but the science was. Against the panic of superstition he opposed the tranquillity of common sense; against Pavor, Veritas, or at least that which seemed truth to him.

There is nothing classic about Lucretius except his materialism. The value of that is slight, but contemporary readers have found themselves startled at the modernity of his sentiments. The cry of disgust which came from him is identical with that which the latest singers have uttered. Their common pessimism has been echoed across the centuries. In many ways Lucretius may be considered Pyrrho's heir as well as that of Epicurus. Between the testators the difference is not wide. One addressed the mind, the other the heart; the ultimate object, the attainment of happiness, was the same. If their dual influence has been unimportant, it is perhaps because the goal is fabulous. In this respect Lucretius may then be considered their direct successor, and one, moreover, who had his own views regarding the possible improvement of the possessions which descended to him. Lucretius not only denied the existence of the gods, he denied the existence of happiness. There was none in this life, and in his negation of an hereafter there could be none in another. As for ambition, what is it but a desire for an existence in the minds of other people—a desire which when fulfilled is a mockery, and unfulfilled a tomb? And besides, to what does success lead? To honor, glory and wealth? But these things are simulachres, not happiness. Any effort, any aspiration, any struggle, is vain.

> *"Nequidquam, quoniam medio de fonte leporum' Surgit amari aliquid, quod in ipsis floribus angat."*

Nequidquam! In vain, indeed! How vain, few knew better than Alfred de Musset, when he paraphrased that immortal, if hackneyed, distich in lines like these:

> *"Au fond des vains plaisirs que j'appelle à mon aide,*
> *Je sens un tel dégout que je me sens mourir."*

But Lucretius' nequidquam applied not only to empty pleasures; it applied to all the illusions that circle life, and to all that drape the grave. His disenchantment needed but one thing to be complete, a visit from that thought which was afterwards to haunt De Vigny:

> *"Seul, le silence est grand, tout le reste est faiblesse."*

Whether or not the influence of Lucretius was great enough to effect a revolution, is difficult to determine. But this at least is certain: he was a popular poet, and the appearance of his work coincided with a great decline of superstition. The dread which had been multiplying temples subsided. Among the educated classes, atheism became the fashion. Those who were less indifferent occupied themselves in cooling their indignation, but believers were infrequent. Varro declared that religion was perishing, not from the attacks of its enemies, but from the negligence of the faithless. The testimony of Lucilius is to the effect that no respect was shown to laws, religion, or to gods. To Cicero the latter were absurd; and the immortality of the soul, which Cæsar denied in the open senate, was to him a chimera. "In happiness," he said, "death should be despised; in unhappiness it should be desired. After it there is nothing." Cornelius Nepos looked back and saw temples in ruins, unvisited save by archaic bats. Religion was a thing of the past. Here and there it received that outward semblance of respect which is the due of all that is venerable, but faith had faded and fright had ceased to build. The Romans, some one has suggested, were not unlike those fabled denizens of the under-earth, who suddenly deserted their subterranean palaces, left their toys, their statues and their gods to the darkness, and, emerging into the light, saw for the first time the pervasive blue of the skies and the magnificent simplicity of nature.

Later there was a revival. The restoration of religion was undertaken as a governmental necessity. The Senate proclaimed the divinity of Augustus, and thereafter the Cæsars usurped what little worship was left. That there was much faith in their divinity is doubtful. Valerius Maximus appears to have had no better argument than that they could be seen, which was more than could be said of their predecessors. Vespasian seems to have taken the whole thing as a joke. "I am becoming a god," he said with a smile as he died. Meanwhile, in the general incredulity, the earlier deities lost even the immortality of mummies. Under Diocletian a pantomime was given with great success. It was called, *The Last Will and Testament of Defunct Jupiter.*

CHAPTER THREE.

The Convulsions of the Church.

THE EARLIEST BARBARIAN THAT INVADED ROME WAS A JEW. He did not thunder at the gates; he went unheralded to the Taberna Meritoria—a squalid inn on the Tiber that reeked with garlic—broke his fast, and then sauntered forth, as any modern traveller might do, to view the city. His first visit was to his compatriots at the foot of the Janiculum. To them he whispered something, went away, returned and whispered again. After a while he spoke out loud. Some of his hearers contradicted him; he spoke louder. The peddlers, the rag-pickers, the *valets-de-place* and hook-nosed porters grew tumultuous at his words. The ghetto was raided, and a complaint for inciting disorder was lodged against a certain Christus, of whom nothing was known and who had managed to elude arrest.

Who was this Christus? Apart from the Gospels, canonical and apocryphal, history gives no answer. He is not mentioned by Philo or Justus. Other makers of contemporary chronicles are equally silent. Josephus makes a passing allusion to him, but that passing allusion is very generally regarded as the interpolation of a later hand. It may be added, that while Justus and Josephus say nothing of Jesus, they yet describe Essenism, and in those days many of the tenets of the early Church were indistinguishable from it. It seems, therefore, not unfair to suppose that either these historians knew nothing of the teaching of the Christ, or else that they considered it too unimportant to be deserving of record.

An early legend has, however, been handed down from Celsus, a Jew who lived about the time of Hadrian. The work containing this legend has been lost, and is known only through fragments which Origen has preserved. In substance it amounts to this. A beautiful young woman lived with her mother in a neglected caphar. This young woman, whose name was Mirjam—Mary—supported herself by needlework. She became betrothed to a carpenter, broke her vows in favor of a soldier named Panthera, and wandering away gave birth to a male child called Jeschu—Jeschu being a contraction of the Hebrew Jehoshua, of which Jesus is the Greek form. When Jeschu grew up, he went as servant into Egypt, which was then the head-quarters of the magicians. There he learned the occult sciences, and these gave him such confidence that on his return he proclaimed himself a god.

The story of Mirjam and Panthera is repeated in the Gemaras—the complements and commentaries of the Talmud—and also in the Toledoth Jeschu, an independent collection of traditions relative to the birth of the Christ. These later accounts differ from that of Celsus merely in this, that Mirjam is represented as a hairdresser, while Panthera or Pandira is described as a freebooter and a ruffian. It may be noted that, in a work on this subject, Mr. Baring-Gould states that St. Epiphanius, when giving the genealogy of Jesus, brings the name Panthera into the pedigree.[*]

The importance of these legends is slight, and the question

---

*   *The Lost and Hostile Gospels.*

of their truth or falsity is of small moment. That which it is alone important to consider is the individuality of the Saviour; and the point whose conveyance has been sought is simply this, that beyond a restricted circle nothing was known of it during the first century of the present era.

Jesus, the Anointed, the Christ, was the flower of the Mosaic Law. The date of his birth is uncertain, and the story of his early years is vague. The picture of his boyhood, in which he is represented as questioning the Darschanim, the learned men, is, however, familiar to us all. In the schools—the houses of Midrasch, as they were called—he heard the sacred books of his race expounded, and learned such lessons in ethics as were obtainable from the moralists of the day. Meanwhile the dream of Israel, the forecast of a triumphant future, the advent of a Messiah, the abrupt upheaval which was to be both the beginning of the end and the end of the beginning, the punishment of the wicked, the sanctification of the faithful, the remission of sins and the magnificence that was to be, were constantly discussed before him. As he grew older, he seems to have placed little credence on these prophecies; he waived them aside, retaining only the lessons in ethics, to which, in advancing years, as his own ministry began, he added an idea which he had gathered from one preaching in the wilderness, an idea which his own originality heightened with a newer force and flavor, and which formed the subsequent corner-stone of the Christian Church.

At that time his belief in himself appears to have been slight. To the title of Messiah he made no claim. It was given to him unsought by his earliest adherents, who later imagined a genealogy which certain fractions of Christianity declined to accept. Among these, the Ebionites and Docetae are the most noteworthy. To the one he was an ordinary individual; to the other, a phantasm.

The story of his birth is one which is common to many religions. In a fragment of Irenæus it is stated that the Gospel according to St. Matthew was written to the Jews, who earnestly desired a Messiah of the royal line of David. To satisfy them that their wish was fulfilled was not an easy matter. The Aramaic Gospel to the Hebrews, as well as the gospel according to St. Mark, offered no evidence that Jesus was the one they sought. But the early Church had the boldness of youth. Against the existing Gospels she opposed a new evangel, one which was more complete and convincing than its predecessors, and one, moreover, which bore the revered and authoritative name of Matthew. St. Matthew, however, had then long been dead, and his ability to write in Greek does not appear to have been suspected.

The Gospel which the Church attributed to him is today very generally regarded as a compilation of its predecessors, with the addition of a genealogy. The Messiah, it had been prophesied, would be of the house of David, and accordingly an effort was made to show that Jesus was of the royal race. The royal race seems then to have been extinct; but that is a side issue. The one point to be noted is that the descent of Jesus is claimed through Joseph, who, it is stated, was not his father.

The genealogy completed, the historian turned his attention to two passages in what is known today as the Old Testament. The first of these passages occurs in Isaiah (vii. 14—16), the second in Micah (v. 2). The first relates to a child that the Lord was to give as a sign, and the second designates Bethlehem as his future birthplace. It may be noted that the term in Isaiah which refers to the child's mother, and which was afterwards rendered into παρθένος, is *olme*, and *olme* means young woman. The pseudo-Matthew, however, preferred a narrower description, and represented the mother as a virgin. In regard to the second passage, there is doubtless some mistake, as all impartial commentators are agreed that the nativity of Jesus took place, not at Bethlehem, but at Nazareth.

There are, however, few great events which have been handed down through history unswathed in fables and misconceptions. The Gospel according to St. Matthew—and the remark holds true of the others—was written without any suspicion that it would be subjected to the scrutiny of later ages; it was written to prepare man for the immediate termination of the world. Such misstatements as it contains may therefore be regarded with a lenient eye.

But to return to the point. However slight was the belief of Jesus in himself, it is tolerably clear that the pretensions of his adherents angered the Nazarenes. They declined to admit the royal and supernatural claims that were advanced in favor of one whose kinsmen were of the same clay as themselves. To them he was merely a graceful rabbi. Yet when he addressed the wondering fishers of Galilee, his success was both great and immediate. His electric words thrilled their rude hearts; they were both charmed and coerced by the grave music which he evoked from the Syro-Chaldaic tongue; their belief in him was spontaneous; they regarded him as dwelling in a sphere superior to that of humanity; gladly would they have proclaimed him king; and it was from their unquestioning confidence that Jesus drew a larger trust in himself. Certainly his personal magnetism must have been very great. There is a legend which represents him as being far from well-favored, and this legend, like the others, is doubtless false. It is probable that he possessed that exquisite, if effeminate, type of beauty which is not infrequent in the East. One may fancy that his tiger-tawny hair glistened like a flight of bees, and that his face was whiter than the moon. In his words, his manner and appearance, there must have been a charm which was both unusual and alluring. Indeed, there were few who were privileged to come into direct contact with him that did not love him at once; but the multitude stood aloof. It refused to recognize the son of David in the mystic anarchist who had no where to lay his head.

The ministry of Jesus did not extend over three years. M. Renan thinks it is possible that it did not extend much over one. But the time, however short, was well filled. On its lessons, races and nations have subsisted ever since. The pity of it is that the purport of the instruction should have been misunderstood.

It has been already hinted that the cornerstone of the Christian Church was formed of an idea which Jesus gathered from John the Baptist. When, therefore, he sent forth his disciples, he gave them no other message than that which he had himself received: "Go, preach, saying, The kingdom of heaven is at hand." And he added: "Verily, I say unto you, Ye shall not have gone over the cities of Israel before the Son of Man be come." "All these things shall come upon this generation," were his explicit words to his hearers and disciples. After the episodes in the wilderness, Jesus went into Galilee, saying, "The time is fulfilled, and the kingdom of God is at hand." And a little later he addressed his auditors in these words: "Verily I say unto you that there be some of them that stand by which shall in nowise taste of death till they see the kingdom of God come with power."

Citations of this kind might be multiplied indefinitely. If the testimony of the Gospels is to be believed, it is evident that the disciples were convinced that the fulfilment of the prophecy was a matter of months or at most of a few years. They lived, as M. Renan has noted, in a state of constant expectation. Their watchword was *Maranatha*, The Lord cometh. In fancy they saw themselves enthroned in immutable Edens, dwelling among realized ideals amid the resplendent visions which the prophets had evoked.

It was this error that formed the corner-stone of the Christian Church. When later it was recognized as such, the Church interpreted the "kingdom of God" as the establishment of the Christian religion.

But Jesus had no intention of founding a new religion, and

still less of substituting a personal doctrine for the Mosaic Law. He came to prepare men, not for life, but for death. The virtues which he praised most highly were those of renunciation and abnegation of self. His one thought was centered in the approaching end of the world. It was on this belief that the value of his teaching rested; viewed in any other light, his continual condemnation of labor would be inexplicable; while his prohibition against wealth, his adjuration to forsake all things for his sake, the blow which he struck at the virility of man, his praise of celibacy, his disregard of family ties, his abasement of marriage, and his contempt even of the dead, would be without meaning

The faith which he inculcated was a necessary preparation for the event then assumed to be near at hand. It was exacted as a means of grace. In it the reason, the understanding, had no part. It was the complete submission of the intelligence, a resolution to accept dogmas without question. In the moral certainty which his believers possessed of the immediate realization of their hopes, it is not surprising that this faith should have been readily accorded. The enigma lies in the faith of the subsequent centuries. It may be, however, that the doctrine which has descended to us was merely the exoteric teaching. Of at least fifty Gospels that were written, four only have been recognized by the Church. Of these, the originals do not exist, and their supposed texts have been so frequently re-touched, that more than thirty thousand variations are said to have been discovered. It may be, then, that there was another doctrine, an esoteric teaching, which was never fully disclosed, or else has been lost in the dust-bins of literature. This possibility is strengthened by the fact that Valentine is recorded as asserting that he had received an esoteric doctrine which Jesus imparted only to the most spiritual among his disciples; and the possibility is further heightened by the incongruity between the sublimity of the genius which was the Christ's and the tenancy of a belief in the realization of the visions of Daniel.

Jesus was in no sense a scientist, but his insight was piercing and his intuitions clairvoyant. He was the most transcendent of rebels, but he was possessed of a comprehension too unerring to be deluded by the utopias of dreams. It maybe, then, that in the solitudes of the desert he conceived some such system as that which was taught by his predecessor in Nepal. To him, as to the Buddha, life was a tribulation. And what fairer paradise could there be than the infinite rest of chaos? Let the sullen rumble of accursed life once be quelled, and God's kingdom would indeed be come with power. What save this could have been that peace which passeth all understanding?

It may be remembered that according to the Hebrew sages man survived only in his children. The doctrine of resurrection, and the attendant theory of rewards and punishments, was unknown to them. But at the time of the advent of the Christ, these ideas were part of the teaching of the Pharisaic party. Where they were gathered is uncertain. They may have been acquired through acquaintance with the Parsis—and certainly Satan bears an astonishing resemblance to Ahriman—or they may have merely represented the natural development of Messianic hopes. In any event they seem to have pre-occupied Jesus greatly; and when questioned about them, he gave answers which, while delicate in their irony, are seldom other than vague.

It is probable that at the time when the questions were addressed to him, his system, which owing to his sudden death was perhaps never fully elaborated, was then merely in germ. But that he reflected deeply over the views of the patriarchs there can be no doubt, and it is equally indubitable that he considered the high-road to salvation to be discoverable, if anywhere, through them. The logic of it amounted to this: Life is evil; the evil subsists through procreation; ergo, abolish procreation and the evil disappears.

Many texts from the canonical Gospels might be given in support of this statement, but to cultivated readers they are doubtless too familiar to need repetition here. For the moment, therefore, it will suffice to quote two passages from the lost Gospel according to the Egyptians, a chronicle which was known to exist in the second half of the second century, and was then regarded as authoritative by certain Christian sects. The passages are to be found in the Stromata of Clement of Alexandria, iii. 6-9. In one, the Saviour speaks as follows: "I am come to destroy the work of the woman: of the woman, that is of concupiscence, whose works are generation and death." In the other passage, Salome, having asked how long men should live, the Lord answered, "So long as you women continue to bear children."

These passages, if authentic, and there is little reason to think them otherwise, seem tolerably conclusive. In any event, it was this idea that peopled with hermits the deserts of Nitria and Scete, and it was this same idea which in its weakened force filled those bastilles of God, the convents and monasteries of pre-mediaeval days. Cerdo, Marcion, and others of lesser note, advocated a doctrine of which it was evidently the starting-point; in many religious communities its influence is still distinguishable; but the question as to whether or not the idea as here represented was really the one on which the thoughts of the Saviour were turned, seems best answerable in the affirmative, if for no other reason than that it is less extravagant and more logical to regard the Christ as a practical philosopher than as an alluring visionary. And if he was not the one, he must have been the other. Certainly no one can claim for him any higher originality than that which was manifested in the form and flavor of his parables. He was the most entrancing of nihilists, but he was not an innovator. Others before him had instituted a reaction against the formalism of the Judaic creed. The austerity of his ethics, the communism which he preached, his contempt of wealth, and his superb disdain of everything which was of this world, were integral parts of the doctrine of the Essenes. The conception of a Supreme Being, differing in benignity from the implacable terrorism which Jehovah exerted, had been already begun by the prophets. Jesus unquestionably amplified the Father of Israel into the God of Humanity, but he did not invent him. It may be further noted that Jesus had no thought of representing himself as an incarnation or descendant of the Deity. To such a title he made no claim, nor except in certain passages inserted in the fourth Gospel, is he ever represented as using it. If Son of God at all, he was so in the sense that might apply to all men, and of which the address beginning, "Our Father who art in heaven," is a fitting example.

Yet this at least may be said. He created pure sentiment, the love of the ideal. He gave the world a fairer theory of æsthetics, a new conception of beauty, and he brought to man a dream of consolation which has outlasted centuries and taken the sting from death. So singular and powerful was the affection which he inspired, that after the crucifixion, Mary of Magdala, in the hallucinations of her love asserted that he had arisen. He arose, indeed, but as elsewhere suggested, it was in the adoring hearts of his disciples. And had it been otherwise, had their natures been less vibrant, their sympathies less exalted, less susceptible to psychological influences, the world would have lost its suavest legend, and the name of the pale Nazarene would have faded with those of the Essenes of the day.

M. Renan says that Rome, through relations with Syria, was probably the first occidental city that learned of the new belief. There were then, he has noted, many Jews there. Some were descendants of former prisoners of war, others were fugitives; but all were poor, miserable and down-trodden. To this abject colony Christianity brought an unexpected hope. The ideal, it is true, had fled from earth; but was it not possible to find it again above?

Many there were that accepted the new creed unquestioningly, but some of their more conservative brethren, disturbed at its dissidence with their orthodox tenets, denounced their compatriots to the government. It is possible that a certain amount of suppression was then exercised, but it appears to have been accidental and momentary. The Romans were familiar with too many deities to be alarmed at the advent of a new one. Their polytheistic tendencies made it quite easy for them to believe in a god, made man, and the suppressions which ensued were ordered in the interest of the public peace. The Christians were evidently regarded as seditious; in denying the divinity of the Cæsars they were guilty of nothing less than high-treason. They were punished accordingly, but their punishment had no religious signification. The Epicureans might easily have been subjected to analogous treatment, but the Epicureans were philosophers, and as such saw no reason for pulling a wry face at harmless mummeries.

Then, too, the early Christians seem to have made themselves extremely unpopular. The Pantheon was most hospitable; its niches were free to every comer. But the believers in the Nazarene would have none of it. They not only refused any allegiance to Olympian potentates, but they would not permit their own God to consort with them. It was tantamount to saying that Jupiter's society was pernicious. There were few indeed that pinned much faith to that opulent divinity; but the open show of respect which was demanded as a governmental necessity was generally accorded, and nothing else was asked. The Christians, moreover, gave offence by their mode of life. They appear to have been a quiet, silent and possibly inoffensive sect, who avoided the forum and the circus, and passed their hours in sullen seclusion. Added to this, they predicted the approaching end of the world, which was obstinate enough to continue to revolve through spacious voids of which they were utterly ignorant; and this prophecy on their part could not have been regarded otherwise than as an open slur on the imperial optimism of the day.

It was doubtless about this time that the edict, *Non licet esse Christianos*, was passed—an edict which with curious clairvoyance appears to have been directed mainly against those Romans who were tempted to embrace the new belief. It is one of the platitudes of history that Rome fell through her rottenness. Yet, as M. Renan has been at no loss to show, Rome fell when her soldiery became converted. The spirit of peace which pervaded the early Church enervated a nation; the virility of the most belligerent of races was sapped. But this is a digression. During its infancy, Christianity was smitten by a disease which has been likened to croup. This croup was endemic in Alexandria, and from there floated over to Rome. It was called Gnosticism.

Gnosticism was a compound of corrupt Platonism, Hinduism and charlatanism. To abandon M. Renan's simile and take another, it was the bridge over which the world passed from paganism. Gnosticism gathered up theosophy, mysticism, rites, ceremonials and art—everything, in fact, which seemed worth the gathering—and passed them all to Christianity, which, thus equipped, set out on its triumphant career. But not at once. The populace, as has been hinted, was not favorably disposed. Tertullian says that a Christian was denned as an enemy of gods, emperors, laws, customs, and Nature itself. To the believers in Jesus was ascribed the influence of that which the modern Roman calls the jettatura. They were held to-be connected with every calamity; and after each disaster the Eternal City echoed with shrieks from uncounted throats, *Christianos ad leonem!* To the circus with the Christians; let them camp with the beasts! It was then that Christianity learned to hate.

Meanwhile, the Ghetto mounted like a flood. Its ascension was favored by many things. The atmosphere of Rome dripped with metaphysics, and through it had passed a new and pervading sense of lassitude. Nero was dead; and Nero, it may be noted, was paradox incarnate. He was an imperial nightmare that was far from unpopular; a drama of the horrible, with a joke for finale; a caricature of the impossible in a crimson frame; a Ceasar whose follies were laws and whose laws were follies; a maniac whose cell was the world and whose delirium was fame; a sceptred acrobat, with a throne for spring-board; an emperor jealous of a tenor; and a cabotin jealous of the gods; in fact, the antithesis of the humdrum. Under him, Rome saw luxury and ferocity hand-in-hand; cruelty married to pleasure. Christians mantled in flame illuminated the gardens of a prince. Intoxication had no frontiers. Life itself was a breathless chase after impossible delights. But now all was quite different, and it was with something of that lassitude which succeeds an orgy that the Romans found themselves tired even of themselves. They could not all have the moon for mistress. What was there left for them to do? Christianity offered itself, and as often as not Christianity was accepted.

After Constantine had used the new belief as a masquerade, its spread was rapid. Julian, indeed, threatened to prevent such of the Galileans from wearing their heads as refused to aid him in the reconstruction of polytheism, but the halt under him was momentary. The impulsion continued unchecked; the intermediate persecutions had made it notorious; the advance continued, but in the advance the watchword, *Martin atha*, had lost its meaning. The end of the world was no longer expected. Fortune favoring, Christianity turned optimist. Yet paganism was not dead; it had merely fallen asleep. Isis gave way to Mary; apotheosis was replaced by canonization; the divinities were succeeded by saints; and, Africa aiding, the Church surged from mythology with the Trinity for tiara.

At the close of the fourth century, the Church was practically mistress of civilization. Her sway was immense and uncontested. And what a sway it was! Temples, statues and manuscripts were destroyed. Bands of monks went about pillaging and demolishing whatever they could. The Bishop Theophilus, after destroying the temple of Serapis, set fire to the Alexandrian library which contained nearly all the literary treasures of the past. But the power of the Church, though magnificent, was brief. At the moment when her glory was most brilliant, when Julian was forgotten and persecution had ceased, a mixed multitude of barbarians beat at the gates of Rome, and in their victorious onslaught swept antiquity away.

When the Church found herself surrounded by unfamiliar kings and chieftains—a set of fair, proud, honest and brutal ignoramuses, who wandered from place to place, or shut themselves up and got drunk in their strongholds, and with whom she had nothing in common—her dominant idea was to govern them. In this she succeeded: strength, however great, is defenceless against cunning, and the Church then was the depository of all the intelligence of the age. But her first act was to save herself from the violence to which society fell a prey. To save herself, she announced the principle of a separation of spiritual and temporal power. This accepted, she announced as corollary the superiority of the spiritual over the temporal. The rest was easy. Free inquiry was condemned; belief was forced; heretics were persecuted; and out of the ashes of imperial Rome a mitred prelate dragged a throne. *L'Eglise, c'etait lui.* Through his influence the barbarians were led to baptism like brutes to the slaughter. Those who objected were baptized by force. Dagobert had all Gaul baptized in this way. Thereafter the Church presided over an eclipse of the intellect that lasted a thousand years. During that thousand years it was blasphemy to think; yet over those ages that are known as dark there hovered that prescience of fairer things which is the accompaniment of night.

Meanwhile, in a corner of the Orient whither some of the flotsam and jetsam of civilization had drifted, a college of charlatans wearied the centuries with abstractions and discussions on words. Their earlier disputes are legendary. One of them concerned the soul. Was the soul round or oblong? This question was never satisfactorily determined. Another proposition which was much discussed concerned the Saviour. Was he, or was he not, co-eternal with God? The Council at Nicæa, to which appeal was made, decided that he was both; and the Church anathematized all those who disagreed with its decision. In spite of the anathema, certain erudites suggested a compromise which involved the acceptance or rejection of an iota: ὁμοούσις signified consubstantial, ὁμοιούσιος signified like as to the substance. If the one term were replaced by the other, the difficulty, it was argued, would be removed. But this solution was too easy to be well received, and the absence of that iota caused the death of several thousand dissenters.

Later, Nestorius, Bishop of Constantinople, asserted that Mary, being of the earth, could not rightly be considered the mother of a God. This assertion was condemned as heretical by the General Council of Ephesus, and it was ordered that those who accepted it should be exterminated at once. Eutyches the archimandrite announced the contrary of that which Nestorius had advanced. He, too, was excommunicated; the true doctrine being that Jesus was both a perfect divinity and a perfect man. Then suddenly the Orient became peopled with heretics; some held to Nestorius, others to Eutyches. In the second quarter of the sixth century, Justinian, an emperor who is said to have been so illiterate that he could not write his own name, and who in consequence was easily bored by subtleties, confiscated the property of all who were suspected either of Nestorian or Eutychian sympathies. In spite of these efforts, heresy was not suppressed; or perhaps it would be more exact to say that when one was suppressed, its place was immediately filled by another. At last, Heraclitus in utter exasperation issued an edict forbidding any one to speak of the single or double nature of Jesus the Christ. This edict itself was regarded as heretical, and continued to be so regarded until Constant published another which forbade any theological discussion, no matter of what kind, nature or description. To this edict, which the Pope Theodore qualified as an abominable subtlety, no one paid any attention. Constant, however, refused to be idle. He tried to check the spread of monachism, which at that time was enormous, and failing, went to Rome and sacked it.

In the eighth century appeared the heresy known as that of the iconoclasts. The Church, as has been hinted, adopted much of the pomp of paganism, and with advancing years made herself gorgeous with crosses, images and tapers; but a particular predilection was manifested in favor of big dolls, whether of marble, bronze or precious metals. To this the iconoclasts objected; with the Emperor Leo for chief, they destroyed the statues of Jesus, of Mary, of the saints and angels, wherever such statues were to be found; and for many years persecuted and massacred the worshipers. Yet when the Empress Irene assumed the purple, the iconoclasts were at once pursued with a vigor that was riotous and avenging. It is just possible that this terrible lady perceived that the destruction of images was the destruction of art. But be this as it may, the Beautiful had been sadly frightened, and thereafter remained invisible until lured to view again by the enticements of the Renaissance.

In Europe, matters were even worse. There was a continual panic, a ceaseless fear. There was no security, either civil or ecclesiastical. Diseases of the mind and body were omnipresent; famine at times was so ruthless that anthropophagy was openly practiced. The only theory of right was might, and of this the Church held the reins. Many of the bishops were little better than bandits. They passed their days in wandering from place to place and in pillaging right and left. In a forgotten tale of Cervantes, one amiable scoundrel hails another, "Does your Grace happen to be a highwayman?" "Yes," the other answers, "in the service of God and honest people." Eliminate the courtesy and replace it with a blow from a bludgeon, and the question and answer may be represented as repeated indefinitely for five centuries.

Those of the clergy whose tastes were less adventurous devoted themselves to study and were looked upon as magicians; others, in the dim recesses of undrained monasteries, weary of all things, and most of life, gave themselves up unresistingly to acedia, the delirious pessimism of the cloister, and shrieked for death.

It was in those days that a demon of uncommon ugliness flitted through the gloom of the abbeys, whispering gaily to the cowering monks, "Thou art damned, and thou, and thou art damned for all eternity!" In the cathedrals, maidens had seen a beckoning fiend, who through shudders of song had called them down to swell the red quadrilles of hell. These visitors of course were legates of Satan. And who was Satan? His biography, though well filled, need not be long.

Satan was Jew from horn to hoof. The registry of his birth is contained in the evolution of Hebraic thought. In early ages, when sabaism, the primitive polytheism of the Semitic tribes, narrowed into monotheism, Jehovah was worshiped as the one real divinity. In his hands were the springs of all that is, of good and evil as well. But this idea was transient. About the Eternal were grouped a number of spirits whose duty it was to supervise the works of man. Among these celestials was one whose rôle was limited to that of accuser. This rôle appears to have been gradually expanded into one of general hostility. Above was Jehovah, below was man; while between the two were the inimical eyes of Satan. In the younger books of the Old Testament, Satan is little more than a detective; in the New Testament he is an inciter to evil. But during the intervening period two things seem to have happened. The Hebrews had communicated with the Parsis, and Satan, banished from heaven, had assumed all the powers and attributes of Ahriman. Thereafter he was hatred incarnate, the spirit that *stets verneint*, the fallen son of a mighty father, a disinherited prince who had founded a rival monarchy and called it Hell.

It is in this guise that he appears in the New Testament, and the delicate moral of the Synoptic Gospels is perhaps little more than the prefigurement of the endless conflict between right and wrong. But be this as it may, it is evident that after Satan and the Saviour had met, the apparitions of the former became a matter of frequent occurrence. Did not his minions the sucubes and incubes haunt with lascivious lips the sleep of holy men and holier women? Was it not through his artifices that St. Victor was seduced by a beautiful girl? Did he not personally menace and threaten St. Maur? The stone which he flung at the inflexible St. Dominick is a matter too well attested to be susceptible of doubt. See how he tempted St. Anthony. In fact, unvisited by him it was difficult to be considered a saint at all. In the middle ages he was everywhere. The atmosphere was so heavy with his legions, that the Messalians made spitting a part of their devotions. From encountering him at every turn, the world at last became used to his ways, and thereupon imagined that pact in which the devil agrees, in exchange for the soul, to furnish whatever is desired. The case of Gerbert is one in point. According to the gossip of the day,* Gerbert, once a Spanish student,

---

*   Michelet: *Historie de France.*

afterwards Archbishop of Ravenna, and subsequently Pope, entered into an agreement of this kind, and one night the devil came in person to claim him. It was the agreement they had made together long before in Cordova, where Gerbert, finding his studies too arduous, had signed the bond in exchange for the royal road. It was the devil who had taught him all he knew— algebra, clock-making, and how to become a Pope. It was clear as day that he would have known none of these things without infernal assistance. Gerbert resists, but Mephisto proves his claim. "You did not think me a logician, did you?" are said to have been his historic words, and, presto! Gerbert disappears in a fork of lambent flame.

When Christianity first raised its head, it viewed the pagan gods as part of the cohorts of Satan. These cohorts Tertullian divided into two classes—the rebels who had been banished from heaven in Satan's train, and the angels who in antediluvian days had fallen in love with the daughters of men. Their queen was Lili Abi (Lilith), Adam's first wife, from whose name our lullaby is said to be derived. The Dusii, a later subdivision who have given us the deuce, were so well known to St. Augustine that he declared it an impertinence to deny their existence. These latter appear to have been a malignant set of incubi who made a prey of women. Mr. Lecky says that but little over a hundred years ago an annual mass was given in the abbey of Poissey that the nuns might be preserved from their wiles.

Satan, meanwhile, lost much of his dignity. Mice, wolves and toads became his symbols, his auxiliaries, and even his momentary incarnations. Throughout the middle ages no sorcerer was considered well equipped without a sleek black cat, an animal to which, like many a sensible mortal, the devil appears to have been greatly attached. It was in the company of the cat that the sabbat was attended. The sabbat was popularly held to be a mass offered to Satan, and any one suspected of attending it, or being in any wise affiliated with Mephisto, was burned. The first punishment for this offence occurred in Toulouse in 1275. During the next fifty years over four hundred people were burned in the neighborhood. In the fifteenth century all Christianity joined in a hunt for witches; and the hunt continued for three hundred years, until every sorcerer had disappeared and Salem put out her bonfires. In each country the warmth of the chase was in direct proportion to the power of the clergy. To spare a witch was considered an insult to the Almighty. Luther was particularly vehement on this point; so, too, was Calvin; and Wesley was as great a fanatic as any. Montaigne was one of the first to laugh at witchcraft; but Montaigne, like all advanced thinkers, was wickedly incredulous. The hunt, as has been hinted, was continued, and it was kept up not only until all the witches had disappeared, but until all belief in the devil had gone with them. Persecution subsided when skepticism began. The history of the Inquisition is exactly analogous. When the world began to think, intolerance ceased.

During this time Satan was not otherwise idle. He continued to appear in the most unexpected and surprising manner, and that, too, up to within comparatively recent dates. His last historical appearance is in a pleasant anecdote in which he is represented as visiting Cuvier. He enters the great man's study with his usual *quærens quern devoret* air. "What do you wish of me?" Cuvier asks curtly, for he is annoyed at the intrusion. "I've come to eat you." But Cuvier's shrewd eye had already examined him. "Horns and hoofs!" he retorts; "granivorous! You can't do it." Whereupon, outfaced by science, Satan vanished through an in-quarto, never to appear again save when, in the garb and aspect of a policeman, he visits the conscience of the misdemeanant.

But to return to the middle ages. The chronicles of Cassien, Vincent de Beauvais and Raoul Glaber, are filled with lurid pictures of those dark days. Disasters followed one another with the regularity of the seasons. The desolation which the Church had sought to stay had increased to terrific proportions. The empire of Karl the Great had been swept away as utterly as that of the Cæsars. Throughout Europe there was a hideous fear, a breathless expectation. The Antichrist had come. His presence was signalled from the pulpit. Churches, monasteries, donjons and burgs, echoed and thrilled with the rumor of his sacrileges. Now he was the son of the Popess Johanna, conceived during a pontifical procession; now he was a ruffian marauder, burning basilicas and violating the tombs of the saints. In the ninth century there was an eclipse of the sun which frightened a king to death. In 945, while a cyclone swept over Paris, monsters armed with battle-axes dropped from the skies, and, rushing into a church, tore down the pulpit, which they used as a battering-ram to destroy a neighboring house. In 988, a wolf entered the cathedral of Orleans, and, seizing the bell-rope in his mouth, rang out the knell of the world. It was evident to everyone that the trumpets of the last judgment were soon to be heard. At once there was a frantic effort to make peace with God; there was a rush for the monasteries, and a general donation of property to the Church. The *dies iræ* was at hand. The exact date was known. It was to come on the 25th of March, A.D. 1000. An hysterical rictus passed over the face of Christendom; the forgotten hope was to be realized! At last the *dies illa* arrived. In the Holy See the Pope sat, enervated and impatient, counting the minutes and awaiting the climax through the succeeding fractions of each hour. In the churches, the crowd, with heads bowed to the ground, felt time limp by and yet saw no sign. The expectation lasted four days and four nights. Then, so runs the chronicle, an immense dragon rushed through the open skies. In an abbey the eyes of a Christ were seen to weep. Yet still the earth remained unsundered and humanity unclaimed.

When the panic subsided, the Church found that her wealth had been largely increased. Her power, too, had developed. The cowl was everywhere, and everywhere it was dreaded. This dread was not unmingled with disgust; the fanaticism, asceticism and illiteracy of the clergy resulted as often as not in delirium and satyrisis. Indeed, their customs were neither amiable nor cleanly. The different bulls which the Popes launched at them make it easy to see of what they were capable, and difficult to fancy of what they were not. But their manners and morals are relatively unimportant; the terrorism that the Church exerted is more to the point.

The chief instruments of coercion of which the Church disposed were excommunication and the confessional. Without confession, no absolution; and without absolution, eternal torture.

There is a quaint little anecdote about the Curé of Mendon, in which that immortal jester is represented face to face with Clement VII. His Holiness having graciously permitted him to ask a favor, Rabelais begged to be excommunicated. Exclamation-points and question-marks shot from the Pontiffs eyes. "Holy Father," said the apostate, "I am a Frenchman. I come from a little town called Chinon, where the stake is often seen. A good many fine people have been burned there: some of my relatives, among others. But if your Holiness would excommunicate me, I fancy that I would never be burned. And my reason is this. Journeying lately with the Bishop from Paris to Rome, we passed through the Tarantaises, where the cold is bitter. Having reached a hut where dwelled an old woman, we besought her to make a fire. She took a faggot and tried to light it, but did not succeed; then she took some straw from her bed, and, being still unable to make it burn, she began cursing, and said, 'Since the faggot won't burn, it must have been excommunicated by the Pope's own jaw.'" This of course occurred after the Reformation, and relates to a man who was a notorious skeptic. It is even probable that the story is a fabrication; but as an anecdote it is serviceable in pointing the moral of the decadence of great things. In the primitive days of the Church, excommunication amounted merely to expulsion. Those against whom it was addressed were shut out of a limited circle; but when that circle expanded until it circumscribed all society, the potency of excommunication was prodigious. If the anathema was launched at a king, his entire monarchy fell under the ban. When Philippe Auguste was excommunicated, neither baptism, marriage nor burial was permitted in the realm. Corpses rotted in the highways. The people became wild with terror. This state of affairs lasted for eighteen months—in fact, until the interdict was removed. But with time, as has been hinted, its potency waned; like other good things, it was overdone; and early in the fifteenth century all those who had the heart to laugh must have been hugely amused at the spectacle of three rival popes excommunicating each other.

During the dark ages, however, amusement was rare. The masses were a prey to all the delusions and depressions that come of poor nourishment. They were ignorant and credulous; their minds were filled with fables and legends; they were terrorized by the dead as well as the living; agonized in this life, they were threatened with everlasting torture in another. It is, therefore, but small wonder that they shuddered at the viaticum and trembled before the priest. It was through his ministrations alone that salvation was obtainable.

At first the priest was merely an intercessor. In return for his good offices, he asked of the penitent little else than fasting, prayer and contrition; but gradually he discovered that these canonical penances were without advantage to himself, and he began to exact payment for the divine forgiveness which it was his privilege to declare. In the course of time, this custom was found so profitable that plenary indulgences were granted. In

1300, pilgrims from far and near flocked to Rome and covered the altars with gold. Every sin, every penalty, was remitted. The claims of purgatory were obliterated. The joy was so great, that the pilgrimage was called a jubilee.

The jubilee was instituted by Boniface VIII, the author of the bull *Ausculta fili*, in which he declared that, as representative of God, he had the right and the power to uproot, tear down, destroy, dissipate, rebuild and raise up in His name. In spite of this fine language, the Avignon Consistory established that he had asserted that the Trinity was an absurdity; that it was fatuous to believe in it; that religion was a lie; that there was no harm in adultery; and that he, the pope, who could humble kings, was mightier than Christ.

The success of the first jubilee was so great that Urban VI held another; only instead of summoning the pilgrims to Rome, he allowed his absolution to be hawked about wherever sinners most did congregate. It had been said that the riches of man are his redemption, and the clergy were very ready to put the saying into practice. Indulgences were not only sold, they appear to have been forced on those who refused them. A dominican, Johan Tetzel, took charge of the sale in Germany of those granted by Leo X. He announced that he had power to deliver a full discharge from the penalties of sin, even *si quis Virginem vitiasset ac gravidam fecisset*. His tariff is still exhibited.

Meanwhile, the General Councils had moved from Constantinople to Rome. The heresies which they were called upon to consider were mainly protestations against the despotism of the Church. First came the heresies of the Petrobusians and the Arnoldists—unimportant, but vexatious; so vexatious, in fact, that their respective founders, Petrus de Brueys and Arnold de Bresse, were burned at the stake. The Petrobusians were followed by the Vaudois, who, although pursued, proscribed and anathematized, maintained a secret continuity until Calvinism offered them a harbor. Another heresy was that of the Albigenses. The Albigenses, who came from a village in Languedoc, at a time Michelet has noted, when Languedoc was a Babel, professed a mixture of Gnosticism and Manicheism. They considered the Saviour to have been a man, like any other, who had suffered the just punishment of his sins. But, what was more serious, they questioned the prerogatives of the Holy See. Innocent III determined to exterminate them. At his commands the King of France and the Duke of Burgundy set out for Languedoc. The query was, how the heretics were to be distinquished from the orthodox. "Kill them all," said Armand, the pope's legate; "kill them all; God will know his own." Sixty thousand are reported to have been killed; and of these, seven thousand were slaughtered in a cathedral that was ringing with a Te Deum. The whole of Provence was devastated; vines were uprooted, harvests destroyed, and houses torn down. As this seemed insufficient, the bishops received orders to visit personally or by delegate any portion of their diocese in which they suspected that heretics might lurk. When this decretal was made, the Inquisition was established. "*Et ardet*," said the pseudo St. John; and those two words were sufficient to send over half-a-million of human beings to the stake.* Yet still heresies continued to appear. There was the heresy of the Dulcinists, the heresy of John Wicliffe, of John Huss, of Jerome of Prague. *J'en passe et des plus exquises.*

From the Crusades, in which nations wrangled over a sepulchre, sprang a new heresy, or rather an apostasy—that of the Templars, whose office it had been to protect pilgrims on their way to the East. It was claimed that, instead of attending to their duties, they had become believers in Muhammad; and, moreover, that they held Salahaddin to be a valiant and courteous knight, which he probably was. Muhammad, who had long been turned to dust, was a well-intentioned visionary, afflicted with what is known to pathology as hysteria muscularis—the

---

*   Michelet: *Histoire de France.* Llorente; *Histoire de l'Inquisition.*

only disease that ever founded a religion. Now if the Templars were apostates, they at least were logical. The Papacy had pitted Christianity against Muhammadanism, and staked the authenticity of each on the result. The result was that the latter proved its claim. This point, however, does not seem to have been advanced in their favor. They were tried, convicted, and many of them were burned.

Meanwhile, the popes and princes of the Church had lost faith, and decency as well. Petrarch, in his letters *Sine titulo*, speaks of the papal court as follows:

"There is here (in Avignon) everything imaginable in the way of confusion, darkness and horror. Avignon is the sewer of every vice, the gully of every wickedness. I know from personal experience that in this place there is neither piety nor charity. Faith is absent; there is nothing holy, nothing just, nothing human. Friendship, modesty and decency are unknown. Houses, squares, temples, courts and pontifical palaces drip with lies. The hope of a future life is considered an illusion; Jesus Christ is looked upon as a useless invention; virtue is regarded as a proof of stupidity, and prostitution leads to fame."

Such is Petrarch's account; but Petrarch was possibly annoyed because his sister had been seduced by the pope.

The Abbé Guyot, author of the *Dictionary of Heresies*, says, though alluding this time to Rome: "The luxury of the bishops, their scandalous mode of life, their ignorance, which is on a par with their vices, have furnished heretics with excellent grounds for violent rhetoric."

Of Sixtus IV, Infessura says, in words that are best left untranslated, "*puerorum amator et sodomita fuit.*" And it would appear, not only that he was guilty of these charming practices, but that he granted indulgences for their general commission. Innocent VIII, his successor, by way of setting a good example to future pontiffs, made public acknowledgment of four sons and three daughters. He established an agency where the remission of sins could be bought as readily as a railway ticket today. Of Alexander VI, the father and lover of Lucretia Borgia, little that is favorable can be said, except perhaps that he was the most magnificent ruffian that Rome had seen since the days when Nero, with a concave emerald for monocle, watched the rape of Christian girls.

If the popes were a bad lot, the clergy do not seem to have been much better. Gerson says that the cloisters were markets, the convents like lupanars, and that the churches and cathedrals were lairs of bandits and thieves. But the mediæval priest was not only a voluptuary and a freebooter, he appears to have been a jocular blasphemer as well. It is a part of history that when Luther reached Rome he heard more than one of them consecrate the Eucharist with a jeer: "*Panis es et panis manebis, vinum es et vinum manebis.*" There cannot have been two hells; and, granting that there was one, the Roman Catholic and Apostolic Church seems to have been built on it.

In the year 1500 the world was very old. The Renaissance had lied. It had promised and not fulfilled. A few years before, Savonarola had sought to reform Christianity, and particularly the pope. He was burned. In words that rise and greet and kiss the eye, Dante had rejuvenated hell. Petrarch had poured the newest of wine into a cup that was gothic. Across the centuries an unterrified spirit of beauty had called to Boccaccio, and he had repeated the message to inattentive ears. There seemed to be no one that cared to blow away the dust of ages. Every germ that promised fruit was neutralized. Yet Italy was peopled with atheists. The jurisdiction of the Orient was lost; England was no longer a vassal. A tottering pontiff anathematized in vain, and, seeing the uselessness of his maledictions, filled Europe with the uproar of his debauches. The world was very old, but in the printing-press it had found the waters of youth. The earth was larger, and soon the skies were to be unveiled.

It was in those days that a German monk threw an ink-bottle at the devil and defied the pope. A little later, Bohemia seceded. Germany followed in the wake, and with her went Switzerland and the Northern States. Luther's heresy became orthodoxy. And yet the newest thing about it was so old that it had been forgotten. Everywhere it was welcomed. The question of its youth or age had nothing to do with it. It was in opposition to the existing order of things, and as such it was a success. Catholicism was a twilight, Lutherism a dawn. Christ said, Prepare; the Church said, Sleep; the Reformation called upon the world to awake. Luther's aim was to lead belief back to the starting-point, but for the time being his aim was overlooked. The heresy which bore his name was considered merely a quarrel between monks. "Bravo!" Hutton said; "let them eat each other up!"

Luther, who was a courageous blunderer and sincere in all his endeavors, did something more than try to change the current of affairs. He created German as Dante had created Italian. It was he who caught and tamed the ringing tongue of the Niebelungen. From the resisting heroes of the Rhine he lured a secret, and first of his race, gave to a nation a language for birthright.

Barbarism, meanwhile, had not absorbed itself. Pyrrho still slept. The reform which Luther instituted aggravated the evils which it proposed to correct. The Protestantism which followed was as intolerant as the mother Church; more so perhaps, for it had the intolerance of youth, and as it broke and scattered into countless creeds, each of the brood, save the Quakers, arrogated to itself the right to persecute and destroy. To Luther, persecution seemed not only lawful but necessary. Calvin, who was as intolerant as the Inquisition and every whit as fanatical, made it a prop of his church. And Knox, to whom one mass was more frightful than ten thousands insurgents, declared that an idolater merited nothing less than death.

But persecution, however endorsed, was not of a nature to resist the influence of advancing thought. As skepticism arose, Intolerance declined; and as belief in future punishment passed away, so did the torture of the recalcitrant. It may be noted that the lamented Ranke estimates the number of human beings destroyed by Christianity as surpassing ten million. And yet there are people who think that Justice merely limps. During ten centuries it sat motionless in a *cul de-jatte*.

Among the first to break a lance in the Lutheran tragedy was Erasmus. No one that has read *The Cloister and the Hearth* will need to be reminded that the story of Gerard and Marguerite is the history of his parentage. As a knight-errant of free thought he went about combating intolerance. In the last pages of the ever-famous *Praise of Folly*, he showed, with exquisite felicity of diction, the folly of creeds and sects. We are wiser now; but the world then was learning the alphabet. Erasmus received his full share of abuse, and, what is more to the point, saw his enemies exhaust twenty-seven editions of his work. Unpopularity has its advantages.

In spite of his intrepidity, Erasmus was as a small boy in comparison to that *abstracteur de quinte essence*, Master Alcofrybas Nasier. Where Dante, Petrarch and Boccaccio had looked into the past, the author of the exceedingly horrifying life of the Great Gargantua pointed to unexplored horizons. The *Praise of Folly* was cold as a rapier; the biography which Rabelais gave to the public was as exuberant, as prodigal and as turbulent as the sea. It was a new praise of Nature. Its appearance marked the beginning of another Renaissance; in all its pantagruelism there was not a single tear. Its philosophy was a commingling of science and satire; it was unexampled in boldness, but it was not dogmatic. Rabelais, who had been educated in a monastery, where the vows were those of ignorance and not of religion, was too wise to be an atheist. He objected mightily to tyranny, but he did not meddle with the unknowable. If he was anything, he was an agnostic. "I am going in search of the great Perhaps," he said on his death-bed. His obscenity is compromising, but it is not blasphemous. The nakedness of his thought extended only to the material.

Another thinker who refused to take a step beyond the actual was Montaigne. Where Rabelais hesitated, Montaigne doubted. He had caught the Isostheneia of Pyrrho, and balanced his thought in a perfect equilibrium. He neither affirmed nor denied. If he fancied that the universe was a foundling, his good taste prevented him from openly questioning the parentage. In this respect his silence is admirable and well worthy of imitation. Christianity he looked upon as a decadence. He noted with mild regret that the high-roads of civilization were moss-grown and abandoned, and that the compass which the Greeks had used was buried under the dust of centuries. But he waived conclusions; his thought was too volatile to convey a decision. Stella said that had Swift so desired, he could have written beautifully about a broomstick. Montaigne wrote about nothing at all with a charm that has never been excelled.

When Montaigne put a question-mark, Charron shrugged his shoulders; the *Que sçay ie?* the What do I know? became, What does it matter? And yet, like many another that affected indifference, Charron was ardent and prone to indignation. In his chief work, *De la Sagesse*, a work undeservedly forgotten, he said many smart things to the orthodox, and he said them, too, in a language which, if antiquated today, was then very virile. He was among the first to note that ideas of right and wrong vary with the latitude. "That which is impious, unjust and abominable in one place, is piety, justice and honor in another. There is not a law, a custom or a belief, that is everywhere received or rejected." Religion, too, he held to be a question of latitude. "Our

religion is that of the country in which we are born and educated; we are circumcised and baptized, we are Jews, Muhammad-
ans or Christians, before we know that we are men." To which
he added: "A strange thing it is that the Christian religion,
which, being the only belief true and revealed of God, ought to
be extremely one and united, because there is but one God and
one truth, is, on the contrary, torn into many parts and divided
into many conflicting sects, to such an extent even, that there is
not an article of faith or point of doctrine which has not been
diversely argued and agitated, and given rise to heresies and dis-
sensions. But what makes it seem still more strange is, that in
the false and bastard religions, whether Gentile, Pagan, Jewish
or Muhammadan, the like divisions do not appear." And much
more to the same effect; concluding that truth is intangible, religions are equally *estranges et horribles au sens commun*, and that
the sovereign remedy for the ills of life is *de se prester à aultruy et
de ne se donner qu'à soy.*

While Charron in this manner was foreshortening Pyrrho,
Sanchez, a Spaniard, was laying the foundations of agnosticism
in a work entitled, *Tractus de multum nobile et prima universali
Scientia, quod non scitur*—"Treatise on the very noble and extremely universal Science, to wit, that we know nothing." This
contribution to literature appears to have created quite a little
commotion; but, strange as it may seem, the commotion subsided, and today, outside the covers of a dictionary of philosophy,
Sanchez, like Charron, is hard to find.

In the course of these international attacks, Rome had heard
Bruno announce that the universe was a living organism whose
soul was God. He was sent to the stake. Vanini had refused to
discuss the immortality of the soul before he was old, rich and a
German. He was burned at Toulouse. Campanella wrote a book
against heresies, and was tortured at Naples seven times for his
pains.

But the fangs of Romanism were being drawn. The Pope Urban VIII had written on his brother's tomb, *Hie jacet pulvis et cinis, postea nihil*, and announced that the world governed itself. Decidedly the influence of the Church was on the wane, and yet the time was still far away when thought was to be disenthralled.

Were it not for a handful of thinkers, the seventeenth century might be cataloged among the dark ages. The intellectual fecundity which was the characteristic of the sixteenth gave way to an era which was largely one of mental stagnation. The world seemed tired of disputes, and inclined, too, to accept old beliefs unquestioned. The hand of scholasticism was still upon it. It viewed speculation with uneasy dread, and kept its anxious eyes fixed upon the past.

And yet there were a few whose instincts invited to other vistas. In Holland was Spinoza; in England, Bacon and Hobbes; in Germany, Kepler and Leibnitz; while in France was Gassendi, Bayle, but first Descartes. "Give me force and matter," he cried, "and I will refurbish the world." Force and matter were not forthcoming, but in that magnificent boast was the accouchement of modern thought. One may even say that its layette was already prepared. A few years before, Europe had listened to Galileo recanting his heresy; but when, before the assembled prelates, the prisoner muttered, *E pur si muove*, a page of history was turned down, and across it was written, Farewell to Rome.

CHAPTER FOUR.

The Dissent of the Seers.

In one of the forgotten plays of Laberius, a jester is represented as recommending a smug-faced companion to get a foretaste of philosophy in the latrinas. In one sense the jester was wise in his generation and clairvoyant too. About philosophy in general, and metaphysics in particular, the impolite have always discerned a bad odor. And this not without reason. In literature there is nothing more unpleasant than an attempt to prove something; indeed, if ever a proper penal code is devised, the dietary products of logic will be declared contraband, and every ergo banished the realm. In the absence of any criterion of truth, such a word as Therefore has seemingly no *raison d'être*. The sum of all the angles of a triangle may be equal to two right-angles, but however amply that fact or any other be demonstrated, it cannot lift the inquisitive beyond the limits of an experience which in itself may be erroneous. Who shall say but that in some other sphere, where perhaps there are now such commodities as square fluids and moral substances,—who shall say but that there the sum of all the angles of a triangle may not be equal to two right angles; or, as Mill has suggested, who shall say but that there is a land where two and two make five? Yet, waiving such magnificent hypotheses, and granting that deductions which follow from experience are not erroneous, it must be admitted that they bring us no nearer the truth; the essence, the reason of things is as intangible as before.

And metaphysics has yet another defect. The eternal questions, What am I? What can I know?—questions which it purports to answer—are left for all response as vague as the enveloping scholia. But the good that comes of evil is ever re-nascent, and out of the questions and answers have sprung the three foremost systems of modern anti-theistic thought. Of these, Pantheism takes the precedence, which is the due of age. Its nominal founder is Spinoza.

The life of Baruch Spinoza should be taught to every schoolboy. It is not only as uninteresting as the ordinary studies of average youth, but it holds a lesson of such gentleness, modesty and abnegation of self, that in a search for a better one the whole parade of history might be reviewed in vain.

Like certain other notabilities, Spinoza was a Jew. His parents were descendants of Portuguese Israelites, who had fled from the Inquisition and unfolded their tents behind the dykes of the Netherlands. Today, in Amsterdam, any valet-de-place will designate the early home of the philosopher, and every valet-de-place will point to a different house. But when the sightseer is tired into satisfaction, discrepancies are of small moment. Moreover, after exhausting his imagination on the Burgwal, any valet-de-place is competent to show the exact spot near the synagogue where a fanatic believer aimed a dagger at the thinker's heart. The aim was unsuccessful, though it rent the coat; and this coat the guide, if he is clever, will tell you that Spinoza kept ever after among his memorabilia. But, clever or not, give him a louis and let him go. Spinoza's life is not such an one as should be listened to in the streets.

In the library at Wolfenbeütel there is a portrait of a grave, olive-skinned Hebrew, who stands in the upright idleness which is peculiar to portraits in oil. The hair falls back and over the shoulders in an expanding flood. The face is nearly oval, and the eyes are large and patient. This portrait, which is of Spinoza, was probably painted toward the close of his life. He died, it may be noted, at the age of forty-four, in the year 1677. As has been hinted, his life is without interest. If there was a tragedy in it, it was, as Oscar Wilde would say, that there was none at all. There is some mention of a little romance with the daughter of his teacher. But Spinoza was poor, and it is said that a wealthier student made diamonds of indifferent water fall in miniature cascades before the maiden's unresisting eyes. It is possible that this legend, out of which Auerbach has weaved one of his charming tales, is not untrue. There is a quotation to the effect that Mammon can win his way where angels might despair; and if an angel, then, *à fortiori*, a philosopher. In any event, Spinoza appears to have been jilted, which probably was the best thing that could have happened. A thinker should have everything, even to sex, in his brain.

Spinoza was educated to be a rabbi, but with increasing years he grew too big for Jewish theology and declined to visit the synagogue. It was then that some zealot tried to stab him. This argument being insufficient, the elders offered him an annual pension of a thousand florins, on condition that now and then he would appear in the synagogue and keep his opinions to himself. Spinoza was very poor, but his opinions were to him more precious than money. He refused therefore, and was excommunicated at once. The great ban, the Schammatha, was publicly pronounced upon him. For half-an-hour, to the blare of trumpets, he was cursed in the name which contains forty-two letters; in the name of Him who said, *I am that I am and who shall be;* in the name of the Lord of Hosts, the Tetragrammaton; in the name of the Globes, the Wheels, Mysterious Beasts and Ministering Angels; in the name of the great Prince Michael; in the name of Metateron, whose name is like that of his master; in the name of Achthariel Jah. The Seraphim and Ofanim were called upon to give mouth to the malediction. Jehovah was supplicated never to forgive his sin, to let all the curses in the Book of the Law fall upon and blot him from under the heavens. Then, as the music swooned in a shudder of brass, the candles were reversed, and through the darkness the whole congregation chanted in unison, Amen!

After that, Spinoza, being no longer a Jew, changed his name from Baruch to Benedictus, and turned his thoughts from the Kabbala to Descartes. The life he thereafter led was one of extreme simplicity. He earned his bread by polishing lenses, and expended on it but a trifle more than the traditional obolus of Epicurus. When his father died, his sisters, arguing that a heretic had no right nor title to the property of the faithful, tried to keep from him his inheritance. Spinoza, however, appealed against them, won his suit, and then gave back as free gift all the contested property except one bed, which his biographer Colerus admits, *était en verité fort bon.* A few other instances of his magnanimity might be given, and a few anecdotes of his gentleness related; but when they were told, the reader would find himself as unacquainted with the man as before. Properly speaking, he had no biography; his life was one of solitude; its essence was meditation; and the Wolfenbeütel portrait would have served its purpose better, had it represented the sombre face of one whose eyes were lost in thought, and whose patient hand polished a concave lens.

Spinoza's fame rests principally on two works which shortly after his death were proscribed as profane, atheistic and blasphemous. These works are the *Tractatus Theologico-politicus* and the *Ethica*. The first in the key-note of rationalism, the second is the basis of modern philosophy. The rationalism of the first and the philosophy of the second stand in the closest connection. In both, Nature is shown to be an omnipotent ruler, in whose court such a parvenu as the supernatural is not received.

Spinoza's negations are three-fold. He denied the existence of an extra-mundane Deity; he denied that man is a free agent; and he denied the doctrine of final causes.

His negation of the existence of an extra-mundane Deity is not always clearly understood. The term *Deus* is strewn through his pages, and its repetition has often misled the unwary. There is, he taught, but one substance, and in this substance all things live, move and have their being. It is at once cause and effect; it is God. But the term thus used has nothing in common with the theistic idea of a Creator, who, having fashioned the world, "sits aloft and sees it go." On the contrary, God and the universe were to Spinoza one and identical; they were correlatives; the existence of the one made that of the other a logical necessity. To him the primordial entity, the *fons et origo rerum*, was God; but God was Nature, and Nature, Substance. The three terms he used interchangeably; the former predominate in his earlier writings, the third in the Ethics. His reason for making use of the first is not entirely apparent, unless it be, as Dr. Martineau has suggested, that even when the sun of Israel had set, he still loved to linger in the mystical penumbra of an earlier faith. But be this as it may, and however his use of the term maybe interpreted, it is tolerably clear that Spinoza, far from lowering the Deity to Nature, exalted Nature to a God. God was everywhere, and every region was filled with the Divine.

Spinoza has been frequently blamed for reading the banns over the unknowable and the known, and perhaps the blame is not altogether undeserved. But in this connection it may not be amiss to call Goethe to his rescue. And Goethe, it may be remembered, is the Spinoza of verse. "To discuss God apart from Nature," said the poet, "is both difficult and dangerous. It is as though we separated the soul from the body. We know the soul only through the medium of the body, and God only through Nature. Hence the absurdity of accusing of absurdity those who philosophically unite the world with God." Voltaire, however, took a different view, the view of an inconsequential historian who relies on his wit. Now wit is little else than the commonplace in fine clothes; and Voltaire, who treated the humdrum with the skill of a modiste, drew the threads of fancy, and worked an elaborate hemstitch:

> "*Alors un petit Juif, au long nez, au teint blême,*
> *Pauvre, mais satisfait, pensif et retiré,*
> *Esprit subtil et creux, moins lu que célébré,*
> *Cache sous le manteau de Descartes son maître,*
> *Marchant à pas comptés, s'approcha du grand Etre: 'Par-*
> *donnez moi,' dit-il, 'en lui parlant tout bas,*
> *Mais je crois entre nous, que vous n'existez pas.'*"

That which is called Free-will had to Spinoza a purely verbal existence. To him, the state of mind at any given moment is the effect of some definite cause, which itself is the effect of a preceding cause, and so on without end. His argument is to the point: "Imagine that a stone which has been set in motion becomes conscious, and, so far as it is able, endeavors to persist in its motion. This stone, since it is conscious of and interested in its endeavor, will believe that it is free, and that it continues in motion for no other reason than that it so wills. Now such is the freedom of man, which every one boasts of possessing, and which consists but in this, that men are aware of their own desires, and ignorant of the causes by which those desires are determined."[*]

---

[*]   Lettre 62. Traduction de Emile Saisset.

This apt negation of free-will in man, Spinoza extended to broader spheres; and in showing that Nature has no alternatives, no standards of comparison of better or worse, and no appreciation of antitheses, of right or of wrong—in fact, that everything occurs in virtue and in accordance with eternal laws which could not be otherwise—arrived at the consoling deduction that he who understands that everything which happens, happens necessarily, will find nothing worthy of hatred, mockery or contempt, but rather will endeavor, so far as human power permits, to do well, and, as the phrase goes, to be of good cheer.

There is something in the foregoing theory that seems to savor of Calvinistic predestination. But it is only a savor. To the Calvinist, predestination is made endurable by the belief that everything is ordained by the highest wisdom; while to the Pantheist, man is never the subject of fate. The laws of necessity are identical with his own nature, and it is through an understanding of them that he finds himself at peace with all the world.

Spinoza held the doctrine of Final Causes to be untenable, because inconsistent with the perfection that resides in God. His argument, which is advanced in the *Ethica*, has the charm which attaches to brevity: "If God acts for a designed end, it must be that He desireth something which He hath not."

Spinoza was neither an optimist nor a pessimist. He neither laughed at life nor grieved over it. It is possible that he understood it. Like many another before him, he had looked about for happiness; and in the search he saw that such simulachres as wealth, distinction and pleasure, even to that *grande dame* whose name is Glory, were smitten with one and the same defect. The desire for them sprang from an archaic source, the love of the transitory. But happiness to be real, he argued, should be imperishable. And where could such happiness be found?—where, indeed, save in the love of the eternal and the unending, in the love of truth, which in purifying and exalting the heart shields it from vain desires? If Spinoza had not been a geometrician, he would have been a poet.

In the *Tractatus Theologico-politicus*, Spinoza noted, with great good sense, that a plain man who does not enter upon philosophy may without harm and even with profit believe whatever he finds most edifying, provided he believes it sincerely. And it is related that his hostess, a simple-minded Lutheran, having asked him whether the religion she professed was capable of assuring her salvation, he advised her to seek no other, nor to doubt of its efficiency. "Do but good works," he said, " and endeavor so far as it is possible to lead a peaceful and virtuous life."

As Heine has well said, wherever a great mind gives utterance to its thoughts, there too is Golgotha. Spinoza was persecuted during his lifetime, and after death his works were condemned as profane, blasphemous and atheistic. And yet it is probable that few men more sincerely religious than he have ever lived and taught. His doctrine was one of abnegation of self and patient devotion to the eternal. He was in love with the Infinite; it was Nature that fluttered his pulse; it was the Spirit of the universe that filled his heart with living springs. Nevertheless there are today many warm-hearted and accomplished gentlemen whose views on Spinoza are a trifle more than two hundred years behind the age. To them he is still the blasphemer. But in all sincerity one may ask which is the more blasphemous, nay, which is the more vulgar, the mind that pictures the Deity as a jealous tyrant who keeps the world as a separate establishment, or the thinker who seeks to banish the dream that veils the part from the whole, and who shows the soul of man and of the universe to be the same?

In attempting to convey the higher view, Spinoza admittedly transcended the limits of experience. Indeed, there are contemporary free-thinkers who are ready to assert that he was sunk in the grossest superstitions. Perhaps he was; yet his superstitions were so refined, that in them there was room for nothing but the ideal.

A few years after Spinoza's death, on the 22nd day of November, 1694, François Arouet and Marie-Marguerite Daumart, his wife, caused to be baptized at the church of St. André des Arcs in Paris, a male child, who, born dying six months before, lived long enough to christen himself Voltaire.

The heart of the eighteenth century was like a *veilliebchen*. As Michelet, who dissected it, announced, it was double. One half was Diderot, the other Voltaire; but Rousseau was wedged between. Voltaire wished superstition abolished and the throne preserved; Rousseau wanted the monarchy abolished and the altar upheld. Diderot sought the overthrow of both.

The united works of Diderot and Voltaire form a library of ninety volumes. But much of their labor is uncatalogued. Their ninety-first achievement is the French Revolution, their ninety-second is Modern Thought. If they are little read today, it is because their ideas have become common property, their daring seems less bold. Concerning Diderot, a word will be said later on; but no conjunction of phrases is rich enough to paint Voltaire. His figure is as familiar as the moon, yet the currents of his thought are almost as intangible. Nature, who, as Malebranche has said, speaks neither Latin nor Greek nor Hebrew, had taught him the nothingness of creeds. He had but one dogma, Reason. When he preached God and liberty, the liberty was freedom of thought, and God the deification of common-sense. In his vague deism there was room for many things. "Believe in God," he said to a questioning rhymster; "believe in God; there is nothing more poetic." But to Madame du Deffand, in whom he confided, he admitted his acquaintanceship with a man who thoroughly believed that when a bee died it ceased to hum. That man was none other than himself. In those days there were not a few who believed as he did. Among them was that most anti-christian of monarchs, the fat Frederick, who played badly on the flute, wrote verses that limp after him through history, but who possessed an enchanted sword, a nimble wit, and a great fund of appreciation for those whose views coincided with his own.

From this monarch there came to Voltaire an invitation requesting the pleasures of his society, and this invitation Voltaire accepted. Voltaire was never young. When he reached Berlin his hair was white, and he looked, Madame de Staël has said, like a wicked old monk come back from another world to visit this; but such a fascinating pagan was he, that in winning him from the fifteenth Louis of France, Frederick valued the gain more highly than a province.

At the historic suppers of the king, Voltaire likened the symposiasts to the seven sages of Greece in a lupanar. "In no corner of the globe," he said, " has liberty of speech been greater, or have superstitions been treated with keener contempt." Beside Voltaire and Frederick, the usual guests were the Marquis d'Argens, Lamettrie, Maupertuis, Algarotti and d'Armand. The last-named gentlemen are relatively unimportant, but the others should not pass unnoticed.

D'Argens was not only the king's guest, he was his nearest friend, a sort of dignified Triboulet. He was a Provencal, an ex-free lance, handsome and dissipated, who after a riotous career, during which he had explored most of the side scenes of life, made love in five languages, and fought over the better part of Europe, retired suddenly to Holland and burned the midnight oil. It was the old story of the devil turned hermit. In Holland in those days, thought was almost untrammelled. When a foreign author was afraid of the printers in his own country, he set those of the Netherlands at work, very much as the ultra-naturalists of contemporary France obtain today the assistance of Belgian publishers. D'Argens therefore went to the Hague, hired an apartment, shut himself up for six months, and then walked out with the *Lettres Juives* in his pockets.

The *Lettres Juives*, which are nothing if not liberal, were read and appreciated by the Crown Prince of Prussia, who at once asked d'Argens to pay him a visit. But d'Argens sent a regret. The throne was occupied by Frederick Wilhelm, and that monarch was not an agreeable person. If he took a walk, everybody took to their heels. Voltaire has given it to history that whenever he met a woman in the street, he sent her about her business: "Get thee hence, thou trull, thou trollope; thy place is at home!"—a remonstrance which was accompanied as often as not by a blow or a kick; and Voltaire adds that whenever a minister of the gospel took it into his head to view a parade, he was, if caught, treated in precisely the same manner.

D'Argens knew him by reputation, and declined his son's invitation with thanks. "To reach Potsdam," he wrote to the prince, "I should have to pass three battalions; and as I am tall, well-built, and not altogether bad-looking, I don't dare." But when the prince became king, there was nothing to fear, and Potsdam counted another guest.

It was not long before d'Argens became the chamberlain, and, as has been hinted, the friend of the king. He was a brilliant conversationalist, epigrammatic, paradoxical, and possessed of great opulence of imagination. And Frederick, who at that time, was possibly the only German in Berlin who knew how to talk, knew, too, how to appreciate that ability in another. The intimacy increased with years. When the king, overcome by public and private misfortunes, doubtful of the morrow and uncertain even of the day, reflected on the advantages which a bare bodkin can procure, d'Argens hurried to the rescue with comforting maxims. The king listened, but would have his say: "Philosophy, my dear Marquis, is an excellent remedy against the ills of the past or of the future, but it is powerless against those of the present." "And what about the impassibility that

Zeno taught?" "Zeno," answered the king, "was the philosopher of the gods, and I am a man." Nevertheless he took heart again, and all thoughts of the bodkin were dismissed. But d'Argens was not always so comforting. On the eve of the battle of Rosbach, Frederick happening to remark that if he lost it he would go and practice medicine in Venice, Triboulet steadied himself against a table and hissed. "Toujours assassin."

D'Argens and Frederick grew old together. They had disputes which made them faster friends. They played practical jokes on one another, and quarrelled noisily over trifles. The king often acted like a school-boy, and d'Argens not infrequently forgot that he was a philosopher. He remembered, however, that he was not born in Berlin. About Sans-Souci there circled at times an icy wind that made him dream of Provence. One day he asked for his passport. Frederick was vexed; he did not like to be deserted; it diminished him in his own esteem. "Bah!" he exclaimed, "what is a prince born for, unless it be to cause ingratitude?" But he gave the exeat, and d'Argens returned to his early home. Soon after he died—a convert, so it was said. When Frederick heard the rumor, he laughed; he knew d'Argens too well to believe any such gossip as that. "If he received the Last Sacrament," he said, "it is because it was given to him by main strength."

"D'Argens," said Voltaire, "has the wit of Bayle and the charm of Montaigne." The doctrine which he displayed in the Philosophie *du bon sens* is a half-hearted Pyrrhonisn. He, too, saw that there was no criterion of truth, but he could not always keep his eyes on the fact. "How," he asked, "can men pretend to know the essence of things when they are ignorant of their own?" That they cannot may be readily admitted, unless it be that they are willing to supersede judgment with faith, which proceeding is the one that d'Argens recommended. He was deeply purposeful, but he was circumspect. What he shook with one hand, he steadied with the other. When he showed the advantages of belief, he was not in a greater hurry to do anything else than to show its disadvantages. First he honeycombed it with doubt and toppled it over completely. Then he set to work and built it up anew. After which he gave it another shake, and so on indefinitely, until his ink blushed and his pen refused its office. The method employed by M. Renan is not dissimilar.

There are few lands in Europe that have been more fecund in myths than Brittany. The belief in that lost city of Is, whose spires the fishers sometimes saw, whose bells, rung by the waves, clang through the winter nights, and whose magnificence was such that for the capital of France no better name could be found than Par-Is, equal to Is—the belief in that lost city was the origin of many beautiful legends. In few other lands has the faith in the weird and the supernatural been preserved with greater simplicity. Yet through one of those paradoxes of which Nature alone holds the secret, Brittany has been as fertile of doubt as of credulity. Many of the foremost of French anti-theists claim it as their home. Between Maupertuis and Renan there is a parade of familiar names, and of these names few are more significant than that of Lamettrie.

Lamettrie appears to have been an unprincipled saint, a rake without vices. He was brilliant and whimsical, an excellent purveyor of the entremets of the imagination; and as it is the individual and not the topic that makes or unmakes conversation, the great Frederick held him in high favor. Some years before Voltaire appeared in Berlin, Lamettrie had written a book, *l' Histoire naturelle de l'âme*, which had created such a stir that he had been obliged to leave France and seek refuge in Holland. There he published another book, *l'Homme machine*, which created even a greater stir; and while he was wondering where he should hide, Frederick, who had read his writings, and who never let slip an opportunity of adding another philosopher to his collection, invited him to Berlin. "He is a victim of theologians and fools," said the monarch; "let him come here and write what he pleases. I am always sorry for a philosopher in difficulties; were I not born a prince, I would be one myself."

Lamettrie was quite willing to accord to a king the pleasures of his company, and took a seat at the royal supper-table without delay. Frederick was so charmed with him that he made him his salaried reader. "I am delighted with my acquisition," he said; "Lamettrie is as light-hearted and clever as any one can be. He is a sound physician and hates doctors; he is a materialist and not material. He says scandalous things now and then, but we weaken his Epicurean wine with the water of Pythagoras."

Like some other gentlemen of a skeptical turn, Lamettrie announced that vice and virtue were purely relative—a platitude which has been running about the book-shelves ever since books were shelved. But he added something which is worth larger attention: "Away with remorse!" he exclaimed; "it is a weakness, an outcome of education." And if virtue and vice are merely questions of surroundings, it is indeed difficult to view remorse otherwise than as a pre-mediaeval emotion. But virtue, to say nothing of vice, is something more. According to the Buddha, virtue is the agreement of the will and the conscience, a definition which would be matchless if the will were free. Marcus Aurelius called it a living and enthusiastic sympathy with Nature; but if the boundless immorality of Nature be conceded, as it should, the fine words of the emperor are as empty as the wind. Virtue, said one who had eyed it narrowly, virtue is a name. Perhaps. Yet virtue declines to be dismissed with a phrase; there is a disturbing magnificence about it which routs the most skillful. In describing it, Raphael is a better lexicographer than Shakespeare, though even Raphael, for all his cunning, could not paint a temperament. And virtue is little else than a question of disposition. It may be sunned and watered by a thousand influences, it may be hedged and fortified, but in its essence it is temperamental. However great the outward success may appear, the lessons and precepts of ages will not suffice to keep it unspotted if the inner spirit be adverse. And as with virtue, so too with vice. Standards may differ with the climate, but in each case, it is the conscience that elects itself judge. It is the heart, memory aiding, that gives us a paradise or a hell. If we could hush the conscience and still the heart, we might afford to listen to Lamettrie; and perhaps in future ages, when through the progress of evolution man will lose the lobes of his ears as he has already lost his tail, when he will be as completely bald as he was once entirely hirsute, perhaps then the conscience will go the way of useless possessions; but meanwhile to declaim against it is as profitable as asking alms of statues. We are perfectly free to enjoy our remorse undisturbed.

Lamettrie admitted no other life than this, and not unnaturally sought to make the most of the worst. His ideas are contained in a treatise on Happiness, which he prefixed to a translation of Seneca's thoughts on the same subject. "Our organs," he said, "are susceptible of sensations which render life agreeable. When the impression which a sensation conveys is brief, it is pleasure that we experience; prolonged, it is bliss; permanent, it is happiness. But in every case it is the same sensation, differing merely in intensity and duration. The absence of fear and desire is happiness in its primitive state; but to possess all that one wishes—to have beauty, wit, talent, esteem, wealth, health and glory—that is a happiness which is real and perfect."

The spectacle of a eudamonist is as charming as that of a ballerina. Both belong to the category of the Delightful. But even though one be pleasured by a Taglioni, there comes a moment when the pleasure palls. Lamettrie, who was fond of adventurous nights and incursions—not perhaps to the unknowable, but to that which he might have known and did not—was wont to please his readers with the *entrechats* of a lawless imagination. As a consequence, his views, if entertaining, are valueless. The real and perfect happiness of which he speaks is a will-o'-the-wisp of fancy. The possession of all that one wishes, whether the possession is concomitant, as in fairy tales, with the wish, or obtained after years of striving, does not and never will constitute happiness. In its essence, happiness is intangible; the desire for it is insatiable; and consequently, and despite every possession, it is ever unsatisfied. There may be a happiness which is transitory and fugitive, but there is none that is permanent. To say to the contrary is to announce one of the most insolent absurdities that has ever been proclaimed in the privileged aisles of the insane. For the sake of example, let it be supposed that in some one person are united all the factors which Lamettrie mentions—beauty, wit, talent, esteem, wealth, health and glory; if these possessions are what may be termed congenital, as in the case of a poet-prince, they are taken by their possessor as a matter of course, and have never served as preservatives from discontent; on the other hand, if their re-union is accomplished after more or less prolonged endeavors, their possessor, in obtaining them, finds himself as poor as before; he might be able to call the world his own, and yet not know what happiness is. The honors, the riches and glory to which he aspired, are as empty as the hands of the dead. If they are magnificent, it is only from afar. The best that can be, the best that ever has been, is in the discovery and maintenance of contentment. Its factors are two-fold—the first is health; the second, indifference.

Lamettrie's chief titles to recognition rest on the *Histoire naturelle de l'âme* and the *Homme machine.* The first-mentioned work is an argument against the belief in the immortality of the soul. With this doctrine ancient philosophy had little to do. With the exception of Pythagoras and Plato, the thinkers of classic antiquity agreed in one particular—the soul was material. Even to Tertullian its immateriality was unestablished. "*Animam nihil est*," he said, "*sed corpus non sit*;" and not a few of the fathers of the Church held the same opinion. The masses of course thought differently. The belief in a future life was by them unquestioned. It probably arose from the re-appearance of the dead in the dreams of the living. But in Greece, as in the Roman Empire, the life prefigured was one in which there was little charm. The neglect of funeral rites turned it into a dull and restless torture. In this particular the observances of believers were little else than precautionary safeguards, and the *Requiescat in pace* which is to be seen on contemporary tomb-stones is but a forlorn survival of their naïve superstitions. Later, when it was taught that the soul was imperishable, not through an inherent indestructibility, but through the influence of grace divine, its materiality was still undoubted. The soul and the body were considered inseparable. There were casuists who thought otherwise, and their disputes are legendary; but their disputes occurred in an era when faith was well-nigh universal. When the distinction between the soul and the body was at last satisfactorily established—that is, to those who were interested in the establishment of a satisfactory distinction—the believer found himself turning back to Plato. The soul was represented as a resultant of the forces of the body, very much as harmony is known to be won from the strings of the lyre. Yet, as Simmias queried, when the strings are broken and the wood reduced to dust, from what shall the harmony be produced?

In the *Histoire naturelle de l'âme*, little is said on this subject. It was not Lamettrie's intention to narrate what had been thought; what he wished to do was to paint the soul's development, and he put forth his best efforts to show that that which is termed soul is but the outcome of the perfectionment and education of the senses.

In *l'Homme machine* it is again a question of the soul, and the conclusion of course is the same. In spite of Descartes, who taught of two substances precisely as though he had seen and counted them; in spite of Leibnitz, who spiritualized matter instead of materializing the spirit; in spite of every one and everything to the contrary, Lamettrie, in broad paragraphs, proved to his own satisfaction that to think, to feel, to distinguish right from wrong as readily as blue from yellow, and to be but an animal, superior, perhaps, but still a brute, is not a bit more contradictory than it is for a parrot or a monkey to be able to distinguish pleasure from pain.

"Man is a machine," he said, "wound up and kept running by digestion. The soul is the mainspring. Both, of course, are material. As to thought, it is as much a property of matter as is electricity, motricity, impenetrability and breadth. To query with Locke whether matter can think, is tantamount to wondering whether it can tell time. In brief, man is a machine, and throughout the universe there is but one substance diversely modified. Such," he concluded "is my idea, or rather such is the truth. *Dispute qui voudra.*"

Another Breton who found a seat at the royal supper-table was Maupertuis. Before he found it, there had been some discussion among the erudite concerning the sphericity of the globe, and two separate expeditions were sent from France to measure different degrees of longitude. One went to Lapland, the other to Peru. Maupertuis, who was a geometrician, was placed at the head of the Polar expedition. He set out at once for Sweden, and after sixteen months of fatiguing adventures, returned to Paris to find himself the hero of the day. But in a city like Paris, a knowledge of the meridian, however exact, is not an attainment apt to make a man ceaselessly admired; and Maupertuis, who had taken the admiration quite seriously, and had had himself painted, mantled in fur, in the act of flattening the globe, soon found that his glory was so much vapor. Now Maupertuis was not only a geometrician, he was a philosopher, and the occupant of the Prussian throne was, as has been hinted, ever ready to add a new one to his collection; consequently, while Maupertuis was wondering at the inconstancy of his compatriots, a note was brought to him from Frederick. "Come to Berlin," it ran. "You have taught the world the form of the earth; you shall learn from a king how much you are appreciated."

The king at that time, however, happened to be in a battle-field; and to the battle-field Maupertuis, with the true spirit of a courtier, directed his steps. Unfortunately for him, Frederick was obliged to retreat, and Maupertuis was taken prisoner. At first it was thought that he had been killed; but when it was learned that he had been conducted to Vienna and there fêted at court, Voltaire took occasion to say a few smart things, and the world smiled with amusement and relief.

At Vienna, the Queen asked him what his philosophy taught him to think of two princes who wrangled over patches of a planet which he had measured. "I have no right," he answered sedately, "to be more philosophic than kings." To change the subject, her Majesty deigned to inquire whether the Queen of Sweden was not the most beautiful princess in Europe. To which Maupertuis, who was nothing if not regence, answered, with his best bow, "I had always thought so until now." After that, he was returned unransomed to Frederick.

At Berlin, a young Pomeranian lady fell in love with him. His conversation, it appears, was so lively, that women never suspected him of being a savant. The young Pomeranian became his bride; while he, through the king's good offices, was made President of the Berlin Academy,—a sort of Minister of Literature, much as d'Argens was Minister of the Stage. Voltaire, meanwhile, was lounging at Sans-Souci. Maupertuis had not forgotten the smart things he had said, and Voltaire was perhaps a little jealous of the favor shown to a rival. But, be this as it may, it is a part of history that no love was lost between them. When Voltaire had the king's ear, he poured into it scurrilous anecdotes about his compatriot; and when Maupertuis enjoyed a similar privilege, the tale of his grievances never tarried. "They take me for a sewer," said Frederick, with the indulgent smile of a man who has said a good thing.

Frederick sided with Maupertuis. It is possible that in some kingly fashion he, too, was jealous, though in his case the jealousy was of one whose royalty threatened at times to overshadow his own. Voltaire was irascible; he was annoyed at the preference; and after brooding over his discontent, he composed and published a pamphlet entitled *Docteur Akakia.*

In this trifle Maupertuis was lampooned as no one had ever been before; his pet theories—to wit, that there is no other proof of God than an algebraic formula, and that nothing which we see is as we see it—were held up to the laughter of the world. Frederick caused the edition to be seized and burned by the headsman. Voltaire, however, was not easily circumvented. A few copies escaped the *auto-da-fe* and went careering over Europe. Maupertuis was forever ridiculous, but Voltaire was still unsatisfied. He kept pricking him with his pen, until Maupertuis, outwearied with his struggle with an ogre, took to his bed and died of mortification—"between two monks," said the relentless Arouet. "What do you think of him?" he asked d'Alembert; "he has been suffering for a long time from a repletion of pride, but I did not take him either for a hypocrite or an imbecile."

Maupertuis was one of the first of the modern thinkers that have ventured to add up the balance-sheet of pleasure and pain, and also one of the first to discover that the latter largely exceeds the former; indeed, so large did the excess seem, that he had no hesitation in announcing that were all that is painful in life suppressed and only the pleasurable moments counted, the duration of the happiest existence would not exceed a few hours.

He had scanned the *paysages de tristesse* as carefully as another, and the fairest vista that he saw was behind the delinquent hands of death. *"Post mortem nihil est; ipsaque mors nihil,"*—After death is nothing; death itself is naught,—said Seneca; and Maupertuis, who agreed with him thoroughly, advocated suicide, and praised the stoics for teaching that it was a permissible remedy, and one that was most useful, against the ills of life. "If," he argued, "a man believes in a religion which offers eternal rewards to those that suffer, and which threatens with eternal punishment those that die to avoid suffering, it is not bravery on his part to commit suicide, nor is it cowardice, it is idiocy. On the other hand, a man who has no belief in a future life, and who is solely occupied in making this one as little unpleasant as possible, sees neither rhyme nor reason in submitting to misfortunes from which he can free himself in a trice." Nevertheless, Maupertuis died a natural death, and, as Voltaire said, between two monks at that.

Maupertuis, Lamettrie, d'Argens, even to the philosopher king himself, were dominated and overshadowed by Voltaire. Though purposeful, their influence was slight; it had barely strength enough to cross the Rhine. But on the other side of that muddy river there was then a group of thinkers whose influence can be felt in some of the currents of contemporary thought, and concerning whom a word or two may now be said.

When the foremost of England's skeptics, David Hume, visited Paris, he found a warm welcome at the house of the Baron d'Holbach. It was there, Burton says, that professing he had never met an atheist, Hume was told that he was in the company of seventeen. Of these, the more noteworthy were Diderot, d'Alembert, Naigeon and the host.

The Baron d'Holbach was a German who had been educated in France. He was a man of large wealth, wise, liberal and charitable. His house in the Rue Royale, which was called the Cafe de l'Europe, was a free academy of the freest thinkers; and of free-thinkers, domiciled and transient, d'Holbach was known as the *maître d'hôtel*. But d'Holbach was something more; he was one of the field-marshals of the little army of materialists who were the forerunners of the Revolution, and a lord in the literature of anti-theism. His erudition is said to have been practically unbounded. There was nothing of value written or suggested with which he was unfamiliar. "No matter what system I may imagine," said Diderot, "I am always sure that my friend d'Holbach can find me with facts and authorities to support it."

The doctrine which d'Holbach advocated was as liberal as the sea. It was a doctrine of freedom in all things—in speech, in thought, in politics and in religion. Its tenets are displayed at length in the *Systeme de la Nature*, a work published in Holland, and, through a literary trickery then not infrequent, attributed to a gentleman who, being dead, could not be prosecuted.

"Lost at nightfall in a forest, I have," said Diderot, "but a feeble light to guide me. A stranger happens along: 'Blow out your candle,' he says, 'and you will see your way the better.' That stranger is a theologian."

This squib might have served as epigraph to the *Systeme de la Nature*.

"Man," said d'Holbach, "is miserable, simply because he is ignorant. His mind is so infected with prejudices, that one might think him forever condemned to err... It is error that has forged the chains with which tyrants and priests have manacled nations... It is error that has evoked the religious fears which shrivel up men with fright, or make them butcher each other for chimeras. The hatreds, persecutions, massacres and tragedies of which, under pretext of the interests of Heaven, the earth has been the repeated theatre, are one and all the outcome of error."

These bold words were the prelude to the frankest exposition of anti-theism that France had ever read. Its audacity terrified, but its austerity repelled. Its paragraphs were as Cimmerian to the chamber-maids and hair-dressers of Paris, as the gayeties of Lamettrie had been shocking to the pedantry of Berlin. Then, too, it was rich and elaborate in its materialism. Today it seems a trifle antiquated; the world has thought more deeply since; but with its general outlines contemporary thinkers have had no fault to find. In these outlines Nature is represented as the one-in-all, beyond which is nothing. The main propositions tend to show that throughout the length and breadth of space there is merely force and matter, the infinite interconnection of cause and effect; and that it is through an ignorance of natural laws that divinities have been imagined and made the objects of hope and fear.

On the subject of hope and fear, d'Holbach had much to say. The gist of it may be summarized in the fatalist axiom, Whatever will be, is. Everything that happens, happens necessarily, and in virtue of immutable laws. As to order or disorder, they are empty terms; like time and space, they belong to the categories of thought; there is nothing outside of us which corresponds to them. It is all very well for man to see order in that which is in conformity with his state of being, and disorder in that which is contrary to it; to call one the effect of an Intelligence acting toward a determined end, and the other the play of hazard. But order and disorder are but words used to designate certain states and conditions of being, which if permanent are called after the one, and if transitory after the other. Beside, Nature can have no aim, for there is nothing beyond it to which it can strive. As to hazard, it is meaningless, save in contradistinction to that Intelligence which man himself has conceived. Now man, d'Holbach explains, has always fancied himself the central fact in the universe. He has connected with himself everything that he has seen, and modelled everything after his own image. In this way he grew to believe that the universe is governed by an intelligence like unto his own; yet, being at the same time convinced of his individual incapacity to cause the multiform effects of which he stood a witness, he was forced to distinguish between himself and the invisible producer, and he thought to overcome the difficulty by attributing to that intelligence an aggrandizement of the prowess which he himself possessed.

The belief in the supernatural, which in man is inherent, d'Holbach regarded as a disease to which humanity's greatest misfortunes are attributable. Truth, he was fond of saying, can never harm. Nor can it. But that does not make it a welcome guest. The whole history of religion goes to prove that man would rather be wrong in his beliefs than have none at all. Then, too, the majority have never been provided with such leisure as would enable them to dispense with illusions. The thinker may wave them away, but his gestures leaves the masses unaffected. Perhaps if the world were merely learned, it would be anti-theistic; But fortunately, or unfortunately, as the actual status of affairs may be viewed, it is something more or something less; there is an unstillable longing, an unconquerable expectation of better things, which so exalts the heart, that the serenest of atheists can never witness its effects without experiencing some sudden pang of envy.

In the polite society in which d'Holbach moved, disbelief was so prevalent that it is possible he had no occasion to experience a twinge. And if he did, the emotion has been unrecorded. He was squarely opposed to the idea of God, and at the same time a living contradiction to the theory that an atheist is necessarily a man of lax principles. Walmar, in the *Nouvelle Heloïse*, is the portrait which Rousseau took of him. Yet, as has been already intimated, it is the temperament, and not the point of view, that guides us into paths that are those of virtue or its opposite. And it was d'Holbach's temperament that made him shame the Jew devil as Satan had never been shamed before. On this point the testimony of his contemporaries is unanimous. The purity of his life, and that, too, in a century when immorality was less a vice than a grace, has never been questioned. He was a simple-mannered gentleman, warm of heart, sweet-tempered, endowed with great delicacy of sentiment, and possessed of such tact that even Rousseau, who would have quarreled with an archangel, was unable to find in him any other cause of grievance than his wealth. "He is too rich for me," he said; but he added, "He is a better man, and one more really charitable than many a Christian. *He does good without the hope of reward.*"

The only immortality in which d'Holbach believed was fame. In life there is certainly nothing more exquisite. As Schopenhauer said, it is the Golden Fleece of the elect. But after death, and true glory comes but then, fame and ignominy are to the recipient equally unmeaning. And even were it otherwise, when it is remembered what are the limitations of fame, and when it is considered how small a value can be accorded to public opinion, the immortality in which d'Holbach believed does not seem worth an effort.

D'Holbach was one of the few writers that have had the courage to advocate suicide, and he advocated it as boldly to those who cowered at death, as he advocated virtue to a century whose vice is historic. His main argument in its favor is to the effect that the engagements between man and Nature are neither voluntary on the part of the one nor reciprocal on the part of the other. Man is therefore in nowise bound; and should he find himself unsupported, he can desert a position which has become unpleasant and irksome. As to the citizen, he can hold to his country and associates only by the mortgage on his well-being. If the lien is paid off, he is free. "Would a man be blamed," he asks, "a man who, finding himself useless and without resources in his native place, should withdraw into solitude? Well, then, with what right can a man be blamed who kills himself from despair? And what is death but an isolation?"

Maxims such as these are considered dangerous and provocative. But maxims have never caused a suicide. A man may cut his throat or hang himself to put an end to the agonies of grief or boredom, but not because he has happened on a suggestive quotation. He will look for the great quietus if he wants to, but not because it is recommended. In any case the contempt of death is a useful possession; and it is well for every one to understand that while virtue and happiness are supposed to go hand-in-hand, and that to do good is to receive it, yet after the loss of any one of us the world will go on in quite the same manner as before.

In the days when d'Holbach was giving dinner-parties in the Rue Royale, the flag of France was noticeably black. Some said that it was from the dye of the cassock; others, that it had caught the grime of medieval institutions. At d'Holbach's dinner-table, however, in the salons of Madame Geoffrin—she who was so plain that Greuze exclaimed, "My God, if she annoys me I'll paint her!"—in the salons of Mesdames du Deffand, de Lespinasse and Necker, there assembled from time to time a handful of thinkers who were determined to give the flag of France another hue. These gentlemen were resolute and aggressive. The century they saw, was hungry for ideas, and it was in an effort to give it food of the right quality that the Encyclopædia was produced.

The Encyclopædia—a name coined by Rabelais—displayed the genealogy of thought. It was at once a storehouse of knowledge, an attack on ignorance, an appeal to common-sense, and a plea for liberty. It opposed every abuse, political, theological, ecclesiastical, industrial, fiscal, legal and penal. It sought to establish toleration, to abolish sacerdotal thaumaturgy, to banish the supernatural, and thwart the subornation of the understanding.

It was in no sense free from error, and its erudition presents today a most mildewed appearance; but it served its purpose, and from out its wide bindings burst the torrents of the Revolution.

In its opposition to everything that savored of the illiberal, the Encyclopædia encountered many an obstacle and not a few embarrassments; indeed, the history of the government and literature of the third quarter of the last century is interwoven with that of its vicissitudes and final triumph. Every man of brains wrote for it, and those who had none and wanted some subscribed. The responsibility of its publication was assumed by Diderot and d'Alembert.

Diderot was a giant, whose head was in the clouds and whose feet were in the mud. He wrote obscene stories and anticipated Lamark, Darwin's precursor. History, art, science and philosophy he held in fee, and yet he was not erudite. He had drunk oft, not deep. "I know a great many things," he said, "but there is hardly a man that does not know some one thing better than I." In the activity of his mind may be found the reason of the admiration of his contemporaries and that of posterity's neglect. He has left us twenty volumes of essays and digressions, but not a single book. Yet no one was ever so prodigal with his pen as he. He gave it to any one that asked, to an enemy as readily as to a friend. Grimm asked his opinion on an exhibition of paintings; he gave it in an in-octavo. "I have written a satire against you," said a young man to him one day. "I am poor; will you buy it?" "Ah! sir," he exclaimed, "what a pitiable vocation is yours! but," he continued, "I will tell you what to do. The Duke of Orleans honors me with his dislike; dedicate your book to him; he will pay you well." "A good dedication is a difficult job," said the young black-mailer. "Well, sit down," Diderot answered, "and I will write it for you." And he did, and the youth received his pay.

Diderot being without ambition was known as the Philosopher, but he was so poor that he could hardly buy the cloak.

When he wished to dower his daughter, he found that he had nothing except his library, and his library to him was life itself. Nevertheless, he determined to sell it. Catharine of Russia learned of the determination and bought the library; but with a true sense of what is royal, she left him the use of his books and made him their salaried custodian beside.

At the beginning of his literary career, Diderot was a sincere deist, which, as some one has said, is a proof of what education may do. It was not long, however, before he saw that skepticism is the first step to philosophy; and when the step was taken, he descended without a compunction the precipitate stair of negation. The stages of his thought are well defined. "Aggrandize God," he shouted in his first enthusiasm; "free Him from the captivity of temples and creeds. See Him everywhere, or say that he does not exist." Later—in the "Letter on the Blind for the Use of those who See"—he manifested a classic indifference on the whole subject. "Ask an Indian how the world is suspended in the air, and he will tell you that it rests on the back of an elephant. 'And the elephant?' 'On a turtle.' You pity the Indian, yet one might say to you as to him, 'Admit your ignorance, and don't bother me with a menagerie.'"

But his indifference was transient. "Among the difficulties (of believing in God), there is one," he noted, "which has been agitated since the world began. It is that men suffer without having deserved to do so. To this there has never been an answer. The existence of a Supreme Being is incompatible with evils, moral and physical. What, then, is the safest course? The one which we have taken. Whatever the optimist may say, we answer that if the world could not exist without sentient beings, and sentient beings without pain, the Almighty would have done better to keep quiet." Thereafter he became firmly anti-theistic. "It is," he said, "highly important not to mistake hemlock for parsley, but it is entirely unnecessary to believe in God." "The

Christian religion," he added, "is atrocious in its dogmas. It is unintelligible, metaphysical, intertwisted and obscure. It is mischievous to tranquility, dangerous in its discipline, puerile and unsocial in its ethics, and in its ceremonial dreary, flat, Gothic and most gloomy... If my ideas please no one," he concluded, "it is possible that they are poor; but if they pleased everybody, I would consider them detestable." Yet as he preached tolerance, he practiced it, and was never known to refuse a crutch to those who had no legs.

Among the Encyclopædists, where Diderot was king, d'Alembert was prime minister, a Mazarin, as one may say; but a Mazarin who grew fainthearted, and, fearing the Bastille, left his monarch in the lurch.

D'Alembert was more a mathematician than a philosopher. His mistress was Algebra. History has given the same title to Mile. de l'Espinasse; but if he was unfaithful, the lady in question appears to have paid him back in a better coin than his own. He was not a cheerful person, yet when alone with his books he was happy as though he were dead. "*Qui est-ce qui est heureux?*" someone asked him. "*Quelque misérable,*" he replied. He was an invalid, too; but he hated medicine, and held a physician to be like a blind man who armed with a cudgel strikes at random, and, according as he strikes, annihilates the disease or—the patient.

As has been hinted, he was timid, or perhaps merely cautious, a trait which found little favor with Voltaire. "Philosophers are too lukewarm," he said; "instead of shrugging their shoulders at the errors of mankind, they ought to wipe them out." But apparently d'Alembert did not agree with him. "Philosophers," he retorted, "should be like children, who, when they have done anything wrong, put the blame on the cat." But if for one reason or another he thought it best to keep his views from the public, he had no hesitation in whispering them to the sympathetic ear of Frederick the Great. The latter had written what he called a refutation of the naturalism conveyed in d'Holbach's *Système de la Nature*. The book had annoyed him; but what probably annoyed him most was not its naturalism, but its attack on the sacred caste of royalty. At the same time, as he himself said, if d'Holbach were condemned to be burned, he would be the first to play the hose on the stake.

In the eyes of the liberal monarch, d'Alembert, when answering the refutation, brandished the historic doubt. "Montaigne's motto, What do I know? seems to me," he wrote, "the answer that should be made to all questions in metaphysics... Those who deny the existence of a Supreme Intelligence advance more than they can prove. In treating such a subject, skepticism is the only reasonable standpoint. No one, for instance, can deny that throughout the universe, and particularly in the formation of plants and animals, there are combinations which seem to reveal an Intelligence. That they prove it, as a watch proves a watch-maker, is incontestable. But supposing that one wishing to go further asks, What is this Intelligence? Did it create, or did it merely arrange matter? Is creation possible, or, if it be not, is matter eternal? And if matter is eternal and needed an Intelligence simply to arrange it, is that Intelligence united to matter, or is it distinct? If it is united, matter, properly speaking, is God, and God is matter. If it is distinct, how can that which is material be fashioned by that which is not? Besides, if this Intelligence is infinitely wise and infinitely powerful, why is the world, which is its work, so filled with physical and moral imperfections? Why are not all men happy? Why are not all men just? Your Majesty assures me that this question is answered by the world's eternity. And so perhaps it is, but seemingly merely in this sense, that the world being eternal, and in consequence necessary, everything which is, must be as it is; and at once we enter into a system of fatality and necessity which does not in the least accord with the idea of a God infinitely wise and infinitely powerful. Sire, when these questions arise, we should repeat '*Que sais-je?*' an hundred times. Then, too, there is a consolation for ignorance in the thought that, as we know nothing, it is unnecessary for us to know more."

To which Frederick, who gave a nickname as readily as a pension, answered:

"But, my dear Diagoras, if you fancy that I can give a detailed explanation of the Intelligence that I marry to Nature, you over-estimate my ability. I can say merely that I perceive it as I would an object of which I might happen to catch a glimpse through a mist."

D'Alembert, however, was not to be played with, and he returned to the charge and routed the fat king with a fresh arsenal of queries.

"With the exception of the animal kingdom, the realms of matter with which we are acquainted appear deprived of sentiency, volition and thought. Is it possible that intelligence resides in them without our knowledge? Of this there is no evidence, and I am inclined to think that the block of marble, as well as the plants that are the most delicately and ingeniously organized, are without thought and feeling. But, it is objected, the organization of these bodies discloses visible traces of an intelligence. This I do not deny; but I would be glad to know what has become of this intelligence since these bodies were organized. If it resided within them while they were being formed and in order to form them, and if, as it is supposed, this intelligence is not distinct from them, what has become of it since its work is done? Has the very perfection of the organization been annihilated? To me, such a supposition seems untenable. If, then, the intelligence whose effects we admire in man is merely a resultant of organization, why, in other realms of matter, may we not admit a structure and an arrangement as necessary and as natural as matter itself, and from which, without the intervention of any intelligence, would result the very effects which surround and surprise us? Lastly, in admitting the doctrine that an Intelligence presided over the formation of the world and still watches over its well-being, it is hard to reconcile the theory of that Intelligence with the idea of infinite wisdom and power. For, to the misfortune of humanity, this world of ours, is very far from being the best one possible. With the best of intentions, we are therefore unable to recognize any other God than one who, at most, is material, limited and dependent. I do not know whether this view is the correct one, but certainly it is not that of the Deity's partisans, who would much prefer to have us atheists than the Spinozists that we are. To mollify them, let us turn skeptic and repeat with Montaigne, *Que sais-je?*"

This amiable agnosticism was shared by few of the Encyclopaedists. To Naigeon, who would have nothing to do with half-way measures, it seemed little less than revolting. Naigeon was a Puritan without beliefs; his atheism was as fervent as his life was austere. When he first sat, a stripling, at d'Holbach's table, he was largely ridiculed. He was a pretty boy, with fair skin and curled blonde hair. Diderot's monkey, La Harpe called him, for it was through Diderot that he was brought into notice. But with age the comely lad developed into a tiger. To him Diderot left the care of his unpublished manuscripts, and these Naigeon edited, together with the memoirs of the author. He, too, was a voluminous writer, and scattered essays and treatises with a prodigality which he had caught from his master. But the work which caused the greatest number of people to turn about and look after him in the street was the *Theologie portative.* In it the beliefs and tenets of Christendom were treated in a manner that reminds one of Col. Ingersoll. In the subsequent *Encyclopédie méthodique* he wrote again on these and adjacent subjects, though this time from a broader and more serious standpoint.

Politically, socially and morally untrammelled, he had,

meanwhile, been keeping a finger on the public pulse, and he felt that some great, if undetermined, change was at hand. So soon, then, as the National Assembly got to work on its declaration of the rights of man, Naigeon issued an address, in which he prayed the Assembly to banish from the proclamation any suggestion of religion, and in its place to assert man's right to entire freedom of thought and speech. But the petition was unnoticed. It is possible that he made a second appeal to Robespierre; but if he did, it was as unsuccessful as the first. And there is an anecdote that one day during the Terror he looked so much alarmed, that some asked him if he were on the list of the condemned. "Worse than that," he cried. "That monster Robespierre has decreed the existence of a Supreme Being!" To Robespierre, an atheist was an aristocrat.

While Naigeon was addressing the Assembly, a young man named Sylvain Maréchal passed out of Saint-Lazare. A few months previous, he had published a little book entitled, *l'Almanack des honnêtes gens*, in which wise men were given precedence over saints. This disregard of etiquette procured for Marechal an opportunity to meditate on the proprieties of life. When the prison-doors were opened, he passed his time in succoring the indigent and housing the pursued. He fed and sheltered priests and royalists alike, and even paid masses for the repose of the soul of an old woman because he knew that such had been her wish.

Yet Maréchal was one of the fanatics of atheism, and as proud of negation as though he had invented it. The devil, one may see, is rarely as red as he appears on the stage. The thinkers with whom this chapter has had to deal were fervent in their disbelief; but in their disbelief there was room for such charity, tolerance and broad good-will, that one looks in vain for a stone that shall hit them. Perhaps, as some one has said, it is only the just that have a right to be athiests. And yet they were not impeccable;

with one exception, they were guilty of a grievous sin against good manners—they were dogmatic. One may fancy that their voices were seldom modulated; it is probable that they shouted, and there are few among us that care to be shouted at. Then, too, there was a confidence and an assurance in their atheism which is as unpleasant as bigotry. They forgot Montaigne, and they let Pyrrho fall asleep. Maréchal was not better than the others; one may even say that he was worse, for he was dogmatic in rhyme. Since Lucretius, atheism had been without a poet. Leopardi's father was then a bachelor. and Shelley was in the cradle. It was Maréchal that the irreverent muse first ordered to hold the lute. And Maréchal kissed the Muse full upon the mouth, and sang loudly in a strain of boyish bravado. Whether or not Maréchal's notes were listened to, is relatively a matter of small importance. A little later, the Being whose existence Robespierre had decreed was publicly deposed. The cathedral of Notre-Dame was consecrated to the worship of Reason, the crosier and the ring were trampled under foot, and an ass, crowned with a mitre, was led through exulting crowds.

CHAPTER FIVE.

The Protests of Yesterday.

THE LIVES OF PHILOSOPHERS ARE DULL. DESCARTES MIGHT figure as the hero of a romance, but Descartes is an exception. Fichte belongs to the rule. The story of his manhood is one of poverty which is not poignant, and of successes which were not great.

In a work on this thinker, Professor Adamson notes one fact which is palpitant in truth and lucidity; it is to the effect that Europe today does not hold ten students of that marvellous sophist. And yet Fichte is one of the most insolent of dissenters. To the ordinary reader his negations are inexplicable; they comprise the denial of the reality of the external world. This denial, which is known as akosmism, is pantheism's twin-sister. Pantheism admits no other reality than Nature; and akosmism, taking one step further, declines to admit any reality at all. Of the two, pantheism has been the more fruitful. It began with the Vedas; ran through Eleatic and Neo-platonic philosophy; was caught up by Scott Erigena and handed to Bruno, who passed it to Spinoza. Another thread or two runs through the Talmud, the Kabbala, the theories of Maimonides, Gerson and Chesdai Creskas; and there are tangles of it in the beliefs of mediaeval communities, in the heresies of the Beghards and Beguines, the Turlupins and Adamites; but with their unravelment the reader need not be wearied. Akosmism has found fewer adherents. Like pantheism, it began with the Vedas, or, more correctly, with the Vedanta philosophy; left broad traces in Greece; revived for a moment during the Renaissance; and then sank back into obscurity until Fichte, Kant aiding, brought it to light anew. Between the two systems there is this cardinal distinction. Pantheism and science have never been other than the best of friends. There is nothing in the one that has ever been seriously opposed by the other. But akosmism and science look at each other askant. They have as much in common as have the poet and the mathematician.

The clearest idea of Fichte's akosmism, or rather the clearest idea of its charm and futility, is conveyed in a work entitled the *Bestimmung des Menschen*, the Vocation of Man. The work is divided into three parts: Doubt, Knowledge and Faith. The first part, Doubt, opens with an inquiry concerning that mystery within us that calls itself "I," and an examination of Nature that vaunts itself real. From this inquiry and from this examination, Fichte discovers that man is but a link in a chain of necessity, a part of that force which, amid the everlasting revolution and mutation of things, is the sum and substance of all that is.

And that chain of necessity! Was there ever anything more delicately interconnected? One has but to look at it to see that its rivets are so neatly joined that they make it impossible for anything to be other than it is. Take, for instance, a single grain of sand on the sea-shore, and fancy that it lies a few feet further inland than it actually does. The mental operation is, admittedly, most easy to perform; but note the consequences. For that grain of sand to be a few feet further inland, then must the wind which bore it have been stronger than it was; then must the state of the atmosphere which occasioned the wind have been different from what it was, and the previous changes different; in fact, it is necessary to presuppose an entirely different temperature from that which actually existed. We must also suppose a different constitution of the bodies which influence the temperature, the barrenness or fertility of countries, on which depend the health of man and the duration of life. Interfere, therefore, with that grain of sand, and it is within the range of possibilities that in such a state of weather as was necessary to move it but a few feet further inland, some one, long ago, may have died of cold or hunger—long ago, before the birth of that son from whom the sophist himself descended; and behold, Fichte would have been spared the trials of life, and prevented, too, from solving every problem, and leaving the student nothing to do but to bore himself to death.

From Fichte's logic, therefore, the necessity which compels everything to be precisely as it is, is amply demonstrated. Nevertheless, doubt is not yet banished. It is true he has proved the existence of man to be but a manifestation of a force whose operation is determined by the whole of the universe, but into the nature of that force he is unable to look. And even could he, of what use would it be? It would not help him to regulate his actions. Nature is the last one to contradict herself, and she allows no one to contradict her. The force that acts on us and in us makes us what we are; and to attempt to make ourselves otherwise than it has been appointed we should be, is a task which may be pleasant, but which assuredly is useless. In the chain of necessity we are all interlinked: fight free who may. They who have done so have reached that bourne from which no traveller returns.

We may rejoice and repent, we may form good resolutions;

but the joy and the repentance and the good resolutions come to us of themselves, and not until it is appointed that they shall do so. When they do come, however sincere the repentance may be, however magnificent the resolutions, the course of things moves on unchanged and changeless as before. We lie in the lap of necessity. Should Nature destine one man to be wise and to be brave, wise and brave he will be. Should she destine another to be scatterbrained and imbecile, scatterbrained and imbecile will he become. There is no merit, no blame, to be ascribed to her or to them. The wishes that throb in our hearts may rebel, but the great Mother snuffs them out like a candle. She is governed herself. Her laws are ours.

It is in musings of this description that Fichte stretches his hand to Spinoza and denies that man is a free agent. At best he is a conscious automaton. But what if he were not even that? Is there any one thing of which he is certain?

"Dreams are true while they last, and do we not live in dreams?"

Fichte asks himself the same question, and looking with introspective eye for an answer, discovers the purely subjective character of all human knowledge. He sees that he has no consciousness of things in themselves, only a consciousness of a consciousness of them. Were he blind, what would he know of color? Were he deaf, what would he know of song? Were he without imagination, doubt, hope and fear would have no meaning. Such knowledge as man possesses is merely a knowledge of himself; beyond it, consciousness never goes. When it seems to do otherwise, when man assumes to be conscious of an object—the sun, for instance—he has merely the consciousness of a supposition of an object, which supposition he identifies with sensation and takes for the object itself.

It has been hinted that akosmism and science are at odds,

but on this point they agree. As a matter of fact, and one admitted by all decorous scholars, we none of us see the sun. What we do see are certain modifications of light in immediate relation to our organ of vision. And in this connection it is not improper to note that no two persons see the same modifications of the same light, and that for the reason that each person sees a different complement of rays acting on his own individual retina.

But to return to Fichte, and to put his idea less technically, it is a self-evident proposition that we neither see our sight, feel our touch, nor yet have a higher sense by which things affecting the organs of sense are perceived. It is therefore not difficult to accept the axiom that our consciousness of external existence is merely the product of our presentative faculty. The difficulty lies in the application, for with it all reality vanishes. In that which we call intuitive knowledge, we contemplate only ourselves, and our consciousness is and can be only a consciousness of the modifications of our own existence. If, therefore, the external world arises before us only through our own consciousness, it follows that what is particular and multiform in the external world can arise in no other way; and if the connection between ourselves and what is external to us is simply a connection of thought, then is the connection of the multifarious objects of the external world simply this and no other.

The whole of the material world is, then, but a cerebral phenomenon. There is no being, no real existence. The only things that exist are pictures, and these pictures know themselves after the fashion of pictures. They are pictures which float past, without there being anything past which they float—pictures which picture nothing, images without significance and without an aim. Reality is a dream, without a world of which the dream might be, or a mind that might dream it. It is a dream which is woven together in a dream of itself. Intuition is the dream; thought, the source of fancied reality, is the dream of that dream.

In this charming manner, Fichte, after divesting himself of doubt and attaining perfect knowledge, mounts into a higher sphere which he terms Faith. Into the austerities of this abstraction it is unnecessary to follow him; and it will perhaps suffice to note that the conclusion amounts to the assertion that where the canaille believe that things are as they appear, because they must, the philosopher believes because he will. After a deduction such as that, one may well exclaim against the uselessness of philosophy in general, and the Fichtean branch in particular.

Fichte's metaphysical hysterics excited the wildest hilarity. His formula I = I, on which in an earlier work he had sounded all the changes, was popularly supposed to mean his own individual ego. Fichte, however, meant nothing of the sort. The "I" he used in the impersonal sense which is conveyed in such expressions as "it rains," "it snows." The "I" represented the force that pervades all things, and which in man arrives at a consciousness of self. But Fichte was not a clear writer—few Germans are; and if he was taken *au pied de la lettre*, the fault was his own. In any event, his philosophy was largely ridiculed. Heine is witness to the fact that a cartoon was circulated which represented a goose whose liver had become so big that the bird was undecided whether she was all goose or all liver. Across her Fichtean breast ran the legend I = I. The reality of his idealism, however, was not taken so easily. The Philistines waxed wroth. Heine represents a burgomeister as exclaiming, "That man thinks I don't exist, does he? Why, I'm stouter than he and his superior, too!" The ladies asked, "Doesn't he at least believe in the existence of his wife?" "Of course not." "And does Madame Fichte permit that?"

But with whatever facetiousness the matter may be viewed, the question of an external world has been, and is still, one of the great battle-fields of metaphysics. The realists clamor that their opponents are colossal in their errors; the idealists answer, "*Tu quoque.*" Among the latter, few have been more vehement than Fichte. He defended his belief with all the heavy artillery of the German dictionary, and entrenched himself with logic. It was, however, merely on speculative principles that he contended that our knowledge of mind and matter is only a consciousness of what Sir William Hamilton has christened "various bundles of baseless appearances." He did not deny the veracity of consciousness; he denied the veracity of its testimony, a distinction as subtle as it is valid. For all practical purposes the material world—including Madame Fichte—was to him not only thoroughly real, but it went spinning through space at the rate of nineteen miles a second. And it was merely the certainty of uncertainty, the haunting conviction of the unreliability of the perceptions which in earlier days led Socrates to maintain that the only thing he knew was that he knew nothing, which caused Fichte to discriminate between what he believed and what he saw.

But however unreal the world might be in theory, he was quite sure that for every-day purposes it was the worst one possible. Indeed, Fichte was not only an akosmist, he was a pessimist too, a combination which seemed so alluring to Lammenais, that after a debauch in Fichteana he was pleased to describe the world as a shadow of that which is not, an echoless sound from nowhere, the chuckle of Satan in chaos.

Fichte's successor was Schelling. In place of the abstractions of his precursor, this gentleman presented an adventurous mysticism. Both were idealists; but where the one extracted the real from the ideal, the other reversed the proceeding. The transcendentalism which they professed in common, is the history of consciousness to the highest degree of its development. Fichte tiara'd his system with faith; Schelling crowned his own with æsthetics. To the latter, the universe was a poem whose strophes were writ in metaphysical formulas, a phrase which may be taken to mean that he was exquisitely alive to the beauties of Nature and yet unable to picture them in readable prose. His real master was Spinoza, and his philosophy in consequence presents some of the serenest forms of pantheistic belief.

The harmony to which he was alive prefigured to him the agency of a supreme Principle; of a Being eternally unconscious; veiled from the sight of man by the purity of enveloping light, and apprehensible only through intellectual intuition. On the skirts of this intuition he suspended knowledge. Above it he poised art—"the revelation of that Absolute in which subject and object coincide; in which the conscious and the unconscious unite."

"That which we call Nature," he said, "is a poem writ in mysterious hieroglyphics, but in which, were they decipherable, whoso lists might read the Odyssey of the Spirit, preyed upon by illusion, ever seeking, ever fleeing itself... Nature is to the artist that which it is to the philosopher; the ideal world ceaselessly appearing in finite forms: the wan reflection of a universe which does not stretch beyond the mind, but rests within it."

The fundamental idea of the entire system amounts in brief to this: earth, sea and sky, and all that in them is, are, in their essence, emanations, or, as Leibnitz has it, fulgurations of an eternal and unconscious activity. Detached from the primordial matrix, these manifestations, though interconnected, are without permanent reality. The finite world is an illusion. The infinite alone exists.

This idea, while not unalluring, is passably vague. But vagueness has no terrors for those who wish to be mystified, and that there were many such is evident from contemporary accounts of the enthusiasm with which it was greeted. The enthusiasm, however, was as impermanent as Schelling's own reality. His disciples flocked to a rival teacher, to Hegel, whose name has the sound of a knell.

The doctrine which this gentleman advanced, and which today is to be sought for in seventeen massive in-octavos, may be regarded as the apotheosis of the *arrière-pensée*. Hegel was the chameleon of philosophy. He believed in nothing; and not only did he believe in nothing, but he possessed no fixity of disbelief. Whenever it is possible to pin him down, it is always on a contradiction that the pinning is accomplished. He was an anatomist of thought, a midwife of paradox. No phase, no flutter of consciousness, escaped his diagnostic. He analyzed and dissected, but he did not build, or at least only on negations. He created doubts, not convictions. He made disbelievers, not converts. It was he who should have said, "*Ich bin der Geist der stets verneint.*"

It may be noted, parenthetically, that the proposition of which Plato caught a glimpse, and which Descartes dimly perceived, the proposition that man is the one centre of thought, formed the sum and substance of Kent's teaching. "Look," he admonished the reader, "look at time and at space. They are but categories of thought. Time is not, nor yet is space. They are appearances which the mind creates, and with which we envelope the universe." This idealism, which in Kant was partial, in Fichte subjective, and in Schelling objective, became absolute with Hegel. To him, illusion was the one permanency, the one cause, and man but the shadow of its effects.

In its widest sense, Hegel's philosophy is an attempt to make the acquaintence of Schelling's primordial entity—the Absolute. As a necessary preparation he annihilated the finite, or, to use his own language, the categories of the finite which stood in his way; and when he had done so, behold, the Absolute had crumbled with them. The heavens were void. There has been nothing, there is nothing, there will be nothing, save a constant evolution, a continuous development, with death for a goal. And, after all, what is the lesson that history conveys? What, indeed, if it be not this, that whatever is born, is born to die.

The idolatry, the infatuation of Hegel's disciples was without precedent or parallel. The streets and beer-halls echoed with discussions on the identity of contradictories. The Idea, the Absolute, the Ich and the non-Ich, were every-night topics. Metaphysics hung over Berlin like a London fog. Hegel was not only a popular teacher, he was a national idol. His dialectic prestidigitations had all the charm which attaches to the unfathomable. That he was a charlatan is clear, but that he was revered is certain. Among the group of mourners that assembled about his tomb, one, a theologian, likened him to Jesus. More recently, Scherer compared him to Napoleon. Yet on his death-bed Hegel was heard to mutter, "Only one man understood my philosophy, and he only half-caught its import."

After such a confession, one might well offer him the viaticum and hum a requiem over his seventeen in-octavos. And yet in vain. Hegel's influence is too substantial to be quieted by any requiescat, however determined. In spite of the hilarity of the impolite, his spectre looms through the most rational forms of contemporary negation. In the core of his philosophy there broods a sphinx that still defies.

When the bewilderment which Hegel excited subsided, the faith which he had inculcated was questioned; belief soon gave way to heresies, and the metaphysical assembly divided itself into dissenting camps. From one of these issued the philosophy which counted Emerson and Carlyle among its exponents. In the uproar of another, Strauss, Feuerbach, Bruno and Stirner have pointed to an eternal grave and taken the nimbus from a god. It is owing to the instruction of a third that Vacherot has occupied his time in showing that the idea of perfection is God, and that perfection does not exist; and it was something of the original spirit that smoothed the way for the amiable fumisteries of Ernest Renan.

In the days when Hegelism was at its apogee, there appeared in Berlin a young man who declined to take any other part in the general intoxication than that of spectre at the feast. His contempt for the sophist, the pachyderm hydrocephali, and all the pedantic eunuchs who made up what he was wont to term the apocalyptic retinue of the *bestia trionfante*, was sumptuous in its magnificence. So sumptuous even, that he took counsel from an attorney as to the exact limit his contempt might reach without making him amenable to a suit for defamation. Then, reassured, he began an attack. "Hegel's philosophy," he said, "is sufficient to cause an atrophy of the intellect. It is a crystallized paralogism, an abracadabra, a puff of bombast, and a wish-wash of phrases which in its monstrous construction compels the mind to form impossible contradictions." For its preparation he offered a receipt which is homeopathic in its simplicity. "Dilute a minimum of thought in five hundred pages of nauseous phraseology, and for the rest trust to the Teuton patience of the reader."

A few years before, this violent yet cautious young man had written a work which he signed in full letters, Arthur Schopenhauer, and entitled, *Die Weltals With und Vorstellung.* This work, which he thought would shake the sophistry of all civilization, had been left unnoticed and neglected on the back book-shelves of its Leipzig publisher. It is said that he smarted at this inattention, and that his aggressiveness and contempt of Hegel, and not of Hegel alone, but of Fichte and Schelling, the three sophists, as he was pleased to call them, was the outcome of envy. Whether or not this statement is true, is a matter of small importance. The point to be noted is, that thirty years later Hegel was largely forgotten, and the works of his obscure opponent were welcomed with an enthusiasm which has been expanding ever since.

The World as Will and Idea is an atheology compounded of Buddhism, Tauism and Epicurism, a mosaic of Oriental and classic negations worked out by an original and brilliant think-

er. If the seventeen in-octavos already alluded to may be regarded as the apotheosis of the *arrière-pensée*, then, in comparison,
this philosophy, together with its complementary monographs,
represents the renaissance of common-sense.

Schopenhauer was not a pantheist. Had he possessed any of
the views of ordinary orthodoxy, the belief, for instance, in

> "*L'univers*
> *Où règne un Jehovah dont Satan est l'envers,*"

he might possibly have read the banns over Nature and Satan,
but he never would have identified the former with God. Nor
was Schopenhauer a materialist. He was a theorematist of force,
but atoms found no place in his system. Yet if he must be cataloged, it will perhaps be safest to say that he was an idealist who
saw the inutility of dream. Kant's *Kritik*, from which all German metaphysics proceeds, had shown him that reason must either be confined within the limits of experience, or else let loose
into an absolute idealism. The three sophists had disgusted him
with the super-sensible, and yet he felt suffocated in the narrow
limits of the real. There was yet a middle course, and that course
he took. It was useless to ask whence the world comes or whither
it tends, but it would not be impertinent to state *what it is;* and
the statement which Schopenhauer made to the public was to
the effect that the world is but the perception of a perceiver, a
simple representation, a mere idea which man carries with him
to the tomb, and which in the absence of a thinker to think it
would not exist at all.

In the *Cogita*, a note-book of which extracts have been selected by Schopenhauer's literary executor,* is the following passage: "Two things were before me, two bodies, regularly formed,
beautiful to see. One was a vase of jaspar, with a border and handles of gold. The other was an organism, a man. When I had admired them sufficiently from without, I begged the genie who

---

*   Arthur Schopenhauer. *Von ihm Ueber ihn.* Frauenstadt.

accompanied me to let me visit within. This permission was accorded. In the vase I found nothing save the pressure of weight, and between the parts some obscure reciprocal tendency which I have heard designated as cohesion and affinity. But when I entered the other object, my surprise was so great as to be almost untellable: in legends and fairy-tales there is nothing more unbelievable than the spectacle which I beheld. In this object, or rather in its upper end, called the head, and which from without looks like anything else, I saw nothing less than the world itself; I saw the immensity of space in which all is contained, the immensity of time in which everything moves, and therewith the prodigious variety of objects that fill both space and time; but, what is most astounding, I saw myself coming and going! That is what I discovered in this object that was barely larger than a large fruit; in this object which the headsman can dissever with a single blow, and that, too, in such wise as to plunge into sudden and eternal night the whole of the world that it contains. And the amusing part of it all is, that if objects of this sort did not sprout like mushrooms, continuously prepared to receive a universe that is ever ready to subside into chaos, and did not give and take like a ball the great idea (Vorstellung) which is identical in each, and of which the identity is expressed with the word objectivity, the world would no longer exist."

Schopenhauer was not far from agreeing with Berkeley that the world is a phantasmagoria, a transformation-scene existing in fancy, or, as the Brahmins declared, a mirage evoked for the entertainment of the Supreme. The source and origin of the exterior world lay in the representative faculty which creates it and with which it disappears. Matter, according to him, is a lie that is truth; it is not an illusion, it is correlative with the intelligence; the two rise and fall together; separated, they could not exist; one is a reflection of the other. Properly speaking, they are the same thing examined from different points. But what is this same thing? Schopenhauer answers with a word. It is Will.

This Will should not be taken to mean the conscious act of a higher Intelligence. It is a force, invariable, identical and equal, of which gravitation, electricity, heat—in fact, every form of activity from the fall of an apple to the founding of a monarchy, from a cataclysm to a blade of grass, from the choir of planets to the invisible molecule—is merely a derivative and nothing more. In Nature, it is a blind, unconscious power; in man, it is the foundation of being.

This theory, which Schopenhauer expounded with a great luxuriance of vivid argument, and in a style that is crystal in its clarity, coincides in the aptest manner with the doctrine of evolution. During the early ages of the world's formation, the objectivity of this force was, he says, limited to inferior forms; but when the conflict of chemical forces had ended, and the granite, like a tombstone, covered the combatants, it irrupted in the world of plant and forest. The air, decarbonized, was then prepared for animal life, and the Will's objectivity realized a new form. Fish and crustaceans filled the sea, gigantic reptiles covered the earth, and gradually through innumerable forms, each more perfect than the last, the propulsion ascended to man.

Schopenhauer declined to believe that either here or in another planet a being superior to man could possibly exist; and that for the reason that with enlarged intelligence he would consider life too deplorable to be supported for a moment. As a consequence, the Will's objectivity can ascend no higher. Its latest manifestation is even the final term of its progress, for with it has come the possibility of its denial, the possibility that some day it may be throttled into extinction and choked back into the chaos from which it sprang.

In all the grades of its manifestations, Will, he taught, dispenses with any end or aim. It simply and ceaselessly strives, for striving is its sole nature. But as any hindrance of this striving, through an obstacle placed between it and its temporary aim, is called suffering, and the absence of any obstacle, satisfaction—it follows, if the obstacles it meets outnumber the facilities it encounters, that, having no final end or aim, there can be no end and no measure of suffering.

That pain does outbalance pleasure is a fact too well established to need discussion here. Pain begins with the lowest types of animal life, becomes acute with the nervous system of the vertebrates, increases in proportion to the development of the intelligence; and as intelligence attains distinctness, pain advances with it, until what Mr. Swinburne calls the gift of tears finds its supreme expression in man. And man is not a being to be envied. He is the concretion of a thousand necessities. His life, as Schopenhauer has it, is a fight for existence, with the certainty of defeat in the end; and even when his existence is assured, there comes a struggle with a shadowy burden, an effort to kill time, and a vain attempt to escape ennui.

Nor is ennui a minor evil. It is not every one who can get away from himself. Schopenhauer could, it is true; but in so doing he noted that its ravages depicted on the human countenance an expression of absolute despair, and made beings who love each other as little as men do, seek eagerly the society of each other. In this way, between effort and attainment, the life of man rolls on. The wish is in its nature pain, and satisfaction soon begets satiety. No matter what fortune may have done, no matter what a man may be or what he may possess, pain can never be avoided. Efforts to banish it effect, if successful, only a change of form. It may appear as want or care for the maintenance of life. If this preoccupation be removed, back it comes again in the mask of love, jealousy, hatred or ambition; and if it gain entrance through none of these avatars, it comes as simple boredom, against which we strive as best we may. Even in this latter case, if we get the upper hand, we shall hardly do so,

Schopenhauer says, without letting pain in again in one of its earlier forms. And then the dance begins afresh; for life, like a pendulum, swings ever backward and forward between pain and ennui.

The one relief, a relief which at best is momentary and accidental, is in that impersonal contemplation in which the individual is effaced, and only the pure, knowing subject subsists. This condition Schopenhauer praises as the painless state which Epicurus described as the highest good, the bliss of the gods. Therein man is freed from the yoke of Will; the penal servitude of daily life ceases as for a Sabbath; the wheel of Ixion stands still. The cause of this he was at no loss to explain, and he did so, it may be added, in a manner poetically logical and peculiar to himself.

"Every desire is born of a need, of a privation or of a suffering. When satisfied, it is lulled; but for one that is satisfied, how many are unappeased! Desire, moreover, is of long duration; its exigencies are infinite; while pleasure is brief and narrowly measured. Pleasure, too, is but an apparition that is destined to be succeeded by another. The first is a vanished illusion; the second an illusion that lingers still. Nothing is capable of appeasing Will, nor of permanently arresting it. The best we can do is like the alms tossed to a beggar, which, in preserving his life today, prolongs his misery to-morrow. While, then, we are dominated by desires and ruled by Will, so long as we give ourselves up to hopes that delude and fears that alarm, we have neither peace nor happiness. But when an accident, an interior harmony lifting us for the moment from out the torrent of desire, delivers the spirit from the oppression of Will, turns our attention from everything that solicits it, and all things seem as freed from the allurements of hope and personal interest, then repose, vainly pursued, yet ever intangible, comes to us of itself, bearing with open hands the plenitude of the gift of peace."

Contemplation is then an affranchisement. It delivers us for a moment from ourselves; it suspends the activity of Will; and in raising man out of misery into the pure world of ideas, brings him a foretaste of that repose which is the freedom of the non-existent. But the liberation from the trammels of Will which is found in art and disinterested contemplation, is a solace that is momentary and accidental. That which is more desirable is a complete and unfettered freedom. The cause of evil is known; it is the affirmation of the Will-to-live. The remedy is its denial. The Will affirms itself when, after an acquaintance with life, it persists as much in willing as in the first moment when it was a mere blind necessity. The Will denies itself when it renounces life, when it frees itself through a persistent abdication, and abolishes itself of its own accord.

In this there is no question of suicide. For suicide, far from being a denial of the Will-to-live, is one of its strongest affirmations. The man who takes his own life really wants to live.

What he does not want are the miseries and trials attendant on his particular existence. He abolishes the individual, but not the race. The species continues, and pain with it. To be scientifically annihilated, life should be abolished not only in its suffering, but in its empty pleasures as well. Its entire inanity should be recognized, and the whole root cut once and for all. In explaining in what manner this is to be accomplished, Schopenhauer carried his reader far off into the shadows of the Orient. On the one side is the lethargy of the Rishis; on the other, the Tauists drugged with opium; while above all rises the phantasy of the East, the dogma of metempsychosis.

As the present writer has elsewhere explained,* Schopenhauer gives the name of Will to that force which in Indian philosophy is held to resurrect with man across successive lives, and with which the horror of ulterior existence reappears. It is from this nightmare that we are summoned to awake, but in the

* _The Philosophy of Disenchantment._

summons we are told that the awakening can only come with a recognition of the true nature of the dream. The work to be accomplished is therefore less physical than moral. We are not to strangle ourselves in sleep; we are to rise out of it in meditation.

"In man," Schopenhauer says, "the Will-to-live advances to consciousness, to that point where it can choose between its continuance or abolition. Man is the Saviour. Nature awaits her redemption through him. He is at once the priest and the victim."

If, then, in the succeeding generations the appetite for liberty has been so highly cultivated that a widespread and united compassion is felt for all things, then through continence absolute and universal, that condition will be produced in which subject and object disappear, and—the sigh of the egotist Will once choked thereby into a death-rattle—the world, delivered from pain, will pass into that peace which passeth all understanding, into the Prajna-Paramita, the "beyond all knowledge," the Buddhist goal where nothing is.

"It is this," Schopenhauer exclaims in his concluding paragraph, "it is this that the Hindus have expressed in the empty terms of Nirvana and re-absorption in Brahm. I am, of course, aware that what' remains after the abolition of the Will, is without effect on those in whom it still works. But to those in whom it has been crushed, what is this world of ours, with its suns and stellar systems? *Nothing.*"

Among thinking people, Schopenhauer's admirers are today sufficiently frequent to defy enumeration. The theory of force, which was his chief originality, has found few serious adherents; fewer still are they who pin any faith to his plan for the extinction of humanity; it is his classic insistence on the immedicable misery of life, it is the pessimism which he expounded, but which was no more his own invention than is atheism, that has multiplied the translations and editions of his works. For thirty years these works were unnoticed. But Schopenhauer, who was very blithe in his misanthropy, snapped his fingers at the inattention of the public; he knew that Time, who is at least a gentleman, would bring him his due unasked. "My death," he said, "will be a canonization, the extreme unction, a baptism." Yet before he died, fame and honors came and found him unsurprised. "Time has brought his roses at last," he said. "But see," he added, touching his silvered hair, "they are white."

The most prominent of Schopenhauer's successors is Dr. Eduard von Hartmann. On many points this gentleman separates widely from the master. In matters ontological and teleological there is a variance that is noticeably large. But their pessimism is the same; if any difference is discernible, it is merely in this, that the tone of the later comer has gained from recent science the steadiness and assurance that comes of broader knowledge.

Dr. von Hartmann, who sits at the head of contemporary metaphysicians, is a transcendental realist. His doctrine is a pantheism, or, as he prefers to call it, a monism, in which nihilism and idealism are found in equal parts, and one which has given to Hegelism a new and unexpected activity. Nature to him is truly divine; but the misery of existence is irremediable, or at least will continue to be so until advancing science has taught in what way the clamor of life may be quelled. That which the Hindu termed Atma, that which Spinoza designated as Substance— in short, the universal and indetectable force which has made all things what they are, is called by him the Unconscious. The Unconscious is sovereignly wise, and the world is admirable in every respect; it is existence that is irreclaimable in its misery.

The originality of this philosophy consists in a theory of optimistic evolution as counterbalanced by a pessimistic analysis of life; but the originality is not lost in its conclusion, in which it is argued that, as the world's progressus tends neither to universal nor individual happiness, the great aim of science should be to emancipate man from a love of life, and in this wise lead the world back to chaos. The interest of the Unconscious is opposed to our own. It is to our advantage not to live; it is to the advantage of the Unconscious that we should do so, and that others should be brought into existence through us. The Unconscious, therefore, in the furtherment of its aims, has surrounded man with such illusions as are capable of deluding him into a belief that life is a pleasant thing well worth the living. The instincts within us are the different forms beneath which the desire to live is at work, and with which the Unconscious molds man to its profit. Hence the energy witlessly expended for the protection of an existence which is but the right to suffer; hence the erroneous idea which is formed of the happiness derivable from life; and hence, too, the modification of past disenchantments through the influence of fresh and newer hopes. But when in the old age of the world, when humanity has divested itself of the belief that happiness is obtainable in this life, when it has lost all faith in the promise of another—in fact, when every illusion has been dissipated, when hope, love, ambition and gold are recognized as chimeras, or at least as incentives to activity which cause more pain than pleasure—then, science aiding, humanity will perform its own execution, and Time at last will cease to be.

Such is Dr. von Hartmann's conception of life, and such is the idea he has formed of the destiny of the world. In regard to the latter, nothing need now be said; but it may be noted that to the general public his theory of pleasure and pain has not seemed wholly satisfactory. There have been many attempts to confute his pessimism, and many attempts, to show that life, so far from being immedicable in its misery, is a well-spring of delight. And to many, doubtless, it has so seemed. But a point of view is not an argument. Whether life is held to be valuable, or whether it is held to be valueless, its nature in either case remains unchanged. To the obtuse it is usually the one; to the sensitive it is generally the other. But to the impersonal observer, the disinterested witness, to him who looks back through the shudders of history, and who gazes into a future that will be as inexplicable as the past, to him who feels some sympathy for the suffering, some compassion for the distressed and some pity for those in pain, life seldom seems other than an immense, an unnecessary affliction.

Why, asked Voltaire, with that leer which de Musset has made immortal, Why is there anything? An answer often given to this question is, that the ultimate reason of things is discoverable only in matter and motion. In theological circles the advocates of this explanation are not in good repute. In polite society it is considered as bad form to hold such theories as it is to carve salad or guillotine asparagus. In fact, beyond the jurisdiction of the scientific world the materialist has a bad name. The pantheist, *passe encore*. Pantheism is vague and poetic, and apprehended with difficulty. But the materialist brings a different guitar. His conception of the universe demands but little study to seem tolerably clear. Besides, in his heart he seems to say, There is no God, and the appearance of that inward speech is not compatible with good manners. Society has a stronger leaning to affirmations than to negations; in fact as Rousseau has pointed out, the average intellect prefers to be wrong in its belief than to have none at all. The materialist, standing as he does in opposition to theological tenets, is therefore eyed askant, and what is more, is called an atheist when his back is turned.

Parenthetically it may be noted that the historical definition of an atheist is a citizen who refuses to worship the gods which the authorities of the state have appointed as worthy of worship.

In modern parlance the word has acquired a sharper tone, and is generally used in reference to whoso disbelieves in the supernatural. In the coming centuries it is possible that it will cease to be a term of reproach. Indeed, its rehabilitation has in certain quarters already begun. But be this as it may, there are still few thinkers who hear themselves called atheists without experiencing some bewilderment. "Tell a philosopher," Heine said, "that his theories are atheistic, and he will be as much surprised as would a geometrician on learning that his triangles were red."

The denomination is as impertinent to the views of the one, as the color is to the triangles of the other. Not every one, however, has had the privilege of sitting at Heine's feet, and the expression continues to be flung, with more or less vigor, at all systems of rationalistic thought, though at none more virulently than at materialism.

As has been hinted in earlier chapters, materialism is as old as philosophy itself. In India, it was a precursor of Buddhism; in China, it antedates Laou-tze. In classic antiquity, Democritus, Epicurus and Lucretius were among its advocates. Arrested by Christianity, it was imprisoned all through the middle ages; but when, over a century ago, it at last escaped, thrones and altars fell before it. It is, however, only within recent years that materialism received the endorsements of science. The standard-bearer of this movement, a movement all the more significant in that it was a reaction against Hegelian abstractions, was Moleschott. His principal work, the *Krieslauf des Lebens*, awoke Germany from her stupor. It was attacked, applauded and abused. The thin king world, which since Hegel's death had been twirling its thumbs, turned toward it expectant eyes. The hypothesis of an indefinite circulation of matter passing ceaselessly from life to death and from death to life, was old enough to seem quite new, and the axiom, Without force, no matter; without matter, no force, was listened to with grave attention.

The *Kreislauf des Lebens* inspired any number of affiliated works. Vogt, Lowenthal, Czolbe and Rudolphe Wagner made themselves prominent in its defense. Old-fashioned methods were abandoned. Psychology was put aside. Since there was no psyche, of what use could it be? Metaphysics was relegated to the night from which it had sprung. Modern materialism determined to support its dogmas with the sciences which are called exact. And Büchner, mailed with astronomy, chemistry, geology, physiology and natural history, produced in *Kraft und Stoff* the text-book of the new belief. Thereafter it only needed a hymnal to be complete. The deficiency has been supplied by Richepin's *Blasphèmes*.

The first principle of scientific materialism is the inseparability of matter and force. Matter is not a vague substance on which force grapples from without. In the absence of the one, the other is inconceivable, save perhaps by way of hypothesis. Without force, matter would enter at once into a formless void. Without matter, force would fade into a region of pure abstractions. Endeavor, for instance, to represent matter without force, that is, without the power of cohesion or affinity, attraction or repulsion, and, presto! the very idea of matter disappears. In like measure, an effort to represent force without matter results in a similar *dénouement*.

The second principle is that force and matter are indestructible. There are transformations, there are varieties in their manifestations, but in the sum of their effects the intensity is undiminished. Burn a log of wood, and the scales of a chemist will show that not a particle of matter has been destroyed. "Annihilate a particle of matter," said Spinoza, "and the world will crumble." Not an atom can lose itself in immensity, and to immensity not an atom can be added. The flux and reflux of things show beneath incessant variations the same persistent and invariable aggregate. There is a circulation of materials of which each fortuitous combination has its beginning and its end, but in some one form or another the materials meet again and interconnect anew.

As with matter, so with force. What disappears on one side re-appears on another. Friction produces fire, motion is obtained by steam. The amount of movement expended is recovered in the amount of heat; the amount of heat dissipated is recovered in the amount of motion. Force, then, like matter, is immortal. It may be transformed, but never destroyed. From these considerations, materialism concludes that, as that which is indestructible can have had no beginning, matter and force cannot have been created. *Ex nihilo nihil, in nihilum nil posse reverti.* The transformation of something into nothing is as inconceivable, says Lebon, as is the creation of something from nothing. And Taine adds, "There is nothing but matter and motion. Space is the infinity of matter, as time is the eternity of motion." Matter and force are, then, eternal. But eternity is shared alone by them. Dust we are, to dust we shall return.

Matter and force being eternal, their laws are immutable. Were it otherwise, the properties of matter would change, and on the tablets of experience no change is recorded. Nature has never varied. Her laws are the mechanical relation of forces which, in disclosing no trace of a higher Will, turn superstition into a vagabond that has not where to lay its head. Time, in which all things unroll, is the great, the one creator.

The novelty of modern materialism, a novelty which distinguishes it from other systems, is that it claims to rest its affirmations on a basis which is strictly scientific. Its explanation of the universe by means of the action of natural forces, its reduction of natural forces to the variable modes of the force inherent in nature, are indeed supported by physics, chemistry and physiology. But into certain regions that it attempts to penetrate, it has not been preceded by any avant-courier that at all resembles exact knowledge.

The hypothesis that the attraction of all ponderable matter which maintains the planets in their orbits, must at one time have been in a condition to mold the universe from the cosmic dust spread through space, is the starting-point of materialistic cosmogony. This hypothesis, hazarded by Kant, signed by Laplace and attested by Herschel, is crowned by another, which is as opulent in vistas as is the retrospect of the first. It is to the effect that the earth, like her lost satellite whose fragments have deluged the globe, will in turn be disemboweled and tossed through space. Historically these hypotheses are not new. Entertaining as the conjunction may appear, they are part of Buddhist lore. But they are a part of Buddhism which is as vague as it is poetic. In materialism, if there is less vagueness, there is also less poetry. Materialism is nothing if not matter-of-fact. Starting, then, from the hypothesis that a mass of cosmic matter originally filled the space which our planetary system occupies, and that, in accordance with the laws of gravitation which draw the parts to the center, the sun was formed by the gradual concentration of its elements, it is not difficult to fancy a fragment of nebulosity detached from the center and shot through space, developing first in a collection of gases, then into molecules that the rotatory movement fused and ignited, and which in cooling formed a crust above an interior furnace. This flight of fancy accomplished, it is yet easier to imagine the condensation of vapors into rain, the growth of plants and the birth of the Monera from which man descends.

And life? Is it then, as Marcus Aurelius in his sceptred melancholy suggested, but a halt between two eternities? Bah! Away with phrases! A bottle containing carbonate of ammonia, chloride of potassium, phosphate of soda, chalk, magnesia, sulphuric acid and silex, is life in its most ideal, in its completest expression.

Some sixty million years ago, when primitive man blinked at a brighter sky than ours, he thought of the archeolithic ape, if he thought at all, as an inferior animal. And, indeed, there could have been little in common between the shuddering orangutan and the speechless yet ferocious troglodyte who with an uprooted tree crushed the skull of a lion and then sucked the fuming brain.

The link between the two was as undiscernible to him as to the theologian of today. And yet, as Huxley has pointed out, the anatomical difference between man and a gorilla is less than between a gorilla and an inferior ape. And, to pursue the same line of argument, the difference between a Shakespeare and a savage is infinitely greater than between a savage and a brute. Why, a magpie is cleverer than the aboriginal Australian; but at the same time the cleverness of a magpie is not a proof of the evolution of man.

The old coquette, this world of ours, conceals her age, but her biography is under our feet. As we read backwards through it, her years mount up into ten hundred millions. The date of that initial catastrophe, her birth, is yet unreached; but we know enough of her past to be sure that it has been long enough and sufficiently immoral for many things to happen of which our philosophy may dream though it cannot prove. Among these things are spontaneous generation and the descent of man. When these are substantiated, materialism will have proved its claims; its sway will be undisputed; but until then, its arguments have as much evidential value as so many astrogals.

In attempting to explain the organic by the inorganic, the main argument was the alleged birth of insects in putrefied matter. This argument was routed by Redi, who enveloped some meat in a light gauze, on which, a little later, eggs were found to have been deposited by passing flies, and at once the mystery was explained. The discovery of the microscope brought new hopes to the materialists. The animalculae which were found in certain infusions appeared to have been produced without the assistance of antecedent germs. The falsity of this conclusion was demonstrated by Schwann, and the hypothesis of abiogenesis was abandoned, until Pouchet brought it again into fashion. But experiments recently made by M. Pasteur contradict those made by Pouchet; and so far as contemporary science is competent to give a decision, the arguments of the anti-vitalists are inadequate to support their case.

But though the theory of spontaneous generation must be abandoned, at least for the moment, the materialists are by no means at their wits'-end. Life has arisen in some manner, and why not from the interaction of molecular forces?

One of the most charming hypotheses on this subject was advanced a few years ago by Sir William Thomson. To this gentleman, life or perhaps it would be better to say a germ potentially alive, that is, having within itself the tendency to assume a definite living form, first visited the earth in a meteor. If it is proper to assume that meteors are fragments of shattered and once peopled worlds, it may be assumed with equal propriety that some of these fragments are partially intact. The moment, then, that it is admitted that beside our own there are a number of life-supporting worlds and that other worlds have existed in anterior epochs, it would not seem improbable that germ-bearing meteors have moved and do still move through space. As a consequence, any germ-bearing meteor which fell upon the earth during the time when it was destitute of life may have been the unconscious cause of the failure which we are now enjoying.

Dr. Zoellner, a German scientist trained in all the illiberalities of official optimism, attempted to refute this hypothesis on the ground that when a meteor enters our atmosphere, the friction of the air makes it incandescent and consequently incapable of preserving and transporting any germ, however potentially alive. To this refutation Helmholtz made answer, that only the surface of meteors becomes heated, and that germs might readily remain unharmed in interior crevices, or if on the surface might on reaching our atmosphere be blown from their conveyance by the wind, and that, too, before the heat was great enough to cause their destruction. But if this solution be accepted, the origin of life on other planets remains still to be explained. It may be then, as Helmholtz has suggested, that life is coeternal with matter, and its germs, transported from one planet to another, develop wherever they find a propitious spot. But this, too, is merely an hypothesis, and one that has not the slightest evidence in its favor. The enigma of life is for the present a part of the unknowable. But whether it will always remain so is another question. The differences which once were supposed to constitute a barrier between the vertebrate and the non-vertebrate no longer exist. The modifications by which the quadrupedal reptile became a bipedal bird have been clearly shown. Forty years ago, there was no evidence that such a demonstration would ever be made. Forty years hence, who shall say but that the missing link may be discovered, or the manufacture of the organic from the inorganic begun? As Professor Huxley has hinted, no one who has watched the gradual development of a complicated animal from the protoplasm which constitutes the egg of a frog or a hen, will deny that a similar evolution of the whole animal world from a like foundation is at least within the bounds of possibility.

Of the various creeds which man has been pleased to invent, the youngest is positivism. The position which this system of thought has acquired is due to its own merit. It cannot, like pantheism, look back through the terraces of time and claim the quarterings of race. Nor can it, like materialism, bedeck itself with Greek insignia. Among philosophies, positivism is a parvenu. As such it is viewed with scorn, enthusiasm and indifference.

Positivism made its début a little over forty years ago. Its name was its fortune. There was in the sound of it an invitation to nearer acquaintance. But when the acquaintance was made, the name was found to partake of the nature of a lure. Relativism, if less attractive, would have been a clearer description. For positivism, if positive at all, is positive that there is nothing positive. Its sponsor was Auguste Comte.

If the realization of the ambitions of youth may be regarded as the criterion of a successful career, the life of this thinker cannot be considered a failure. At a comparatively early age the outlines of his doctrine appear to have been clearly denned. The outlines sprang of a suggestion of Saint-Simon, who was wont to declare that all knowledge should be co-ordinated into one vast and comprehensive synthesis, but their development was accomplished without material indebtedness. In synthetizing knowledge into a single system of thought, Comte proposed nothing less than the abolishment of theology and metaphysics, and the re-organization of the Occident through a philosophy of his own manufacture. In 1842, the sixth and last volume of this philosophy was given to the public, and with it the knell of all religions was supposed to have been rung. Ten years later, to the utter bewilderment of his disciples, Comte proclaimed the necessity of founding a new religion, of which the sovereign pontiff was to be none other than himself.

In an earlier paragraph it has been hinted that positivism is positive that there is nothing positive, a phrase which, from a Comtist stand-point, may be taken to mean that the essence of things escapes us. We can understand the interconnection of facts—that is, their direct antecedents and immediate sequences—but the initial causes and ultimate results are inaccessible to the intellect. In a word, there is nothing except material phenomena and the laws thereof. As this principle is the pivot on which the entire philosophy turns, a momentary examination may not be without benefit.

Many a skeptic has filled his hours in showing that things are not what they seem, but none of them, however revolutionary, has disputed the reality of consciousness, or denied the phenomena that are manifest in thought, feeling and volition. In affirming, therefore, that the objects apprehended by the senses are the only apprehensible phenomena, positivism apparently displays a radicalism which is as audacious as it is novel. It is of course possible and even proper to regard thought, feeling and volition as products of the body, but it would be a misuse of language to assert that they are material phenomena; and, as positivism's first tenet is that there is nothing except material phenomena, it would seem that, like any other screw, the before-mentioned pivot is loose. On the other hand, it may be objected that the phenomena called internal are unobservable, and that any attempt to distinguish them from their external elements results merely in demonstrating the vainness of the endeavor. If this view be accepted, positivism is found less rickety than it first appeared, and the introductory statement may be welcomed at once and without further hesitation.

If, then, as positivism asserts, the essence of things escapes us, any speculation on the origin and purpose of the world is profitless. On such and kindred subjects the mind should be without conjecture. It is only natural that man should have been on the *qui vive* in his effort to discover efficient and final causes, but his effort has never been successful. "If God did not exist," said Voltaire, "the world would have invented him." "Which," a wit replied, "is precisely what the world has done."

The mobility of phenomena, the fugitiveness of sensations,

the impermanency of the actual, the real which each moment ends and begins anew, have, in all ages, incited to a knowledge of the unknowable. But the knowledge has not been obtained, and it was in view of the impracticability of the attempt that Comte ventured to suggest what may be termed a middle course. In the effort to pierce the impenetrable, humanity, he said, has passed and is still passing through certain stages of thought which correspond to those of childhood, adolescence and maturity. The first is the age of theology; the second, of metaphysics; and the third, of science. This doctrine, which is known as the law of the three states, conveys the suggestion alluded to, together with a theory which is as liberal as the sea. It runs somewhat as follows:

In the infancy of thought, Nature is dowered with the same illusions to which man himself is subjected. Every object is animated, and the government of the universe is ascribed, not to invariable laws, but to sentient and intelligent beings. In everything that occurs is seen the manifestation of a direct intention, and each particular event is attributed to forces which are but the aggrandizements of those of man. In the advance of thought, these forces, whose prowess is discernible in effects which man is impotent to produce, become the gods, invisible yet multitudinous. Then, gradually, as arises the capacity of co-ordinating phenomena into separate groups, the number of divinities diminishes, until, through processes of generalization, they are reduced to one, and behold, man has passed out of fetishism into polytheism, and from thence to a belief in a unique Creator.

But there is a further advance of thought, and in its train comes the suggestion that the uniformity noticeable in the universe is incompatible with the theory of an arbitrary Will. The initial conceptions are dismissed, the celestial and inaccessible reason of things is banished, and realized abstractions are accepted instead. Nature is governed, not by an external power, but by internal and occult qualities. The reign of dryads and nymphs is passed, and their place is usurped by entities, by theories which deal with a plastic force and a vital principle. This is the second, or metaphysical state, which is of advantage in being a negation of the first and a preparation for the third, which latter is reached when men, weary of explanations that explain nothing, discover that what is necessary for the mind is not obligatory for things, and that a cause which is conceived by the one need not have a place among the others. Such is the positive, or scientific state of mind, to which, according to Comte, all humanity tends; and such, too, is the middle course which he recommended to thoughtful and decorous persons.

Stripped of its verbal husks, the law of the three states may be reduced to a truism. In seeking the reason of things, men look first above, then within, and finally confess themselves vanquished.

The law of the three states which Stuart Mill called the backbone of the entire philosophy, but which is not particularly new nor particularly convincing—not new, because sketched by Kant in outline, and not convincing, because Comte himself declined to be bound by it—is supplemented by a classification of sciences from out of which was drawn a fresh one, called sociology.

In the study of facts, the interpretation of the experience which is written between the lines of history, sociology was to be the lever in the substitution of science for religion. It was to terminate the conflict between theology, which demands order without progress, and metaphysics, which aims at progress and turns its back on order. It was to arrest the retrogression of the one, and still the anarchy of the other. In the government of life it was to replace religion with science, and give to intelligence the guiding-strings of the world.

In mapping this programme, Comte fancied that sociology could be raised to the level of an exact science, and that through its influence all enlightened nations would join hands in the profession of identical doctrines. In the Utopias in which he then lost himself, he planned a reorganization of society on a basis which, if suggestive of Plato's Republic, is otherwise without value or allurement. There is, he pointed out, no such thing as liberalism in astronomy, physics or chemistry; and if it be otherwise in ethics and politics, it is because neither of them possess established principles. When they acquire them, as they will do when positivism begins its sway, the force of public opinion will disappear. A corporation of philosophers, salaried by the State and treated with the greatest respect, will have the entire charge of education, together with the right to counsel and direct each citizen in his private and public life, and enjoy, moreover, such an amount of authority over students and thinkers as will enable them to prevent the latter from squandering their time and knowledge in speculations that are valueless to humanity, and oblige them to apply themselves to such investigations as may be deemed most important to general prosperity. The decrees which the corporation may formulate are not to be questioned, and, as the idea of the sovereignty of the people is one of the most pernicious that civilization has advanced, but slight attention will be paid to the inclinations of the masses. In each nation there will be a governing body and a body governed, in which latter the citizen will occupy the position for which his abilities have fitted him. Thereafter religion and metaphysics will disappear. Scientific dissidence will be effaced, and an invariable and uniform political dogma will at last be accepted by united and peaceful nations.

To the clear-headed and matter-of-fact audience which was Comte's, theories such as these were viewed with suspicion. The idea that there is no God had in it nothing that was alarming; the prophecy of the overthrow of superstition and the general adoption of positivist tenets seemed not unreasonable; the prohibition against idle speculations and the complimentary recommendation to treat only with the real were received with open favor; but the sturdiest could not look without terror on a future governed by philosophers.

When this horizon was disclosed, it is probable that Comte had already entered into what is known as his pathological period. In earlier years he suddenly lost his reason, and as suddenly recovered it. The border-lands of genius and insanity are never well defined, and it is not unlikely that before the *Cours de philosophie positive* was completed, something of that of which he had too much, something of that weight of thought which obscures the vision and tips the scales of commonsense, was again at work, though this time more dumbly and dimly than before. Thereafter the champion of the actual who had wished to lead God to the frontiers, and there thank him kindly for his provisory services, lapsed into a morbid mysticism. The sceptre of the world which he had given to intellect was transferred to sentiment. It was for the heart to rule and for the intellect to obey.

The *Philosophic politique*, in which his ideas on this subject are conveyed, shows, even amid the luxuriance of luminous thought, the same evidence of mental decadence as is noticeable in Kant's *Kritik der Practischen Vernunft*. Both belong to the senilia of great minds. During the year that intervened between its appearance and the publication of his chief work, Comte conceived what his biographers term a platonic affection for a lady whose influence over him was of such a nature, that, aided by the historical meditations in which his life had been passed, he dreamed of a happiness that should be universal, and of a world that should be ruled, not by a corporation of salaried philosophers, but by love in its purest and most disinterested form.

The pompous Religion of Humanity which he then evolved, and which has no more connection with positivism than an *opera-bouffe* has with logarithms, saddened the boldest among his adherents. It found adepts—what vagary has not? The altruism which it inculcated is certainly not without charm; but the deification of humanity past and future, the transformation of earth into a fetish, space into fate and numbers into virtues, are among the most deplorable instances of the aberrations of genius. After shutting out the unknowable, the door was opened to superstition; after banishing metaphysics, sentiment was beckoned in to occupy its place; religion was superseded by idolatry; and the heavens, that no longer told of the glory of God, were set ablaze with the memories of great men,

In its uncorrupted form, positivism is a modification of materialism. Among theologians there is a disposition to regard both in the same light. But no positivist likes to be called a materialist. He shows as much displeasure at the term as he would were he called a theist or a pantheist. And, indeed, the lines of demarcation, if not always broad, are none the less apparent. At the origin of things, theism places a personal and infinite Being; pantheism sees in all things the immanency of a Being that is infinite but impersonal; and materialism asserts that the cause of all things lies in the arrangement and properties of force and matter. Positivism, on the other hand, knows nothing of an infinite Being, whether personal or impersonal; in the spheres that are inaccessible to it, it recognizes nothing but matter and the properties of matter; but, unlike materialism, it draws no conclusions. According to Littre, positivism is simply a methodical, hierarchic arrangement of the general facts of science, excluding every subjective element, and accepting nothing that is not drawn from experience.

A positivist; moreover, shows no evidence of delight at being called an atheist. As Littré has described him, an atheist is in a certain measure a theologian. He is not entirely emancipated. He has his explanations of things; he knows how they began.

He believes in the chance clash of atoms, or in occult forces, or in a first cause. Of all this the positivist knows nothing. He ignores productive atoms as well as a creating and ordaining force. But whoso thinks that history follows a development that is obedient to a natural law—whoso thinks that the origin of societies, the establishment or mutation of religion, the founding of empires, cities, castes, aristocracies, governments, oracles, prophecies, revelations, theologies, arts and industries, are due, one and all, to the faculties of man—whoso accepts this view has fully accomplished the cycle of mental emancipation. The moment that he leaves no place for the supernatural either in the organic or the inorganic, either among cosmic phenomena or among those of history, that moment he passes initiate into the brotherhood of positivism.

The charm of positivism is the matter-of-fact position which it assumes before the insolvable. If it cuts no old knots, it brings no new tangles. It treats metaphysics with the respect which is due to all that is venerable; in the presence of religion it puts the dialectic broadsword softly back in its sheath. It leaves the great query where it found it. And in this is its wisdom; its agnosticism is its strength. Clamor as we may, there is no answer to our whys and wherefores. There is in us, about and beyond us, an enigma that will defy the Champollions of the future as it has routed the seers of the past. The reason of things lies beyond the sphere of knowledge, and the nearest approach that can be made is in a suspicion that all is relative.

CHAPTER SIX.

A Poet's Verdict.

THERE HAVE BEEN DAYS IN THE HISTORY OF THE WORLD when the poet was regarded with respect that approached ven-eration. He was considered the oracle of the gods, and his voice was listened to with reverence. This pleasant custom has fallen into disuse. The gods have disappeared and carried the divine afflatus with them. In an age like the present, the demand for poets is slight. Their titles have been examined, and it has been found that to be useless is their one patent of nobility. As a con-sequence, the poet's vocation has seemed to many a synonym of the ridiculous. And yet, as Gautier with a charming affectation of naïvete remarked, an inability to write in verse can scarcely be considered as constituting a special talent. But there is an-other inconvenience: a poet is never rightly appreciated save by his peers; and as his peers are infrequent, the majesty which re-sides within him often lacks the trumpetings of a herald. Then, too, in an era of remorseless activity, it is only quiet people who live in the country that find leisure to listen to the footfalls of

351

the Muse. For the benefit of such as they, verse may be divided into three broad classes: that which pleases the author's enemies, that which pleases the author's contemporaries, and that which passes unobserved to pleasure the idlesse of posterity. Of these classes, the verse of Leconte de Lisle belongs to the third.

Any one who has taken an interest in French literature during the last decade can hardly have failed to notice the number of new writers that have come into being, and more particularly the inferiority of their work. In explanation of this surge of mediocrity, many theories might be advanced; but perhaps the most palpable would be that the literature of our expiring century, after having passed from youth to virility, has begun to experience the maladies and garrulities of old age. But however the subject may be viewed, it is at least evident that the paladins of 1830, who were as revolutionary in literature as their ancestors were in religion, have passed away, and also that their methods have so far disappeared with them that the day before yesterday Victor Hugo seemed like a living anachronism. Readers latterly have refused to be interested in the phantasies of the romantics, and perhaps their pages were a trifle over-colored; but their excuse lay in the fact that literature had become impoverished through conventionalities; there were synonyms instead of words; and in place of ample vocabularies there were small niceties of expression. All this the romantics did away with. They breathed health and vigor into an enervated dictionary, and startled Europe with the opulence of their adjectives.

It was in those victorious days that Gautier threw aside his brush and went in a famous red waistcoat to guy the philistines at the birth-night of Hernani. In graver years Gautier complained that in the eyes of the bourgeois he had never ceased to wear that crimson garment, and somehow, save among the liberal few, he has always been looked upon more or less askant. It has been said that it was his purpose to seek the hazardous and display it, but it must be admitted that what he had to say he told with a grace such as had been seldom heard before. He chose his words for their color, for their aroma, as one may say; and it is related that he objected now and then to an accent because it took away something from the charm which the grouping of certain letters otherwise conveyed.

Through those days, too, Alfred de Musset passed with the indolence of a dissolute young god. He joined the ranks of the romantics, as did all men of talent, but he joined them more as an amateur than a professional: the familiar ballad in which the moon is represented as suspended over a steeple like a dot over an *i*, opened for him the doors of the cénacle without even giving him the trouble to knock. In a subsequent poem he asked forgiveness for that misdeed; and though he boasted that his Muse went bare of foot like Truth, she might still have been pictured as shod with buskins of gold.

Another of the heroes of this epoch was Alfred de Vigny. Someone has said that the face of a poet is never known until years and sorrow have marred its original beauty; but to this rule de Vigny was an exception. He was famous when quite young, and his bust, as it stands today in the lobby of the Théâtre Français, arrests the attention even of the indifferent. At the time to which allusion is made, he mingled but little with his fellows, appearing only when the moral support of his presence was needed. In later years, in spite of his talent, his beauty and his position, de Vigny, devoured by melancholy, turned his back entirely upon the world, and retired into what Sainte-Beuve has termed his *tour d'ivoire*.

In the wake of these poets came the familiar figure of Charles Baudelaire. Recently he has been described as having had the appearance of a delicate prelate, a trifle depraved. This description might be suggested by the mere reading of his verse. In the work of every poet there is something of the individual, and it is probable that few have studied the chiseled lines which he worked up with even a shrewder eye for the Satanic than that which was given to Edgar Poe, without calling up some such picture of their author. Baudelaire entered the ranks when the battle was won, but nevertheless he managed to flaunt a standard that has troubled the vision of many an after-comer.

So swiftly does time go by, that of these writers little more than tradition now remains. In the eyes of contemporary critics, de Musset is a dislocator of Alexandrines, de Vigny is a memory, Baudelaire a curiosity, and Gautier a model. Yet each of them left a legacy that is still disputed. From de Musset descends the gift of eloquence; in Baudelaire's testament is the heirloom of lurid effect; de Vigny has devised his morbidity; while Gautier's bequest is perfection in form. Taken together, they were the poetic embodiment of the agitation of which Voltaire, Holbach and Diderot were the heralds. *"Je ne crois pas, ô Christ, a ta parole sainte,"* cried de Musset, and the cry was echoed by his fellow-workers.

In a literary sense, these poets were, on their first appearance, very generally looked upon as impertinent innovators, and in their assault upon the classicists they caused much rage and rhetoric. Viewed at this distance, the disturbance seems unnecessary; for, after all, what is romanticism but the art of pleasing one's contemporaries, and what is classicism but the art which delighted earlier generations? Turn about is always fair play. In a little while Hugo will be a classic, precisely as Racine is beginning to be considered a romantic. But be this as it may, the seething passion which in 1830 seemed more alluring than the chill restrictions of former years, gradually disappeared, and its place was taken by the serene impassibility of another group of poets who were called the Parnassians.

The advent of this new school was necessarily less boisterous than that of their predecessors: for that matter, they excited more ridicule than anger; and it is related that a cabman in a street row, after having called his adversary everything that was unpleasant, hurled at him with withering contempt as last and supreme reproach, the unavengeable insult, *"Parnassien, va!"*

Of the poets who made up this group, the better known are MM. Sully-Prudhomme and François Coppée. Sully-Prudhomme is an avowed materialist and frankly pessimistic. His poems may be summarized as a series of very delicate impressions intermingled with a fair amount of philosophic suggestion. His repertory is not extensive. It consists in three or four themes and their variations—such, for instance, as the familiar aspiration toward the infinite, man's sentiment of nothingness before the immensity of the universe, the agony of doubt, and the usual communion with Nature. The limits of this range do not necessarily imply a lack of ability. The art in any form of verse consists merely in the skill with which one or more of half-a-dozen old-fashioned sentiments is rendered, and in this respect the work of Sully-Prudhomme is generally irreproachable. In his treatment of purely personal dramas, the mental and moral combats which we all of us wage with ourselves, he leaves little to be desired, and it would be difficult to mention a poet who has entered more deeply than he into the psychological developments of the century. For all this he has received much praise, and if his verse is ever criticized, it is because it is at times a trifle vague. Sully-Prudhomme has been as honestly puzzled by the discord between the real and the ideal as any writer of his class; but in his perplexity his thought floats away to uncertain heights, and there disappears with a flutter of restless inquietude. To put the matter briefly, Sully-Prudhomme very often seems as though he were about to say something well worth the telling, but before he has gotten it safely on paper the force of the idea has vanished.

François Coppée is another of the dispersed Parnassians.

His negations, if more carefully veiled than those of Sully-Prud-homme, are none the less discernible. He is at times dramatic, but his sadness is always insistent. To be sad is admittedly the poet's privilege; yet to be simply sad, and to express such a state of being as who should say, "I hunger" or "I thirst," is not necessarily poetic; rather is it commonplace. To be worth the telling, grief should express a thought that is neither humdrum nor familiar; it should lay bare fresh possibilities or set new limits to resignation: if it does not do this, then, however readily the tears may flow, however gracefully the grief be told, it is what a boulevardier would call *le vieux jeu*—the old story, of which we are most of us thoroughly tired. It is this old story that M. Coppére tells; and though the telling is managed with much refinement, it is impossible to call it novel. M. Coppée has also much to say about his boredom. Boredom, however, is not a flexible topic; indeed, unless it is handled with unusual dexterity, there is a danger that the reader will find it even more irritating than the writer, and thereupon withdraw his attention and support. Boredom also is more of a fine art than is generally supposed, and not to every one is it given to disentangle original ideas from that which is flat and unprofitable. Leopardi and Baudelaire have done so, it is true; but between them they managed to throttle the subject and share the booty. For a later comer like M. Coppée, nothing was left.

MM. Prudhomme and Coppée have both sat at the feet of Leconte de Lisle. Today they are better known than he, but neither of them has ventured to rate his work above that of the master. In this modesty much good taste is shown. He has none of their faults, and, moreover, he has genius, which both of them lack. In comparison with him they are as concettists to Dante.

Laconte de Lisle is perhaps the most perfect poet of France. It is he who is the rightful heir to the legacies of the romantics, and these possessions he has rounded and improved with an erudition which embraces history, philology, archaeology, anthropology, and doubtless much more beside. In spite of this, or perhaps on that account, his literary luggage is scant. He has translated a few ancient authors, written a drama or two, and published three compact volumes of verse. In speaking of the latter, it is difficult to describe them in a phrase, though this perhaps may be accomplished in saying that they do not contain a commonplace line. The three volumes are respectively entitled, *Poèmes antiques*, *Poèmes barbares*, and *Poèmes tragiques*. The first division, which is largely made up of Vedic hymns and Greek idyls, is one in which the characteristics of the author are best displayed, and in which his impersonality is most strongly marked. Many of the poems in this series bring with them a haunting impression that they are translations from some unknown Valmiki, while others might be taken for the work of Max Müller turned poet.

When these poems were first published, they created among the lettered an intense admiration. It was admitted that lines of such splendor and impersonal serenity had never been hewn before; and certainly, after the ardor of the romantics, their impassibility could not have been other than a refreshing change. It was, however, the fortune of the book to appeal only to scholars; to the newspaper public it was unintelligible; the author had made no effort to please; and, moreover, he had declined to make any concessions to the ordinary reader. The result might have been foreseen; Brahma was declared to lack actuality; and it was held to be tiresome to construe a modern poet with a Greek dictionary. What, it was asked, has Juno done to be called Héré, and why must the sky be ouranos?

As was the case with the series just mentioned, the *Poèmes barbares* found favor only with the few. To the general public they seemed very subversive. They displayed a pessimism which was new to France, and which, being new, was eyed with suspicion. Then, too, Leconte de Lisle was calmly anti-theistic. The bravado of Marechal is boyish in comparison to his grave disdain of things celestial. In the Poemes barbares there are lines that startle and coerce, lines in which the horrible is expressed with such color and yet with such austerity that the reader shudders as he reads and admires as he shudders. Beside them, the declamations of that dissolute Greuze of literature, Alfred de Musset, sound cracked and thin—like a man's laughter, as Mr. Swinburne has it, heard in hell.

The *Poèmes tragiques* are not as satisfactory as are the others. They are made up of a dozen or more recitals which have much to do with the shedding of blood, a few ballads, villanelles, pantoums and sestines, together with a bar or two of pure harmony.

Leconte de Lisle is the Goya of verse, and yet, through a delicious contradiction, one of the most noteworthy characteristics of his work is its constant evocation and suggestion of the beautiful. No other modern poet, except perhaps Mr. Swinburne, has shown a better acquaintance with the road to Paphus. And it would be a task full of charm to follow him from the jungles of the Indian peninsula to the cool lakes of Norway, to fan Leïlah and kiss Glaucé. Unfortunately, the purpose of these pages will not permit of such pleasant digressions, and the beautiful must be neglected that the poet's anti-theism may be the more quickly understood. By way of introduction, a momentary examination of the poem *Qaïn* will not, it is imagined, cause any after reproach of time misspent.

The scenario is simple and audacious. The son of Elam, Thogorma the seer, a captive among the Assyrians, dreams of a night in the mysterious ages when the voice of God echoed through the universe, and in his dream he sees Henokhia, the city of giants, in whose highest tower is the tomb of Cain. Cain's descendants are wending their way homewards from the chase. Thogorma sees them disappear in the immense orb of the ramparts, while night, bringing a vague terror and dumb dread, mantles the great stairways that turn in red broad spirals to the winds. He hears the roar of lions, chained on the ascending steps, and beneath the porticos the clamors of crocodiles rise from the reservoirs. Then, abruptly, from the confines of the outlying desert, a spectre, loosed from Gehenna, surges through the shadows, and Thogorma hears the spirits anathematize Cain and all his race.

Cain awakened, stands upright in the granite sepulchre where for ten centuries he had slept with his face to the sky. His eyes, haunted by one supreme remembrance, contemplate through the preceding epochs the vanished days when the world was young; and with his thoughts rich with the memory of the earth's primal innocence and beauty, he calls to the phantom to be silent and narrates his sombre history. Conceived while his parents were laboring under the divine malediction, his mother, Eve, swooning in the brambles, gave birth with a shriek of horror to Jehovah's victim, to him who was Cain. Nursed with tears, his boyhood knew no smile. What had he done, he wondered, to be punished too? And so, later, in the knowledge of his exile he accosts the angel on guard at the gates of Eden, and learns that on the morrow he is to know the reason of his birth. On the morrow the reason is made apparent. Jehovah arms his hand against Abel, and incites him to kill the brother whom he tenderly loved.

Here ends Cain's account of his life; but immediately, in his awakened thirst for vengeance, he prophesies that when Jehovah is wearied with the world and shall seek by means of the deluge to destroy it, he, Cain, will save the ark—which the poet represents as constructed in spite of Jehovah—whereupon man, no longer brave, but cowardly and envious, will rise from the flood with its mud in his heart. Cain, the avenger, continues:

"Dieu triste, Dieu jaloux qui dérobes ta face,
Dieu qui mentais, disant que ton œuvre était bon,
Mon souffle,ô Pétrisseur de l'antique limon,
Un jour redressera ta victime vivace.
Tu lui diras: Adore! Elle répondra: Non!

.   .   .   .

Afin d'exterminer le monde qui te nie,
Tu feras ruisseler le sang comme une mer,
Tu feras s'acharner les tenailles de fer,
Tu feras flamboyer, dans l'horreur infinie,
Près des bûchers hurlants le gouffre de 1' Enfer:

Mais   .   .   .   .

.   .   .   .

Je ressusciterai les cités submergées,
Et celles dont le sable a couvert les monceaux:
Dans leur lit écumeux j'enfermerai les eaux:
Et les petits enfants des nations vengées,
Ne sachant plus ton nom, riront dans leurs berceaux!

J'effonderai des cieux la voûte dérisoire.
Par delà l'épaisseur de ce sépulchre bas
Sur qui gronde le bruit sinistre de ton pas,
Je ferai bouillonner les mondes dans leur gloire:
Et qui t'y cherchera ne t'y trouvera pas.

Et ce sera mon jour! Et d'étoile en étoile,
Le bienheureux Eden longuement regretté
Verra renaître Abel sur mon coeur abrité;
Et toi, mort et cousu sous la funèbre toile.
Tu t'anéantiras dans ta sterilité."

.   .   .   .

Apart from the wonder and majesty of the language, and apart, too, from the intuition which in earlier stanzas enabled the poet to call again into being the life of the past, *Qaïn*, on a first reading, seems to be merely a work of cultured and harmonious blasphemy, and, indeed, so far as the blasphemy is concerned, nothing more vehement has been penned since Æschylus; but yet on a re-reading *Qaïn* is found to be little else than an allegory of the protestation of the intellect against the unintelligible, a revolt at the mystery of pain.

This protestation, which is as old as philosophy, and which in recent years seems to have increased in volume and significance, has been conveyed by Leconte de Lisle in other poems with great originality, and with particular power in the parable of the *Corbeau*. Through this poem, as through *Qaïn*, there is a running accompaniment of muffled discontent, which in other verses finds a clear and decided note. Something of this same dissatisfaction was expressed by de Vigny and Alfred de Musset, and yet in their case one is inclined to fancy that the grievance was less reasoned than instinctive; they were at odds, so to speak, with the inevitable; life failed to hold what it had seemed to promise, and in consequence their complaints were more or less personal. But in Leconte de Lisle there is no evidence of personal disappointment, and nothing that can be construed as the outcome of an individual grievance. It is a part of his doctrine that an expression of pleasure or pain deforms the human visage, that the poet's correct attitude is the one which most nearly approaches the impassibility of the statue, and it is this theory which he has carried into his work.

It is difficult to say to what category of antitheism Leconte de Lisle belongs. His pantheism is too evident to permit of his being called a materialist, and yet his materialism is so marked that it is difficult to suspect him of any other sympathies with the ideal than those which are purely poetic. He is too aggressive for an agnostic, and yet there are moments when he might be taken for a positivist. Perhaps if will be safest to say that he is a theoretic pessimist, a denomination which is broad enough to include any of the others, and at the same time is serviceable in conveying the exact shade of his thought.

The pessimism which is manifest in the verse of Leconte de Lisle has nothing of Renan's serenity, and none of the calculations of Von Hartmann. In his case it is the formal protest against the enigma of grief which characterizes the philosophy of the earliest thinkers, but one which is entirely free from the shackles with which they delayed the hope of ultimate emancipation. It is not that the idea of absorption in Brahm, or the extinction in Pari-Nirvana, is disagreeable to him; on the contrary, they are dreams through which he lovingly trails his verse, but they are dreams.

> *"Pleurez, contemplateurs! Votre sagesse est veuve*
> *Viçnou ne siege plus sur le lotus d'azur."*

That of which he seems best convinced is the irremediable existence of what apparently has no reason for being. History is little else than the tale of an uninterrupted shudder; chronicles of private life are merely accounts of combats that individuals have waged with fate: and Leconte de Lisle, who is a patient student, has noted compassionately in both the persistence of the law of evil. He should not, however, be considered a follower of Schopenhauer; the majority of his poems were published before the *Welt als Wille und Vorstellung* had crossed the Rhine; moreover, Schopenhauer did not invent pessimism; Kapila was as much occupied with pain as was that Emerson in black; indeed, it is curious to note that the first metaphysician as well as the latest of great poets are agreed that life is an affliction, and it is also curious to note that the tendency of modern thought is to an agreement with their views.

The soul, whose immortality Robespierre decreed in the law known as that of the 18th Floréal, year II; the soul, which all antiquity, Plato included, accorded to beasts, but whose possession Christianity has limited to man; the soul, which is reported to come no one knows whence, and to depart no one knows whither, has for Leconte de Lisle a purely verbal existence. Robespierre, it is true, knew nothing about primitive man; but Leconte de Lisle does, and he knows, too, that a gorilla to which a soul is refused today is not a whit more elevated than was man in the sylvan age—in that age, in fact, when he had no other weapons than the branches which he tore from a tree. And if a soul be refused to primitive man, at what epoch was the gift bestowed? Is it a result of evolution, or, as certain theologasters have asserted, is it naturally one with the body, and only separable and capable of immortality through the influence of grace divine? The last century combatted these theories with logic. Leconte de Lisle has at his disposal not alone the logic of yesterday, but the science of today, and to him the soul is a phantom evoked by the conscience.

"If you do not believe in a soul and in a future life," said some one to Goethe, "what do you consider to be the object of the present?" To which Goethe, with Olympian egotism, answered tersely, "Self-improvement." One may fancy that to Leconte de Lisle the object of life is none other. He was born in the Isle de Bourbon something over sixty years ago, and came to Paris when quite young. From his early home he brought little else than memories of the beauty of Nature and the invincible immensity of her forces, memories that have since served as frames and backgrounds to his verse. In Paris he followed the developments of science, and studied history, religions and life. From them he learned that man has two antagonists, himself and the exterior world; he found, too, that man is a prey to influences which mould him to their profit, and that humanity had aggravated its misfortunes by inventing explanations which it termed beliefs. Since then, in the quietest ways, he has passed his hours in satiating that vague curiosity which besets even the most indifferent, and in convincing himself not only of the nothingness of creeds, but of the nothingness of life. Life, he says:

> "La vie est comme l'onde oil tombe un corps pesant:
> Un cercle etroit s'y forme et va s'elargissant,
> Et disparait enfin dans sa grandeur sans terme.
> La Māyā te seduit, mais, si ton cœur est ferme,
> Tu verras s'envoler comme un peu do vapeur
> La colere, l'amour, le desir ct la peur,
> Et Je Monde illusoirc aux formes innombrables
> S'ecroulera sous toi comme un monceau de sables."

Gibbon, who was fond of fine paragraphs, declared all religions to be equally true to the vulgar, equally false to the philosopher, and to the statesman equally useful. But Gibbon omitted the poet; and to such an one as Leconte de Lisle no religion can be true, if for no other reason than that there is no criterion of truth; no religion can be wholly false, for every religion has enjoyed an hour of undeniable actuality; and no religion can be deemed useful if the need of it has disappeared. To his thinking, religions have served their purpose. Compounded of fables more or less absurd, and of ethics more or less wholesome, in their obscure origins they were intended to be explanations of natural phenomena with which today we are better acquainted. As to Christianity, it is to Leconte de Lisle an artistic creation, powerfully conceived, venerable in its antiquity, and one whose place is now marked, in the museum of history.

It has been objected, that should this view be accepted, no one would turn to the Bible for instruction, and as a consequence the gateways to immorality would be opened wide. Now Plato said that we should esteem it of the greatest importance that the fictions which children first hear should be adapted in the most perfect manner to the promotion of virtue. There are, however, not a few grave thinkers who have asserted that the Bible is inapt to serve such an end. Admittedly the morality which is displayed in the Synoptic Gospels is admirable, but it is sometimes forgotten that it is an integral part of the teaching of Socrates and the Socratics. M. Havet has shown its sweetest precepts flowing from their lips. In other portions of the Bible there are verses that exalt the spirit like wine; there are delicacies of thought and felicities of expression that both soothe and charm; but one must needs be a paradoxist to claim either as an aid to the promotion of virtue. Beside, as has been hinted in earlier pages, morality is more a question of temperament than of instruction. For that matter, we are most of us well aware that the instruction sometimes defeats its aim. Mr. Froude relates that when St. Patrick preached the gospel on Tarah Hill, the Druids shook their heads. The king, Leoghaire, marked their disapproval wonderingly, and asked, "Why is it that that which the cleric preaches seems so dangerous to you?" "Because," they answered, "he preaches repentance, and the law of repentance is such that a man shall say, 'I may commit a thousand sins, and if I repent it will be not worse with me; I shall be forgiven; therefore will I continue to sin." Leconte de Lisle has therefore put the Bible reverently aside, and in looking back through the dreams from which it came and into the visions which it has evoked, he has murmured with the sadness of the tender-hearted:

"*O songe, ô désirs vains, inutiles souhaits,*
Ceci ne sera point, maintenant ni jamais."

There is no help there, nor is there any elsewhere. The Orient is asleep in the ashes of her gods. The star of Ormuzd has burned out in the skies. On the banks of her sacred seas, Greece, hushed for evermore, rests on the divine limbs of her white immortals.

In the sepulchre of the pale Nazarene, humanity guards its last divinity. Every promise is unfulfilled. There is no light save perchance in death. One torture more, one more throb of the heart, and after it nothing. The grave opens, a little flesh falls in, and the weeds of forgetfulness which soon hide the tomb grow eternally above its vanities. And still the voice of the living, of the just and of the unjust, of kings, of felons and of beasts, will be raised unsilenced, until humanity, unsatisfied as before and yet impatient for the peace which life has disturbed, is tossed at last, with its shattered globe and forgotten gods, to fertilize the furrows of space where worlds ferment.

On this vista the curtain may be drawn. Neither poet nor seer can look beyond. Nature, who is unconscious in her immorality, entrancing in her beauty, savage in her cruelty, imperial in her prodigality, and appalling in her convulsions, is not only deaf, but dumb. There is no answer to any appeal. The best we can do, the best that has ever been done, is to recognize the implacability of the laws that rule the universe, and contemplate as calmly as we can the nothingness from which we are come and into which we shall all disappear. The one consolation that we hold, though it is one which may be illusory too, consists in the belief that when death comes, fear and hope are at an end. Then wonder ceases; the insoluble no longer perplexes; space is lost; the infinite is blank; the farce is done.

Made in the USA
Coppell, TX
30 June 2024